DOS 5.0
for beginners

Manfred Tornsdorf
Helmut Tornsdorf

Abacus
A Data Becker Book

First Printing,
Printed in U.S.A.
Copyright © 1992

Abacus
5370 52nd Street SE
Grand Rapids, MI 49512

Copyright © 1991, 1992

Data Becker, GmbH
Merowingerstrasse 30
4000 Duesseldorf, Germany

Edited by: Gene Traas, Scott Slaughter, Robbin Markley

This book is copyrighted. No part of this book may be reproduced, stored in a retrieval system, or transmitted in any form or by any means, electronic, mechanical, photocopying, recording or otherwise without the prior written permission of Abacus Software or Data Becker, GmbH.

Every effort has been made to ensure complete and accurate information concerning the material presented in this book. However, Abacus Software can neither guarantee nor be held legally responsible for any mistakes in printing or faulty instructions contained in this book. The authors always appreciate receiving notice of any errors or misprints.

DOS, MS-DOS, MS-DOS Editor, QBasic, Microsoft Word, Microsoft Multiplan and Microsoft Windows are trademarks or registered trademarks of Microsoft Corporation. dBASE IV is a registered trademark of Ashton-Tate, Inc.

```
Library of Congress Cataloging-in-Publication Data
    DOS 5.0 for beginners / H. Tornsdorf, M. Tornsdorf.
        p.  cm.
    Includes index.
    ISBN 1-55755-112-X : $18.95
        1. Operating systems (Computers)   2. MS-DOS (Computer file)
I. Tornsdorf, M. (Manfred), 1960-   .  II. Title.  III. Title: DOS
five point zero for beginners.
QA76.76.O63T675  1991                                      91-28272
005.4'46--dc20                                                  CIP
```

Table of Contents

Introduction 1

1. Getting started 5
1.1 What is MS-DOS? 6
1.2 Innovations in MS-DOS 5.0 13
1.3 PC close-up 15
1.4 What you need to use this book 21

2. A journey through your PC 23
2.1 Viewing your PC as a company 23
2.2 Switching on the PC 30
2.3 The MS-DOS Shell screen 31
2.4 In the main building 41
2.5 Room contents 42
2.6 Changing the building directory 48
2.7 A path to a different building 51

3. Your first corporate tasks 55
3.1 Setting up a workroom 55
3.2 Sample boxes 57
3.3 A closer look at the boxes 61
3.4 Renaming and removing boxes 62
3.5 What's in the boxes 64
3.6 Packing slips 66
3.7 Access to tools 67

4. Expanding the company 71
4.1 Outfitting a truck 71
4.2 Using the loading dock 73
4.3 Building the fleet 76

5. Getting organized 77
5.1 Creating new directories 77
5.2 Removing and renaming directories 78
5.3 Planning for organization 79
5.4 Moving quickly between rooms 80

6. MS-DOS Shell extras 83
6.1 Limiting file display 83
6.2 Rearranging files in a directory 84
6.3 Listing all files 85
6.4 Searching for files 86

7.	Keeping things simple	87
7.1	Program items and groups	87
7.2	Groups	88
7.3	Existing programs and groups	90
7.4	Expanding a group	94
7.5	Program parameters	99
7.6	Renaming and deleting program lines	100
7.7	The MS-DOS Shell in practice	101
8.	The command interpreter	103
8.1	Hiring an assistant	103
8.2	How the assistant works	105
8.3	The assistant is quicker	116
8.4	Changing corporate structure	123
8.5	Formatting and copying diskettes	133
8.6	The assistant calls his friends	136
9.	Theft and disasters	143
9.1	What can go wrong	143
9.2	Backing up data to diskettes	145
9.3	In case of emergency	151
9.4	A much quicker way	154
10.	MS-DOS Editor: More than a notepad	157
10.1	A paperless office	157
10.2	Better than a typewriter	160
10.3	Opening and saving finished texts	165
10.4	Cursor movement	169
10.5	MS-DOS Editor keys	170
10.6	MS-DOS Editor menus	171
10.7	Text editing in MS-DOS	173
11.	Hiring experts	175
11.1	Continuing education	175
11.2	Off to the shop	179
11.3	At no extra charge	183
11.4	The boss goes on vacation	188
12.	QBasic	199
12.1	Programs supplied with QBasic	203
12.2	Writing your own programs	205
12.3	Dollars and cents	208

Appendices..**215**
Appendix A: Non-hard drive systems 215
Appendix B: Troubleshooting 217
Appendix C: Glossary...225

Index..**241**

Introduction

Congratulations, you're now the proud owner of a PC. Now you need to learn the basics of your personal computer and MS-DOS. If you've never heard of MS-DOS before, you bought the right book. Using a computer can be confusing to the beginner. Most new users wish they had an experienced friend or teacher to help them through the first steps of using a PC.

This book is here to help. We don't have any more time available than others, but we felt that our own experiences would be helpful to you. This book should put you on the way to knowing your computer more quickly and with less effort, while enjoying the process.

This book deals exclusively with the MS-DOS 5.0 operating system.

Before we start, we want to tell you the structure of this book, and how it will help you feel comfortable when computing:

1. Step by step learning. We start with the simpler aspects of a command, then introduce more complex issues. There will be some repetition, but this happens in any learning process.

2. Reference. After working with us step by step through your new equipment and its capabilities, you will occasionally want to

Introduction

look up something. The alphabetized glossary will help you quickly find command words. The reference section means this book will be of use to you long after you've passed beginner's status.

3. Practical experience. You'll get actual "hands-on" experience working with commands. There's only so much book learning you can do; we show you how to apply your knowledge.

4. We want to save you, as much as possible, from the frustrations that beginners experience.

We've included a section on troubleshooting in case you get discouraged the first time an error message appears on your monitor. You can refer to this section whenever a program or a command doesn't have the desired effect. We included a list of typical beginner's problems and the errors we made when we started. Although the list is incomplete, we hope it will help you make some progress. We're always open to suggestions.

This book deals with PC-DOS from IBM and MS-DOS from Microsoft. Since IBM is a licensee of Microsoft, the differences between both variants are slight. To simplify matters, we only talk about MS-DOS. We'll describe any differences between PC-DOS and MS-DOS at the proper time.

The structure of this book This book considers the "conflicting nature" of MS-DOS. MS-DOS 5.0 allows you two methods of operation: the MS-DOS Shell and the system prompt or command interpreter.

The MS-DOS Shell is a graphically oriented interface for performing DOS commands. The system prompt or command interpreter is a command line on your screen where you type MS-DOS commands from the keyboard. If these terms are new to you, don't panic—we'll describe them later.

Although the MS-DOS Shell the easier and "safer" of the two interfaces, we can't ignore the system prompt. There are a few processes that you cannot access from the MS-DOS Shell. Or you might someday use an older version of DOS that only has the system prompt available.

The structure of this book is problem oriented. We introduce you to basic functions of MS-DOS in the chapters, step by step. We start with

Introduction

	the information you need first and introduce commands as needed in each chapter.
Installation	We hope that your system already has MS-DOS installed. However, if you didn't buy a PC complete with MS-DOS on the hard drive, the installation is easy. Run the SETUP program from Disk 1 of the MS-DOS 5.0 diskettes and follow the instructions.
Chapter 1	This chapter introduces the terms MS-DOS and PC. You'll learn what these terms mean and what they have to do with you. This chapter also tells you what you need to use this book.
Chapter 2	This chapter shows you some elements of PC operation and DOS. These include switching on your PC, starting the MS-DOS Shell, *directories* (contents) and *files*.
Chapter 3	This chapter takes you through the basics of disk files and directories—creating directories, copying files, renaming and deleting files, and starting programs.
Chapter 4	Here, we discuss *diskettes* and how you can manage them. Topics include formatting diskettes and copying files to diskettes.
Chapter 5	This chapter describes directories in more detail. You'll learn how to create, remove, rename and change to directories.
Chapter 6	This chapter explores some of the MS-DOS Shell's more interesting features. These include rearranging files in a directory, sorted file display and searching for files.
Chapter 7	This chapter discusses program management. You'll read about programs and groups, and you'll learn about managing these programs and groups.
Chapter 8	This chapter introduces you to the command interpreter, which you can access through the system prompt mentioned earlier in this introduction. You'll see how the system prompt acts in file management.
Chapter 9	This chapter describes a very serious issue—data security. You'll learn how to copy data in case something goes wrong with DOS or a diskette containing data.
Chapter 10	This chapter discusses the MS-DOS Editor, used for creating and editing text files.

Introduction

Chapter 11   This chapter contains some handy hints for optimizing your operating system. You'll find discussions of *RAM disks* and *cache programs*, as well as the use of *batch files* for automating some tasks.

Chapter 12   This chapter describes the elements of QBasic, the programming language included with DOS 5.0. We'll show you the elements of writing QBasic programs, if you've never written a program before.

Appendices   The Appendices contain valuable extras that weren't described in detail elsewhere in the book.

Icons   Throughout this book you will notice icons, small descriptive pictures, in the left margin. These icons tell you what to do, whether you should read, note important information, or type something on the keyboard.

The reading icon shows that you should read the following section of the text.

The note important information icon points out paragraphs that contain important information.

The computer keyboard entry icon shows that you would be entering something directly at your computer's keyboard.

The mouse entry icon shows that you would be selecting commands or performing operations using the mouse.

We hope you'll have as much fun learning MS-DOS as we had writing about it.

H. and M. Tornsdorf and Staff   June 1991

Editor's Note: We suggest that you read this book in chronological order because the chapters build on one another. This will help you understand the concepts presented in each chapter.

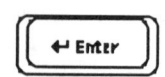

1. Getting started

You probably had the same experience we had some time ago when we became involved with the PC for the first time. We met people who were very familiar with the equipment, while that same equipment was new to us. They often used buzzwords like *operating system*, MS-DOS, *compatibles*, and others. If these terms sound like another language to you, this book is for you—an easy to understand introduction to the world of MS-DOS 5.0 and PCs.

Then again, it's possible that you've already been using a PC for some time. Perhaps you use a word processor to do your business or personal correspondence. Now you find that you need to actually place your word processing files elsewhere or make copies to give to a colleague at work.

For example, you may have found that starting your word processor required entering cryptic phrases like C:\APPS\WORDPROS\WORD5\PROGRAM\WORD. Then someone may have suggested you "make a path" or "create subdirectories" for more organized file storage. When you heard about potential data loss on your hard drive, they told you to do a "total backup". You had the feeling that you simply lacked the important basic knowledge about how a PC works. That's where this book comes in, because it shows you more ways to protect yourself from breakdowns and problems.

If you already have experience in MS-DOS you'll frequently use this book as a reference. At the end of the book you will find an MS-DOS reference that will be useful for a long time.

1. Getting started

1.1 What is MS-DOS?

MS-DOS is the abbreviation for MicroSoft Disk Operating System. Microsoft Corporation manufactures MS-DOS. A disk operating system does just what its name suggests—controls disk operations.

Since the computer is more advanced than the user on what it understands, it serves the inexperienced users as well as computer scientists. Therefore, we must create a bridge of understanding between the PC and us.

Not long ago, the only bridge was a list of commands that the computer understood. These commands are short programs *executed* (run) by the computer.

The *system prompt* was the method by which these commands were entered by the user (more on the system prompt later). The commands were then sent to the *command interpreter*. This command interpreter read and executed the command.

Efforts to make the interaction between the user and computer have been very successful. Special programs called *interfaces* were developed, which displayed the various options and functions of the operating system on the screen. All you have to do is select the function you want. MS-DOS 5.0 has one of these interfaces, which saves you the trouble of committing commands to memory.

The basic functions of the operating system include:

- Testing characters and numbers entered from the keyboard. The operating system determines whether these characters make up a command which must be executed, or data that must be stored (for example, text).

1.1 What is MS-DOS?

- Store data on disk.
- Recall stored data from disk.
- Assign a name to a *file* or set of data on a disk.
- Allow the renaming, copying or deletion of a file.
- Recognize date and time and store this data in files.

As you can see, not much can happen in a computer without an operating system.

One important task that users don't usually notice until something doesn't work is that the operating system makes certain that the individual parts work smoothly. This includes working smoothly by themselves and with other parts. For instance, the operating system sees to it that the keyboard input or mouse movement is visible on the screen. It then makes certain that this movement has an effect on the computer.

Users have much more to do with the special options of the operating system. In MS-DOS 5.0, there are two different variants:

1. A collection of commands that you can type in at the system prompt using the keyboard.
2. A user interface through which you can select certain functions and tasks.

However, users will frequently use one function which appears to make the operating system disappear. This function enables you to start and run applications (programs such as word processors), then disappears for the duration of the work. The operating system remains in the background until you exit the application properly.

Before continuing, we should take a look at Microsoft. This corporation manufactures computer programs and operating systems, including MS-DOS. In August of 1981, IBM (International Business Machines) introduced the first IBM PC. This computer was intended for use by an individual (hence the PC, for Personal Computer). IBM needed an operating system for the new computer, and favored a proposal written by Microsoft Corporation.

Much has happened since 1981. Perhaps you've wondered about the strange numbers that appear after MS-DOS. For example, right now

1. Getting started

the current number is 5.0. These numbers are the version numbers. Normally, higher version numbers refer to newer versions of MS-DOS.

In a way, you could compare it to the number of editions of a book. A higher edition number refers to a newer version of the book. However, in the book publishing world there are sometimes new editions that have not been revised. This is seldom the case with operating systems. A new version of an operating system is released only when updates are required.

In 1984, Microsoft released Versions 3.0 and 3.1 of MS-DOS. They were capable of operating the new, bigger brother of the PC, the AT (see the glossary). The AT (Advanced Technology) features a more powerful microprocessor, a higher processing speed in most cases, greater memory capacity, and higher disk storage capacity.

MS-DOS 3.3 was the standard for a long time. Even today, with the latest version, MS-DOS 5.0, PCs are still sold with earlier versions of MS-DOS.

With the arrival of MS-DOS's successor, the new OS/2 operating system, many people thought it meant the end of MS-DOS. However, OS/2 placed such high demands on the PC system that it was often too expensive to use.

Therefore, in 1988 yet another new MS-DOS version appeared: MS-DOS 4.0. This new DOS worked better with hard drives over 32 *Meg* (megabytes) and with memory over 640K.

For the first time, MS-DOS had a new user interface, the MS-DOS Shell, which made it much easier to operate a PC in DOS. However, there were also some drawbacks to this new version (for example, less memory available for working with application and programs), which often resulted in some rather difficult problems.

That's why MS-DOS 4.0 wasn't a big success. Most PCs were still sold with MS-DOS 3.3. Also, it appeared that development was leaning more toward Windows (a graphical user interface sold by Microsoft, with some good selling points). Then came another very positive surprise:

After the competition, Digital Research, had developed an impressive competitor to MS-DOS (DR DOS 5.0), Microsoft found it necessary to

1.1 What is MS-DOS?

further improve MS-DOS. In mid-1991 MS-DOS 5.0 became available.

If you're interested in an overview of the new version's options (perhaps because you've worked with an older version and are already familiar with some expressions and features), refer to Section 1.2. However, if you're still not quite sure what MS-DOS actually is, we would rather give you a few more basic terms and characteristics here first.

We provided this brief history of MS-DOS to show you both its evolution and that more than one version of DOS exists. There's a second and even more important reason. You should know the following important information:

- You cannot intermix versions of DOS. That is, if you boot your computer with DOS Version 5.0, this is the version of DOS you will use until you switch off your computer.

- MS-DOS is *upwardly compatible*. This means that all applications and programs which ran under DOS 3.3 should also run with DOS 5.0. The other way doesn't hold true, however.

In short, MS-DOS is an operating system. This operating system gives the computer basic instructions about disk and file management and allows communication between the computer and user.

In the beginning, it's difficult for a user to understand the basic capabilities of an operating system completely. Since this understanding has an effect on how you use your computer most effectively, we want to name the most important characteristics. Then we can briefly describe the information we already mentioned.

An operating system makes the necessary options and functions available for operating the computer. For example, it checks the parts of the computer to determine whether they are in working order. If any serious problems are present, the operating system may refuse to run. There are certain basic settings that you only do once, or that you do by hand. Setting the current date and time and selecting the color of the screen are a few of these basic settings.

Other applications, such as a word processor, perform the actual work. However, these applications work only because the operating system provides them with a portion of the computer's brain (random access memory or RAM), as well as enabling them to start and run. Aside

1. Getting started

from that, the applications have to follow the operating system rules exactly, even if the user doesn't directly see this.

You can recognize the MS-DOS files by their short filenames. For instance, a letter to a life insurance company—no matter what word processing application you use—can only be called LIFEINS1.DOC or something similar. There's no file called "First letter to life insurance company."

For the user, however, an operating system is most important for managing memory. You use MS-DOS to prepare storage media, find, copy, rename, delete files, etc.

An operating system is not directly responsible for the actual work you perform. It's not there to write texts, manage addresses, or search for the largest possible prime numbers. Other applications were developed for these purposes.

Probably the clearest way to summarize this characteristic is this: You can't operate a PC without an operating system. The computer would refuse to run a short time after you switched it on. Even with an operating system, you won't have many tools to work with. You can't really perform any practical work with your PC until you install the proper applications, such as a word processor or a database.

When you start an application, it's important that MS-DOS give it complete control. MS-DOS doesn't regain control until you exit the application.

The limitations and starting point of the operating system are the user's ideas or tasks. With the help of the operating system, you start the PC and load the application that you need for the task. Although the operating system seems to disappear, the application is constantly referring to it. A user may believe that only the word processor is functioning.

After you have the finished product, you ordinarily quit the application, restoring control to the operating system. For example, you could then use the operating system to copy your letter to a diskette.

The MS-DOS Shell and the system prompt

Now we want to describe the differences between the system prompt and the graphical user interface (MS-DOS Shell). We mentioned the system prompt earlier. If you ran a PC with an older version of MS-DOS, the screen would appear similar to the following:

1.1 What is MS-DOS?

```
C:\>
```

The system prompt and the MS-DOS Shell are two different views of the same screen. Both enable you to input commands and work with MS-DOS. However, the two are very different from each other. Once again, a brief look at history may help us better understand.

Earlier, the only way you could work with a computer was to give it commands that it understood. For example, if you wanted to see the contents of the current directory you had to know the DIR command, to copy a file from the hard drive to a diskette you had to put together COPY C:FILENAME.EXT A:. Learning MS-DOS was nothing more than a question of learning vocabulary.

Apple Computer Inc. had taken an entirely different route. They had discovered (or at least helped) the idea of an *intuitive user interface*. The Apple Macintosh's operating system displayed the computer as a desk with folders and pictures. This interface offers objects and tools that are easy to understand and control.

You use a *mouse* to work with these objects and tools. Named for its size and tail-like cable, the mouse moves a *pointer* across the screen. You use this mouse pointer to select objects and choose from different options.

Earlier we mentioned a system prompt command—COPY C:FILENAME.EXT A:. With the simple user interface of the Apple, all you do is move the mouse pointer onto the file with the mouse, press and hold the mouse button, and move it to a different area (for example, a picture of a disk drive).

When Microsoft Corporation released the MS-DOS Shell with MS-DOS 4.0, learning MS-DOS became easier. Beginning with the version we describe in this book, learning MS-DOS is no longer a problem.

The MS-DOS Shell of MS-DOS 5.0 displays PC data in an easily understood manner. You can use commands from existing lists or use the keyboard or mouse to change the data (such as, copy, delete, etc.).

The following illustration shows the differences between the two forms of the operating system:

1. Getting started

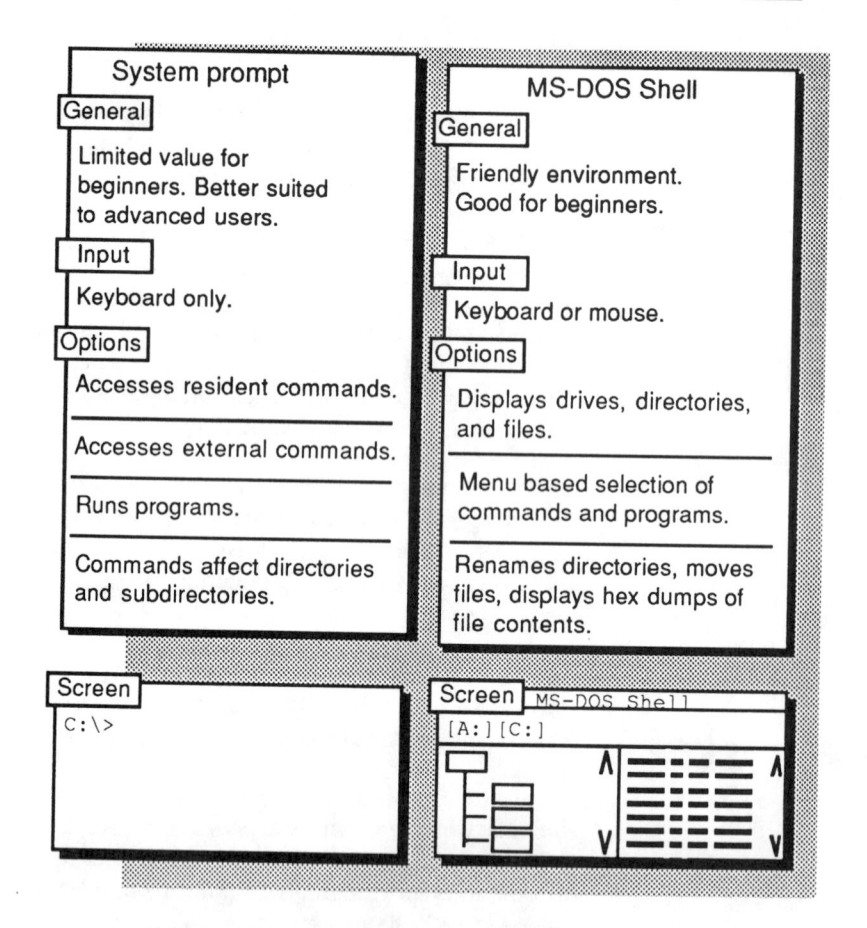

System prompt

General
Limited value for beginners. Better suited to advanced users.

Input
Keyboard only.

Options
Accesses resident commands.

Accesses external commands.

Runs programs.

Commands affect directories and subdirectories.

Screen
`C:\>`

MS-DOS Shell

General
Friendly environment.
Good for beginners.

Input
Keyboard or mouse.

Options
Displays drives, directories, and files.

Menu based selection of commands and programs.

Renames directories, moves files, displays hex dumps of file contents.

Screen
MS-DOS Shell
[A:] [C:]

The system prompt and the MS-DOS Shell

On the left, you see the system prompt. You type in commands after this prompt. The PC either responds with a message that it is executing the command or displays an error message.

On the right you see the same action with the MS-DOS Shell. You don't need to know any special command words. All you need to know is how to select a file, a menu, and various options.

We'll describe the MS-DOS Shell and the system prompt later.

1.2 Innovations in MS-DOS 5.0

If you are already familiar with a different version of MS-DOS (for example, 3.3 or 4.0), then we'd like to give you a short overview of the most important innovations in MS-DOS 5.0.

Easy installation

Installation is extremely simple. MS-DOS 5.0 can automatically back up all the important data of the hard drive to a backup diskette. This means you can put data back the way they were before installation if necessary.

Also, instead of overwriting the existing version of DOS, MS-DOS 5.0 copies it to a special directory. This guarantees a maximum amount of security.

All you need to know about installing MS-DOS 5.0 is one word: SETUP. Running the SETUP program from Disk 1 of the MS-DOS 5.0 diskettes takes you step by step through installation.

The MS-DOS Shell

You can set up the MS-DOS Shell during installation to start automatically in the program list area and file list area of the Shell.

There are many other improvements to the new MS-DOS Shell. Besides colors, you can now set different screen displays. It's easier to arrange different tasks, since you can create new groups for programs. This allows you to create special "default screens" that make your work on the PC a lot easier.

Along with the program list area, there is also the file list area which you use to manage your files and directories. It displays the directory tree on the left and the files of a particular directory on the right. You can divide the screen into two halves with a directory tree and file display in each half. This makes processes, such as copying or moving files, especially easy.

You can also assign file extensions to programs and have the program automatically start when you select a file with the program's extension. Ordinarily the file list area starts the DOS Editor automatically when you open text files, but you could change this and use a word processor such as Microsoft Word 5.5.

In the file list area, a "+" next to a directory in the directory tree shows that the directory contains subdirectories. You can also display these

1. Getting started

subdirectories by selecting them with the mouse. Clicking the parent directory causes the subdirectories to disappear again. If you don't have a mouse, you can also move the highlight to the directory with the arrow keys and use the [+] and [-] keys.

QBasic

MS-DOS 5.0 includes QBasic, an easier version of Microsoft QuickBASIC. Since QBasic's editor supports a mouse, program development is fairly easy.

New full screen editor

If you've worked with earlier versions of MS-DOS, you may have had experience with EDLIN, the line editor included with those versions of DOS. The MS-DOS Editor EDIT is a full screen editor that's included with MS-DOS 5.0.

Help

MS-DOS commands now have an integrated Help screen that you activate from the system prompt by entering the command and the /? *switch*. There is also a new HELP command which displays a list of all the commands with brief explanations of their functions. Help is available for *external* commands (those stored on disk) and *resident* commands (those commands stored in the command interpreter).

MS-DOS 5.0 is "more"

A series of new commands increases the performance of MS-DOS 5.0: You can use UNFORMAT to return a hard drive that you accidentally formatted back to its old status. Use SETVER to trick programs into thinking they're running on a different version of DOS. SETVER has a list stored in the MSDOS.SYS system file. Any changes you make don't go into effect until you reboot the computer. Several programs are already included in this list. You can display this list by typing SETVER without any parameters.

The DOSKEY command lets you redisplay and edit commands previously typed in. DOSKEY also has a built-in language that you can use to assign extensive command sequences to a new command. Microsoft refers to these command sequences as *macros*.

One bigadvantage over similar utility programs is if you assign the name of an internal MS-DOS command, such as DIR, to a macro, the macro is called first. It then replaces the original command with its own version. This allows you to create your own "personal" DOS.

MS-DOS 5.0 is "less"

Due to the HIMEM.SYS extended memory manager, MS-DOS uses the first 64K of extended memory (called High Memory). This provides programs with about 50K of additional RAM. Starting MS-DOS without a driver program leaves about 620K of memory for programs.

1.3 PC close-up

Let's examine our equipment more closely. This examination must be kept generalized. Many PC compatible computers are on the market, in many different configurations, so we can't single out one particular model. However, most of the descriptions in this section apply to your PC.

What is a PC?

The terms PC and personal computer once applied to machines that we now call the *home computer*. Some home computers today actually pack more power and features than the original 1981 IBM PC. Today, PC refers to IBM and IBM compatible computer systems used by individuals, either at home or in the workplace.

Compatibility is the important distinction between the home computer and the PC. This means that the computer's basic appearance and brand name are unimportant. A PC compatible can be manufactured by a small company in Minneapolis or a huge Asian conglomerate. The main requirement of a PC compatible is that it be able to execute all the programs and applications that execute on a true IBM PC. Slight differences occur from computer to computer, which may improve on the genuine IBM product. These same differences may mean that some software won't run on some compatibles.

In the meantime, there are some tremendous differences in performance and equipment. For example, you could be talking about a PC/XT. A PC/XT has an 8088 or 8086 microprocessor. The microprocessor is a micro chip that performs the actual data processing.

Intel manufactures these microprocessors and uses numbers to identify them. Perhaps you have an AT or 286 with an 80286 processor (286s have been available since 1984). Since then there have been some changes in the way you work with diskettes, the date and time, etc. Or you might have a 386 or 486 (80386 or 80486).

Fortunately, these differences won't have any effect on the information we desscribe. All these microprocessors work according to the same standard and all use MS-DOS. To make it easier, we will always talk about the "PC" in general, pointing out the little differences that result from different performance capacities.

1. Getting started

So let's remember that it doesn't matter what your computer looks like. The deciding factor is that it is IBM compatible and uses MS-DOS as its operating system. That means that you can essentially run any application or program on it that would also run on an IBM PC. And you have a wide variety of working options available.

However, in the past there have been small restrictions in specific cases. If you want to be 100% safe, ask questions before buying. Make certain your computer includes a guarantee. In any case, a PC by our definition uses the MS-DOS operating system and can process data created by other compatible PCs.

Let's look at the individual parts of the system. We'll describe each part as non-technical and as general as possible.

The computer itself

The basis of a PC system is a metal or plastic case about the size of a drawer. Usually this case has one or more horizontal slots in front of it. The front of your PC may also include different lights. These include a power light to tell you the PC is on. Addtional lights may be present next to large horizontal slots.

These horizontal slots are *disk drives*, designed to accept diskettes. Another form of disk drive is the *hard drive*. This is a self-contained (sometimes called fixed or non-removable) disk. The following illustration shows the front of a typical desktop PC:

PC case and drives

1.3 PC close-up

At the upper-left corner you should see two LED displays. This displays show that the computer is ready to operate and that MS-DOS is accessing the hard drive.

Below the LED displays is another light which shows the current clock frequency. This tells us how fast the computer is working.

Then comes an on/off switch, used for switching the computer on and off. Frequently the same switch also switches on the monitor.To the right of this switch is a key switch for locking the keyboard, preventing unauthorized use of the computer.

You can use the switch to the right of the key switch to change the processing speed of the PC. The reset button restarts the computer.

On the far right you see two disk drives, one in the older 5-1/4" format and one in the more modern 3-1/2" format. The hard drive underneath is inaccessible from the outside.

The case contains the computer itself. This consists of a set of electronic circuit boards which hold several *chips* (black rectangular components). These chips include the circuitry which drives the PC, *memory* (electronic storage areas) and other items.

Data storage

The horizontal slot or slots on the front of the case are important to us. These are the doors to the *disk drives*, which are used for reading and writing data from and to *diskettes*. These disk drives handle two different sizes: 5-1/4" and 3-1/2". These diskettes and disk handling are discussed below.

AT 286, 386, and 486 disk drives can fit two to three times as much data on a diskette as their XT counterparts.

You will need some blank diskettes for your work with this book. This is especially true in the sections on performing hard drive backups. Remember to have extra diskettes available in advance. If you were working through a part of the book and didn't have any diskettes, you wouldn't be able to finish some of the examples.

Hard drives are becoming more popular. Usually, they're mounted inside the computer case. Unlike diskettes, hard drives can store far more information. However, hard drives cannot be exchanged, are more expensive, and are sensitive to shock and other outside influences.

1. Getting started

The hard drive is the only choice for storing larger amounts of data. The average hard drive holds 20 *Meg* (megabytes)—over 20 million characters, or about 10,000 typewritten pages.

The monitor

Your computer system could not effectively read, store, or process data without the ability to display that data. PCs use monitors for data display. The monitor, which is often *monochrome* (single-color, usually amber or green), normally sits on top of the PC case. The colors vary—the monitor could be color, amber, green or paper-white.

The printer

Another method of displaying data is to use a printer. Although a printer is not a necessity, you'll find very few PCs without printers. They're useful for printing letters, graphics, program listings, disk directories, and much more.

The keyboard

The keyboard lets you enter (type) data. The PC keyboard looks basically like a typewriter keyboard, but has a few more keys. The keyboard arrangement can differ from manufacturer to manufacturer.

The following illustration shows a typical PC keyboard:

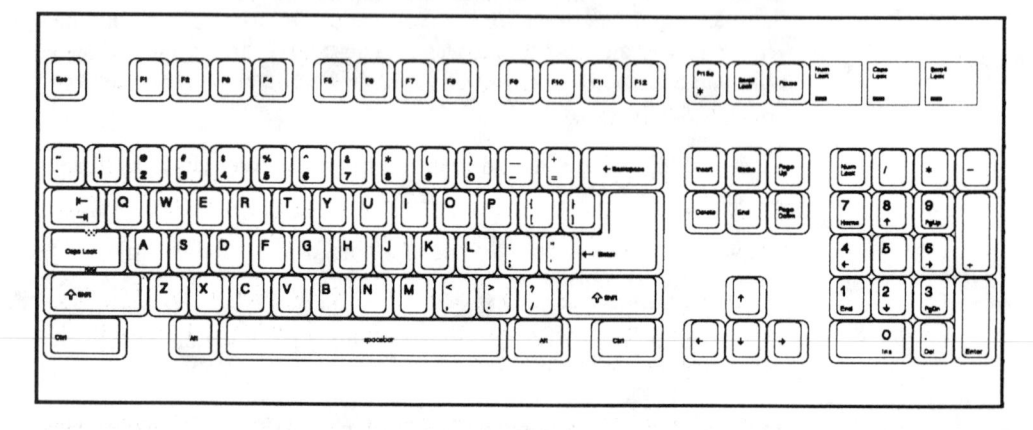

We use a special notation to help distinguish keys from regular text. When we talk about a key, we display a key as it might look on your keyboard. For example, ③ represents the key with the number 3 embossed on it.

18

1.3 PC close-up

Function keys The most obvious difference from a typewriter is the set of keys numbered from [F1] to [F10]. These *function keys* perform different functions, depending on the application in use on the computer.

Keypad Most keyboards include a square block of numbered keys. This block, or *numeric keypad*, allow fast number entry, similar to a calculator keyboard. Similar to the function keys, how the numeric keypad is used varies between programs and applications.

Arrow keys Some of these numbered keys also have arrows embossed on them, with each arrow pointing in a different direction (usually the [8], [4], [6] and [2] keys). These are the *arrow keys* or *cursor keys*, which let you move the *cursor* in certain programs. This cursor marks the current location on the screen. If you press a key, a character appears at the current cursor location.

[Enter] The [Enter], [Return] or [←] key is the one you'll probably use most often. Pressing this key on a typewriter advances the paper to the next line. This also occurs in some PC programs. However, the primary function of the [Enter] key is data entry. That is, the [Enter] key tells the computer to store or execute the text entered up to the [Enter] key. Although the terms [Enter] and [Return] are used interchangeably, we use [Enter].

[Ctrl] The [Ctrl] key is an abbreviation for Control. It helps send *control characters*, used in telecommunication, text editing and other features. DOS uses the [Ctrl] key frequently, as you'll soon see.

[Alt] The other key is the [Alt] key, short for Alternate. Like [Ctrl], the [Alt] key is used with other keys to produce many additional commands and inputs (more on this later).

[Esc] In the top left-corner of the keyboard or on the numeric keypad, note the [Esc] key. Many programs and applications (such as the MS-DOS Shell) use the [Esc] key to cancel commands or options.

You will use other keys in the MS-DOS Shell, such as the [Tab] key, which may appear as [⇥] on your keyboard. This key is located on the left side of the keyboard.

Your keyboard or computer user manuals may use different names than what we use in this book. The following chart shows how the names for the common keys may appear on your keyboard and in this book:

1. Getting started

Keys	Keys in this book	On other computers
Alt	Alt	ALT
1/End or End	End	END
7/Home or Home	Home	HOME
Ctrl	Ctrl	CTRL, CONT
./Del or Delete	Del	DEL, DELETE
0/Ins or Insert	Ins	INS, INSERT
Enter	Enter	RETURN, ENTER
Esc	Esc	Escape, ESCAPE, ESC
← or ← Backspace	Backspace	BACK
⇧ or ⇧ Shift	Shift	Shift, SHIFT
Tab or Tab	Tab	TAB
9/PgUp or Page Up	PgUp	Page Up
3/PgDn or Page Down	PgDn	Page Down

The mouse

A *mouse* is a small box connected to the PC through a cable. Mice control cursor movement on the screen. An average mouse has a ball poking out underneath it. When you place the mouse on a table with the ball touching the table top and you move the mouse, the *mouse pointer* moves on the monitor screen. Many programs support the mouse, including the MS-DOS Shell.

The mouse requires a special program, called a mouse driver, before you can use it. The mouse driver tells MS-DOS that you're using a mouse. It's usually provided with the mouse.

1.4 What you need to use this book

After explaining some of the basics, we want briefly to review the prerequisites for working with this book.

PC with a hard drive

We'll assume that you have a PC with a hard drive and a disk drive. Most of the descriptions in this book refer to or require at least a hard drive. This is especially true with our descriptions of commands.

If you own a PC with two disk drives, but no hard drive, please refer to the Appendix where we describe the most important differences and special features.

By the way, it doesn't matter whether you have a PC/XT, an AT, or a 386. The only effect this will have on our examples is whether the computer reacts to your commands and instructions in a half or a tenth of a second.

Knowledge of possible problems

PC is the abbreviation for personal computer and quite often means that someone has a "personal" computer. Therefore, many users believe they can do what he/she wants with it. However, this is not always the case.

Perhaps you want to learn on a friend's computer. Or you are practicing on a company computer at your place of employment. In both cases the idea of a personal computer no longer applies, and you must be very careful with the computer. This doesn't just apply to the hardware, but also to changes you make to data stored on the computer.

Ask the owner or person in charge of the computer what to try and what to watch out for. One good method is to practice and experiment on a working diskette instead of the computer hard drive. Not too much can happen then.

Even more frequently, another situation arises: Many small companies or freelancers purchased a PC with software and have been using this system for a long time. Now they want to use the PC for other tasks as well, or become more familiar with the existing options. If this applies to you, then you also must be very careful with the computer, because you certainly can't take the liberty of endangering what computer capacity you've been using up until now.

21

1. Getting started

Once again, it's a good idea to take your first steps and do your experiments on a diskette, not the hard drive. It's also a good idea to back up your data. Most of the complete packages installed can transfer the data to diskettes so you can preserve the status. Complete the examples and commands only if you are certain that no damage will occur.

MS-DOS 5.0 installed MS-DOS 5.0 comes on several diskettes (depending on the computer system) that you cannot use directly. If you bought a computer that doesn't have MS-DOS 5.0 installed, then you must install the diskettes. Installing means copying the data and programs to the hard drive of the computer and simultaneously "unpacking" them. The data are stored on the diskettes in a format that saves space, but is not suitable for direct use. Running the SETUP program on disk 1 takes you step by step through installation.

Solving problems We've included some solutions to problems that may happen to the new MS-DOS user.

2. A journey through your PC

Do you have MS-DOS 5.0 installed on a working PC system? If you do, then we're ready to start. This section includes:

- How to switch on and start the PC.

- How to make sure that you end up in the MS-DOS Shell.

- What a PC consists of, or better yet: How a PC actually stores data (texts, addresses, numbers) and how to tell them apart.

- How data are kept in special areas (directories) and how to get to these different areas and drives.

If this is your first time in front of a PC, you may not recognize some of the terminology used here. That's why we added a short section with an illustration of the structure and important basic concepts surrounding a PC.

If you are familiar with the PC and its terminology, you can still skim over this section. We'll return to some of the elements of the illustration as we go along until there are no longer any problems understanding.

2.1 Viewing your PC as a company

In the following sections we will familiarize you with the most important basic concepts of MS-DOS. Among these are storage medium, directory, file, program, and many others. These concepts usually give beginners the most trouble.

Instead of giving you definitions here, we're going to explain important elements of a PC system using the example of a company.

So let's consider your purchase of a PC as the PersComp company. This company, consisting of a big factory, is concerned with manufacturing computers. The best way to get acquainted with the company is to look at the blueprints and go on a tour their headquarters.

The following illustration shows how MS-DOS processes data and keeps order:

2. A journey through your PC

Rooms
(subdirectories)

Areas
(directories)

Main office
(root directory)

Production area
(chips)

Loading dock
(disk drive)

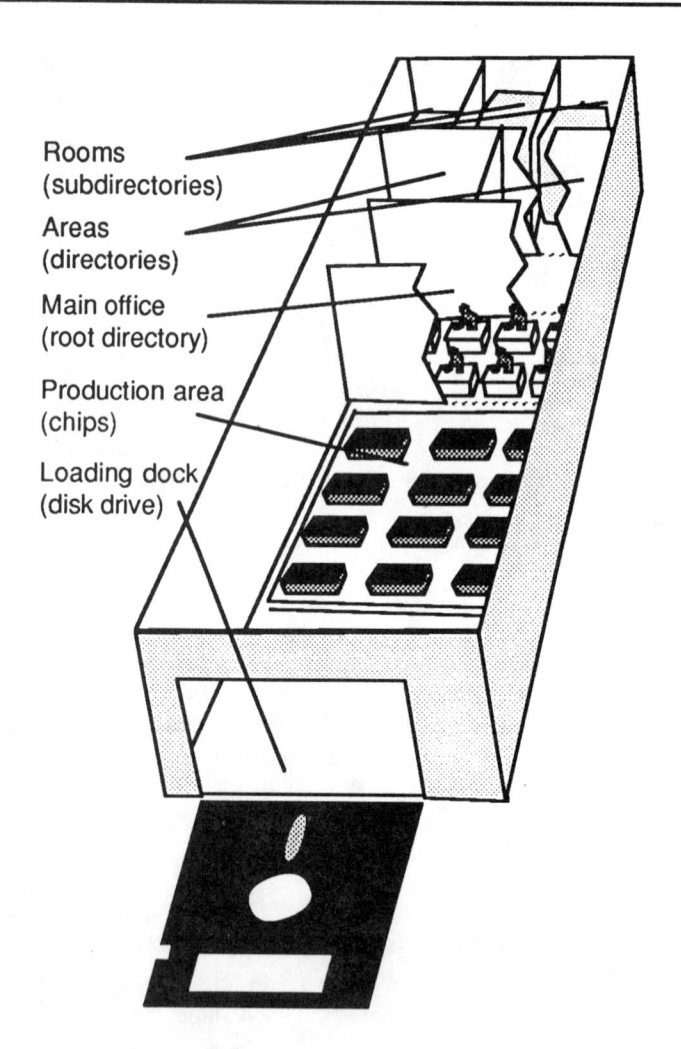

The PC as a company - how MS-DOS keeps organized

We can compare how a computer processes data to how a factory that processes its products. For example, most factories use warehouses to store material. Likewise, the hard drive in a computer system can be considered a warehouse.

Since the production area contains the machinery necessary to assemble the final product, it's the center of the factory. The electronic parts inside your PC correspond to these machines. The machines in the factory require raw material to process into finished products. The raw material in a computer system refer to the data.

2.1 Viewing your PC as a company

Since data always come as a group, rather than single parts, think of data being stored in a box. The machine opens the box, changes the contents and repacks it. Now, where do the data boxes come from, and where do they go? There are two possibilities:

- The data boxes could come from the outside. A factory must have a loading dock so material is delivered and shipped quickly. In our illustration, the disk drive acts as a loading dock so data are transported easily and quickly in and out of the computer. For a factory, a truck delivers materials to a loading dock. In a computer system, a single diskette can deliver data to the disk drive.

    Similar to a delivery company driving a truck to a loading dock, you would insert a diskette in the slot of the disk drive. Then the boxes of data are taken to the production area and processed. Then you load the boxes back on the same truck and store them somewhere outside of the factory (in a diskette storage case). You could also bring them to another partner who continues processing the data.

- Another possibility would be to keep many data boxes in a large hall right next to the production area. A data box is taken from the warehouse to the production area, processed there and returned. Such a warehouse corresponds to the hard drive of a PC system.

Because materials can be easily misplaced in a big warehouse, a factory must use a method to keep losses to a minimum.

PersComp divides their warehouse into different areas. For example, they store monitors, keyboards, printers, etc. in separate areas of the warehouse.

However, even these subdivisions aren't enough. It would be inefficient to store paper-white monitors, amber monitors, and color monitors in the same area. These single areas must be further divided into smaller rooms. Now things are in order.

If necessary, you can partition these rooms even further. Place the simple color monitors in the front of the room while keeping the more expensive monitors in the back of the room.

2. A journey through your PC

☞ The only other important item is to have a layout map or building directory. The best place for this is in front, right at the entrance. Otherwise you wouldn't know where to find it. It should be shaped like a tree, because the tree makes the path descriptions to the different areas easy to understand.

The following illustration shows the division of a hard drive based on the example of a company that manufactures computers and accessories:

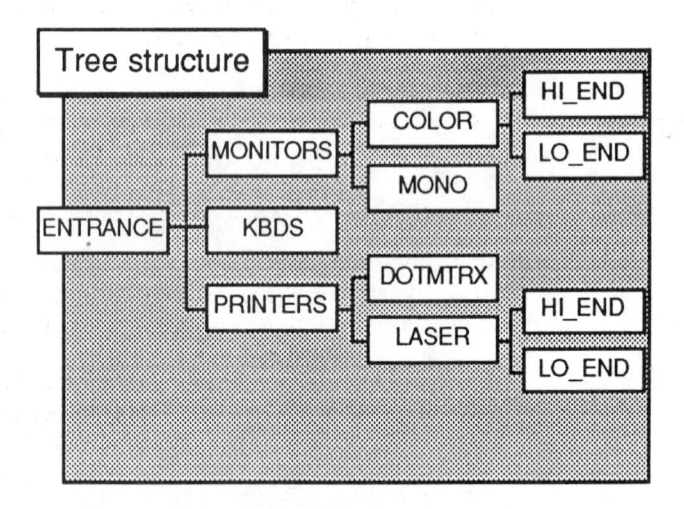

```
Tree structure
                              ┌─ HI_END
                   ┌─ COLOR ──┤
          ┌ MONITORS ─┤       └─ LO_END
          │        └─ MONO
ENTRANCE ─┼ KBDS
          │            ┌─ DOTMTRX
          └ PRINTERS ──┤       ┌─ HI_END
                       └─ LASER┤
                               └─ LO_END
```

Hard drive division into a tree structure

Notice that everything is displayed in the shape of a tree. Therefore you can easily recognize the general division into the main room, the areas for monitors, keyboards, system cases, and their subdivisions.

The starting point is the entrance (left side of the illustration). It represents the root of the tree.

From the root, the illustration goes to the individual areas (MONITORS, KBDS or keyboards, and PRINTERS). From there, the plan branches into rooms (for MONOchrome monitors, COLOR monitors etc.) and sub-rooms (for LO_END or inexpensive and HI_END or expensive color monitors).

If you want to make clear where a certain box is located, you can specify a "path" description (a set of directions):

```
- Go from the main office of the warehouse
- to the "MONITORS" area,
```

2.1 Viewing your PC as a company

- then to the "COLOR" room
- then to the "HI_END" partition.
- Then please bring back the "MULTSYNC" box.

A shorter, more precise path specification would look like:

\MONITORS\COLORS\HI_END\MULTSYNC

Now we'll describe the technical terms for the single components so you can start understanding them:

The production department corresponds to the computer/processor with its "volatile" RAM. When you turn off the lights in the factory, the production area has to be free of data boxes. If not, everything is lost or mixed up. This holds true for the computer. All the data that are still in this area when you switch off the computer are irretrievably lost.

As mentioned earlier, the warehouse corresponds to the hard drive. Material (data) stored in the warehouse (disk drive) are protected even after you turn off the lights (switch off the computer).

The office with the building directory corresponds to the root directory. The most important element is the building directory. There can also be some important boxes (i.e., data groups) here such as the office control computer and a fire extinguisher. Since everything must be within easy reach, it is located right after the entrance.

The individual areas (for monitors, keyboards, etc.) are called *directories*. So if there is a special directory for texts on a hard drive, it only means there is a special area where all the boxes of text are located. If it's a question of the first subdirectory, then it means you can get there directly from the root directory. So, it's right after the entrance. If there are more directories branching off from a subdirectory, these are classified as subdirectories or sub-subdirectories.

What is important to know is the exact location of a directory. A path specification describing the exact path you take from the root directory (office) to get to the target directory. This also makes it clear that these directories themselves are only rooms. The processor, the machines, can't do anything with them directly. The processor works with the boxes of material, referred to as *files* in computer language. The files come either from the central warehouse (hard drive) or are delivered by trucks (diskettes).

In concluding our factory example, let's go into a little more detail about the data boxes. You distinguish between two basic types:

27

2. A journey through your PC

There are the actual data boxes for one. You might be talking about a letter, a statistical table, a graphic or a collection of addresses. They all have one item in common; they're finished products that you must create.

Applications are responsible for creating these data products. The term *programs* is also used instead of applications. We'll use applications when referring to word processors such as Microsoft Word, spreadsheets such as Microsoft Multiplan, graphic programs like PC Paintbrush, and databases like dBASE IV. You use these applications to create the finished product. Applications let users edit their finished products, such as adding addresses, revising a letter and reprinting it, etc. So in our example, along with data boxes (letters, tables etc.), there are also application boxes.

Both types of boxes have much in common. The names have the same structure. The "first name" can be up to eight characters in length. This name is followed by a period which is followed by a "last name". The last name can be as long as three characters in length.

For example, WORD.EXE is an application file and the main part of the word processor Microsoft Word. The last name after the period shows that this is an application file. All documents created with WORD have eight characters for first names and a last name of DOC. INSUR1.DOC, INSUR2.DOC, INSUR3.DOC etc. could be different letters to your insurance company, while the numbers would help you tell which letter was which. To be 100% accurate you would have to specify the path along with the filename (i.e., the description of the distance from the entrance to the data box). In our example using Word, the description could look like this:

```
C:\APPS\WORD\WORD.EXE
```

This tells us the WORD.EXE file is in warehouse C. From there, you would go to the APPS (for application) area and then to the WORD sub-area. You could put your letters to your insurance company in the PERSONAL sub-area of the TEXTS area. This area could be a sub-sub-area called INSUR. Here's the complete name:

```
C:\TEXTS\PERSONAL\INSUR\INSUR1.DOC
```

Don't worry about this long string of words. As a rule it's enough to specify the filename itself or just click it (more on this later).

There's one more thing data files and application files have in common. In both cases, the size of the file, the date and time the file was created, or the time of the last save appear with the filename. The following illustration shows two areas of a hard drive:

2.1 Viewing your PC as a company

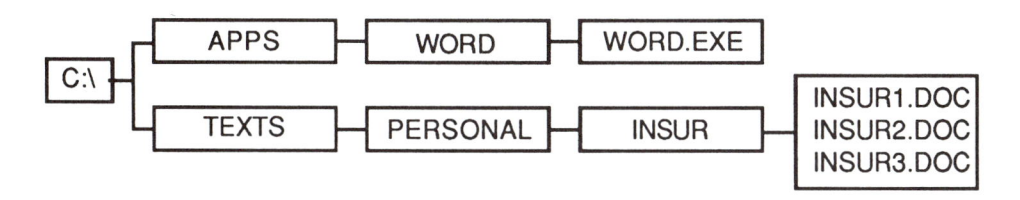

```
C:\ ─┬─ APPS ─── WORD ─── WORD.EXE
     │                              ┌─ INSUR1.DOC
     └─ TEXTS ── PERSONAL ── INSUR ─┼─ INSUR2.DOC
                                    └─ INSUR3.DOC
```

Data and program files

The upper set of directories reserves space for a program (in this case, WORD.EXE). This area contains all the data needed by Microsoft Word, from the program itself to auxiliary files, dictionaries, etc.

The lower set of directories reserves space for documents created by Word. The person who is using the word processor determines what this area looks like and what it will contain.

You also use the same procedure for copying, deleting, renaming, etc., program files and data files. The main difference is that, unlike data files, you cannot change the contents of program files.

2. A journey through your PC

2.2 Switching on the PC

You can now *power-up* (switch on) your computer. If possible, switch on the monitor first—this is usually better for the system. Now switch on the computer.

The monitor displays a few lines of text describing the manufacturer of the device's internal system. Our screen displays the following information (yours may look different):

```
Phoenix ROM BIOS Ver 2.27
Copyright (c) 1984,1985,1986 Phoenix Technologies Ltd
All Rights Reserved
YANGTECH.INC
```

At some point the computer may count quickly through a set of numbers. This *memory test* checks to see how much memory (electronic workspace) is available. Usually this number is between 256K and 640K. One K, or kilobyte, equals 1,024 bytes. One byte equals one character.

If the system prompt (a C or an A with some other characters) appears instead of the MS-DOS Shell, then you must start the MS-DOS Shell from the system prompt. Type DOSSHELL on the keyboard and press the (Enter) key. The MS-DOS Shell should now appear.

We can actually start working now and take a closer look at the information displayed on the screen. However, if you get an error message, it could be for one of the following reasons.

- You may not have installed the operating system on your computer. Run the SETUP program from Disk 1 of your MS-DOS 5.0 diskettes and follow the instructions displayed on the screen.

- You can receive an error message even if MS-DOS is installed. If there is a diskette in your drive, remove it and press any key.

- If you didn't install the operating system on your hard drive, then you have to insert the start diskette in your disk drive when you start your computer. Otherwise you get an error message. Then insert the diskette labelled MS-DOS Shell or SHELL in the drive, type DOSSHELL and press the (Enter) key. The MS-DOS Shell starts and the screen appears.

2.3 The MS-DOS Shell screen

Before we can take a look at everything in the computer, we have to first understand the information displayed on the MS-DOS Shell screen.

Cursor and work area

After you start your PC (or after you call the MS-DOS Shell), a new screen is displayed. This screen has a window (closed area on the screen) in the middle. This window contains information about the hard drive or diskette that is important to the user (Reading Disk Information...).

Below this line are two more lines telling you how many files (data or application boxes) and directories (rooms in the warehouse) the MS-DOS Shell is reading. The details are not important right now: For now, we could say the MS-DOS Shell is taking inventory of available materials.

```
Reading Disk Information . . .
Files Read:            366
Directories Read:       12
```

The MS-DOS Shell reading information

The window disappear when the MS-DOS Shell is finished reading disk information. The screen displays the information (similar to the illustration above). In the following section we'll describe this information in more detail.

Let's familiarize ourselves with the entire MS-DOS Shell screen:

```
                    MS-DOS Shell
File Options View Tree Help
```

Title bar and menu bar

Title bar

At the top of the screen is a *title bar*. It shows the title (subject) of the area (such as **MS-DOS Shell**). Below the title bar is a *menu bar* with five menus (**File**, **Options**, **View**, **Tree**, and **Help**). We'll describe these menus in more detail later.

31

2. A journey through your PC

It's possible that because **Tree** is missing, you may have only four menus in the menu bar. The screen is divided into different work areas. The appearance of the MS-DOS Shell can change depending on which one you use.

Drive icons The letter of the current drive appears under the menu bar. In PC language. A drive can either be a PC warehouse (hard drive) or a loading dock (disk drive). The current drive is from where you start your PC. Usually it's the hard drive, labelled C:\

The MS-DOS Shell displays all the available drives as icons with letters directly underneath. The letter A is usually displayed along with C. If any other letters appear, for example B, then this represents a second disk drive. Any letters above C show that the computer has additional hard drives.

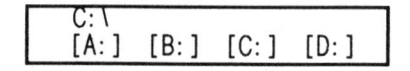

```
C:\
[A:]  [B:]  [C:]  [D:]
```

Drive icons

File list area and Directory Tree area The center of the MS-DOS Shell screen displays the contents of a hard drive or diskette (in our case, drive C:). In the left half of the screen you will find the Directory Tree area. You can see the different directories (rooms) into which the diskette or hard drive is divided. Either square brackets [] or a folder icon precedes each directory name.

The files of a particular area or directory are displayed to the right of the directory name in the file list area. Filenames, such as AUTOEXEC.BAT, appear with numerical values. Notice the filenames still follow MS-DOS rules.

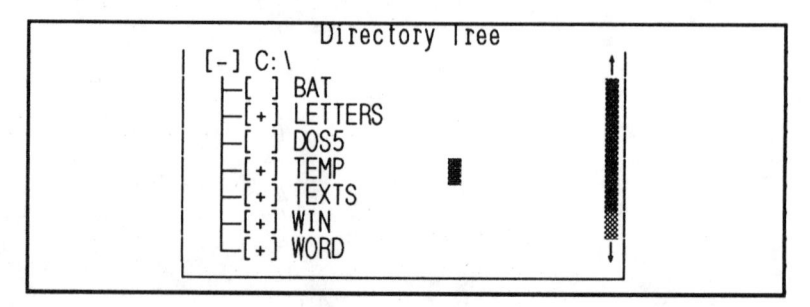

```
            Directory Tree
 [-] C:\                         ↑
  ├[ ] BAT
  ├[+] LETTERS
  ├[ ] DOS5
  ├[+] TEMP       ■
  ├[+] TEXTS
  ├[+] WIN
  └[+] WORD                      ↓
```

Directory Tree area

32

2.3 The MS-DOS Shell screen

However, if you select a different element in the Directory Tree area (for example, another directory), the information in the file list area automatically changes. To test this, do the following:

Directory Tree First, you must press the [Tab] key to get to the Directory Tree area. The [Tab] key moves the *selection cursor* on the screen. This highlights or activates the area. The area that stands out is called the *active* area.

So now we would like you to select the Directory Tree area (move the selection cursor to it using the [Tab] key). Then you can use the [↑] and [↓] keys to move the selection cursor within the Directory Tree area.

When you start, the root directory with the label, C:\ and a DOS directory containing the most important files for operating the PC (operating system) is displayed. In the illustration on the previous page, note the root directory and directories from BAT to WORD.

If you aren't the only one who works on this computer, then the Directory Tree area might look different. The elements with a plus sign next to them could be opened, thus appearing in the display as minus signs. Later we will learn the proper commands for switching back and forth to these different options.

The file list area From the Directory Tree area you can press the [Tab] key again to go to the area on the right. This area, called the file list area, displays the files. The files are the actual contents on a diskette or hard drive. For instance, a text is a file and a program consists of one or more files.

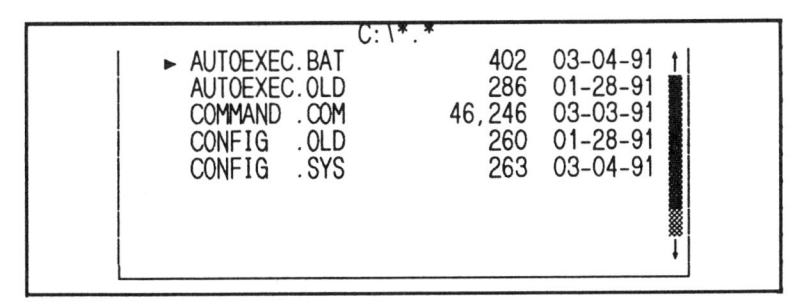

```
                    C:\*.*
        ► AUTOEXEC.BAT        402  03-04-91 ↑
          AUTOEXEC.OLD        286  01-28-91
          COMMAND .COM     46,246  03-03-91
          CONFIG  .OLD        260  01-28-91
          CONFIG  .SYS        263  03-04-91

                                             ↓
```

File list area

Once the file list area is active, use the [↑] and [↓] arrow keys to move the selection cursor in the file list area. The current file is always marked.

The *file* consists of two parts. The first is the name itself and a three character extension. The second is the size of the file and the date it was last saved.

2. A journey through your PC

As you move the selection cursor within the Directory Tree area or the file list area, perhaps you have noticed there is more information than what is displayed. As soon as you move past the selection cursor at the bottom edge of the area, the contents begin to move. This is called *scrolling*. Also, the slider bar changes position in the scroll bar on the right edge of the *window*. We'll describe scrolling in more detail later.

The program list area

The program list area is located in the lower area of the screen. There are four different programs available in the program list area (**Command Prompt, Editor, MS-DOS QBasic,** and **Disk Utilities**).

The program list area is where you'll create your program.

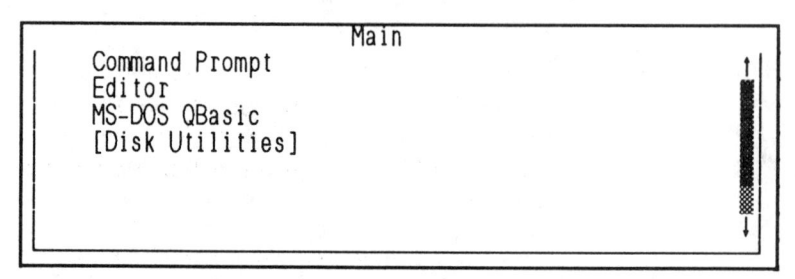

```
                              Main
    │  Command Prompt                                          ↑
    │  Editor                                                  ▓
    │  MS-DOS QBasic                                           ▓
    │  [Disk Utilities]                                        ▓
    │                                                          ▒
    │                                                          ▒
    │                                                          ↓
```

Program list area

To get to this area from the file list area, press [Tab] and use the [↑] and [↓] keys to select from the different programs. We'll describe these lines in more detail later. For now, it's important that you understand the following basic terms:

Programs available

Command Prompt (the command interpreter) lets you temporarily leave the MS-DOS Shell. The MS-DOS system prompt will appear on your screen. You can return to MS-DOS Shell any time by typing EXIT and pressing [Enter].

Editor is a small program you can use to create, view, and change text files. It's comparable to a simple word processor.

MS-DOS QBasic starts the QBasic program. QBasic is an easier version of MS-DOS QuickBASIC. It lets you create your own BASIC programs. We'll describe QBasic in more detail later.

2.3 The MS-DOS Shell screen

Disk Utilities includes options that you could use for working in the MS-DOS Shell. For example, to format a diskette (**Format**) or copy diskettes (**Disk Copy**). To return to the main group of the program list area, select the item at the top (**Main**).

```
[Main]
Disk Copy
Backup Fixed Disk
Restore Fixed Disk
Quick Format
Format
Undelete
```

Disk Utilities

The menu bar in the MS-DOS Shell

Up to this point we've talked about the the four screen areas of the MS-DOS Shell. As a reminder, this included the drive icons containing letters for the drives, the Directory Tree area, the file list area, and the program list area. We still haven't moved the selection cursor to the menu bar.

In the PC world, a *menu* is a list of options for performing tasks. Selecting a *menu command* activates it. For example, first you select a file, and then copy or delete it by selecting the respective menu command. These menus greatly influence your work with the MS-DOS Shell.

Press [Alt] or [F10] to get to the menu. The program then selects the first word in the menu bar—**File**. Then you can use the [↓] or [Enter] keys to open a menu with different commands, all of which belong to **File**. We also refer to these new options as a submenu. The contents of the submenu depend on where you selected the menu (for example, from the Directory Tree area, the file list area, or the program list area).

35

2. A journey through your PC

```
                    File  Options  View  Tree  Help
                   ┌─────────────────────────────┐
                   │ Open                        │
                   │ Run...                      │
                   │ Print                       │
                   │ Associate...                │
                   │ Search...                   │
                   │ View File Contents    F9    │
                   ├─────────────────────────────┤
                   │ Move...               F7    │
                   │ Copy...               F8    │
                   │ Delete...            DEL    │
                   │ Rename...                   │
                   │ Change Attributes...        │
                   ├─────────────────────────────┤
                   │ Create Directory...         │
                   ├─────────────────────────────┤
                   │ Select All                  │
                   │ Deselect All                │
                   ├─────────────────────────────┤
                   │ Exit              ALT+F4    │
                   └─────────────────────────────┘
```

Complete File menu

Use the ⬅ and ➡ arrow keys to move among the different choices in the menu bar. For example, to get from **File** to **Options** you would press the ➡ key once. Pressing it a second time takes you to **View**, and so on. Pressing ⬅ moves you backwards. You can also use the ➡ arrow key to move from an open menu (for example, **View**) to a command displayed in **Options** or **Tree**.

You can move the selection cursor between different menu commands (for example, the commands in the **File** menu) with the ⬆ and ⬇ keys. After selecting a command, press **Enter**.

Press **Alt** to quit a menu. You could also use the **Esc** key, which prematurely quits a process or cancels it completely.

The MS-DOS Shell and the mouse

The mouse makes it possible for you to move a selection cursor or arrow across the screen easily. To activate an area of the MS-DOS Shell, move the mouse pointer to that area. Then *click* (press and release) the left mouse button.

The MS-DOS Shell processes we just finished describing are much easier to perform with a mouse. Therefore, you no longer have to use the **Tab** key to move the selection cursor between different areas.

2.3 The MS-DOS Shell screen

To select an element from one of the areas, move the mouse pointer to the element (directory or filename). Then click (press and release) the left mouse button. This automatically activates both the element and the area of the screen. To activate one of the areas without selecting an element, click on the title bar of the area (for example., Directory Tree).

You can also use the mouse to activate the menus. Move the mouse pointer to one of the menu commands and click the left mouse button to open the menu. From there you can select one of the commands in the menu. You can only get to another menu by first selecting the title of the menu to which you want to go. To exit the menu with the mouse, just click an open spot somewhere on the screen (i.e., anywhere the menu doesn't cover).

Moving the contents of the areas

Perhaps you have already noticed that the MS-DOS Shell displays a lot of information on the screen. For many of the areas it reserves just one part (area) of the screen for an area. For example, there is an area for the Directory Tree area, another for the file list area, and so on. If there are more elements there than can fit in the area, you can scroll (move) the contents of the area.

Use the [↑] and [↓] arrow keys to move the contents of an area by selecting the lowest visible element in the area. Then continue to press the [↓] key. As the elements in the area move up, a new element appears at the bottom of the area. You can continue doing this until the last element appears in the bottom of the area. You could also move the selection cursor up until the first element of the list appears in the top of the area.

Scroll bars

In addition, there is a scroll bar at the right edge of each area. Notice the grey *slider bar* inside the scroll bar. It shows the size and position of the visible area compared to the entire area.

For example, when the slider bar is located at the top of the scroll bar, then the top portion of the information is displayed. If all the information fits in the area, the slider bar takes up the entire area of the scroll bar. If the slider bar is located at the bottom of the scroll bar, then the bottom portion of the information is displayed.

It's even easier to scroll the contents of the area by using a mouse. For example, you can use the two arrows at either end of the scroll bar. The arrow at the bottom takes you farther down, while the arrow at the top moves you farther up the area.

37

2. A journey through your PC

You can also use the mouse to move the scroll bar directly. Clicking once below the slider bar scrolls the window down while clicking above the slider bar scrolls the window up. If you click the slider bar itself and hold down the left mouse button, you can move the slider bar anywhere you want.

Text or graphics mode We haven't yet described certain details of the screen display. This is because the screen can look very different, depending on which mode you use. In text mode, the PC is only able to display complete characters on the screen. It has access to a total of 256 characters, including arrows and frames. Nevertheless, this display mode is limited to the 256 characters.

In text mode, the MS-DOS Shell is also limited to using these characters in its display. That's why certain displays are somewhat simpler in text mode than they are in graphics mode:

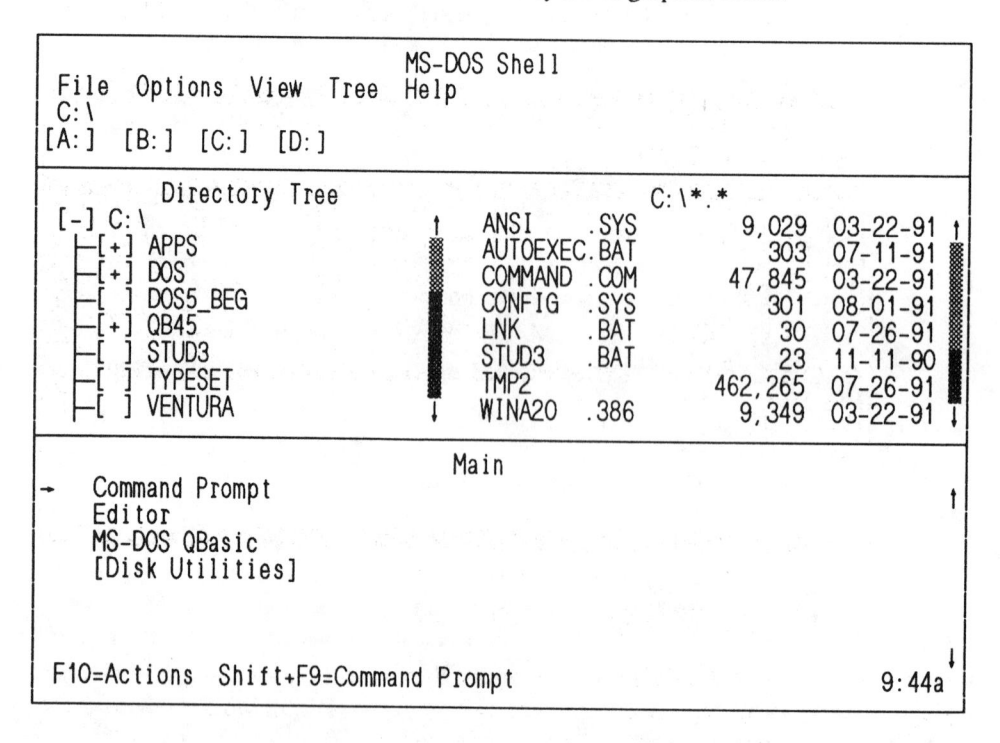

```
                           MS-DOS Shell
 File  Options  View  Tree  Help
 C:\
 [A:]   [B:]   [C:]   [D:]

           Directory Tree                        C:\*.*
 [-] C:\                           ↑  ANSI     .SYS      9,029  03-22-91 ↑
    ├[+] APPS                         AUTOEXEC .BAT        303  07-11-91
    ├[+] DOS                          COMMAND  .COM     47,845  03-22-91
    ├[ ] DOS5_BEG                     CONFIG   .SYS        301  08-01-91
    ├[+] QB45                         LNK      .BAT         30  07-26-91
    ├[ ] STUD3                        STUD3    .BAT         23  11-11-90
    ├[ ] TYPESET                      TMP2              462,265  07-26-91
    ├[ ] VENTURA                   ↓  WINA20   .386      9,349  03-22-91 ↓

                                Main
 → Command Prompt                                                        ↑
   Editor
   MS-DOS QBasic
   [Disk Utilities]


                                                                         ↓
 F10=Actions  Shift+F9=Command Prompt                             9:44a
```

The MS-DOS Shell in text mode

2.3 The MS-DOS Shell screen

On the other hand, in graphics mode, the PC uses *pixels* (individual points of light) to display numbers and letters. This allows more flexibility in how the MS-DOS Shell is displayed on the screen.

A disk drive in text mode consists of the letter and two brackets. In graphics mode, a disk drive appears with the drive slot and the lever. The display of a hard drive in graphics mode is slightly different from the display of a disk drive (see illustration below).

The same is true for the files displayed in the file list area. In graphics mode, files have different icons before their filenames to show if the file is a data file or an executable (program) file. Whether you can use graphics mode (and its appearance) depends on your computer system.

In the following section we'll describe the graphics mode. This mode is much more accurate and provides more information. If you must run the MS-DOS Shell in text mode, your screen display will be a little different.

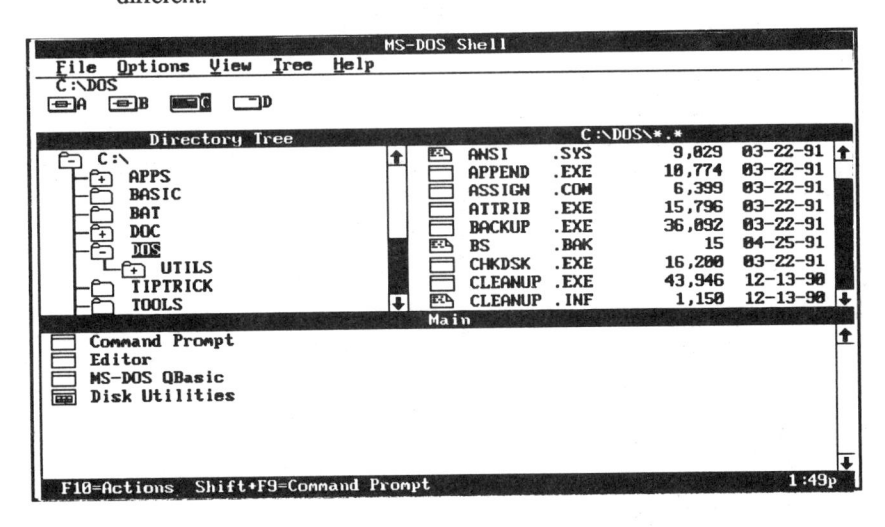

The MS-DOS Shell in graphics mode

Switching display modes

You should be able to tell the current display mode of the MS-DOS Shell by referring to the two previous illustrations. To change the setting, use the following procedure:

- Press [Alt] to highlight **File** in the menu bar.

- Use the [→] arrow key to move the selection cursor to **Options**.

39

2. A journey through your PC

- Use the ⬇ key to pull down the menu and move the selection cursor to **Display...** and press [Enter].

- A window appears with the different possible display modes for text and graphics. Which modes are possible depends on the kind of computer you have. The current display setting is selected.

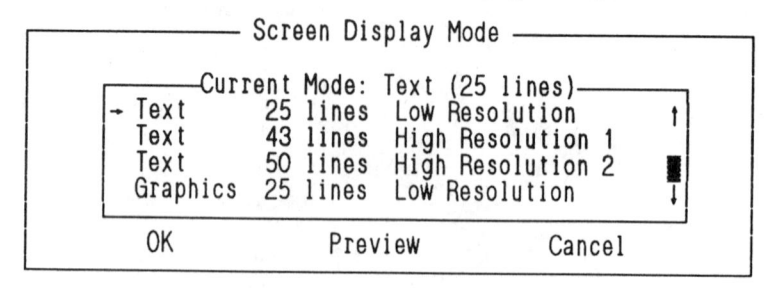

```
┌─────────────── Screen Display Mode ───────────────┐
│          ┌─Current Mode: Text (25 lines)─┐        │
│       → Text       25 lines   Low Resolution    ↑ │
│         Text       43 lines   High Resolution 1   │
│         Text       50 lines   High Resolution 2 ▇ │
│         Graphics   25 lines   Low Resolution    ↓ │
│                                                   │
│        OK             Preview           Cancel    │
└───────────────────────────────────────────────────┘
```

Possible screen display modes

- Use the arrow keys to select a graphics mode with 25 lines and press [Enter]. The MS-DOS Shell then changes the screen display to graphics mode.

If you share a computer with others, the screen display might be different from our illustrations. There could be more lines in the lower screen area, or a part could be subdivided into a program list and a list of "active" programs.

Summary

Now you know the basics of the MS-DOS Shell. For example, you know the three important areas of the MS-DOS Shell—the Directory Tree area, the file list area, and the program list area. You also understand menus and menu commands.

If you decide to interrupt your work and want to switch off the computer, activate **Exit** in the **File** menu.

Press [Alt] to activate the menu bar and press [Enter] to pull-down the **File** menu. Now use the ⬇ arrow key to move to **Exit** and press [Enter] again. The MS-DOS Shell screen disappears and you find yourself in the DOS command interpreter.

You can recognize the command interpreter by the system prompt, such as C:\ or C:\>. Now you can safely switch off your PC.

2.4 In the main building

The contents of drive C:

After getting our first look at the display and operations options of the MS-DOS Shell, we would now like to go into more detail about the structure of our imaginary company.

Different areas of the PersComp company

When planning our warehouse, we placed emphasis on order. It was obvious that you simply couldn't find information fast enough in a gigantic warehouse. So, we immediately divided the warehouse into different areas. In addition, we made certain that each of these areas was divided into many smaller areas, so we could adapt the division of the warehouse to current needs and circumstances.

To give you an overview of the current division of the company, there's a building directory, from which you can find the location of any area.

The Directory Tree

The MS-DOS Shell also has one of these building directories. It's on the left side of the screen, in the middle under the heading Directory Tree. There is a difference between the different directories (warehouses) and their representation in the building directory, the Directory Tree.

You could change the display in the building directory (e.g., show more details) without changing the division of the warehouse. You could also make changes to the areas in the warehouse and forget to update the building directory. Both are possible in the MS-DOS Shell. We'll describe this in more detail later and also remind you of the difference.

At any rate, the building directory provides you with some very good information about the contents of the hard drive. However, the building directory alone won't give you enough information about the contents of the hard drive.

You must thoroughly check for details, which are in the rooms of the warehouse. In our example, the PersComp company has the boxes with the materials here. In PC language, these boxes are referred to as files.

2. A journey through your PC

2.5 Room contents

Files

We have described how you can use MS-DOS to format diskettes, create directories, copy, or delete files. However, MS-DOS was not developed for the purpose of <u>creating</u> files. What creates the files that are kept on diskettes and the hard drive? It depends on which application you're using on your PC.

For example, if you use a word processor to create a file, then the finished product remains in the PC's memory until you choose to store the file. On the other hand, if you are managing addresses on the hard drive, then the files necessary for file management remain there.

To find out which files are located in the PC depends on the tasks performed by the computer. However, there must be some data that should be in the computer to use in illustrating the basic data found on files.

To find out which files are in the root directory of the hard drive, first look in the root directory. You should still be in the root directory. If you're not sure, you can easily find out by checking whether the character string "C:\" is between the menu bar (with **File**, **Options**, etc.), at the top, and the drive icons (the letters [A:], [B:], etc.). If this is the case, then you're at the root directory.

However, if there are some other characters after this character string, such as "C:\DOS", it means that you're in another directory or subdirectory. To return to the root directory, use the arrow keys to activate the Directory Tree. Then move the selection cursor next to "C:\" (all the way to the top).

Move the `Tab` key until the title bar in the area of the Directory Tree area is selected. Now use the `↑` key to move the selection cursor to the top position, the root directory.

How do you recognize files?

Many DOS beginners have trouble telling the difference between files and directories. If we stick to our example of the PersComp company, then the difference becomes clear and easy to understand. Directories are the rooms in the factory, while files are the boxes containing the actual materials.

Although this example also works for the MS-DOS command interpreter (see Chapter 8), it's easier in the MS-DOS Shell. The left half of the Directory Tree consists of directories, while the right half consists of files.

If you set the root directory in the Directory Tree area, you should have at least one file that is common with MS-DOS: the AUTOEXEC.BAT file. We're going to use this file to help explain the basic elements of files:

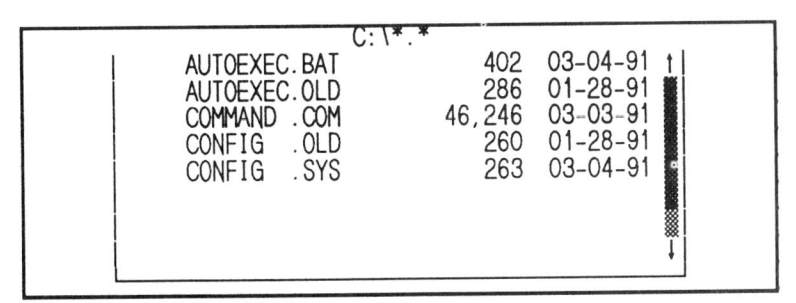

```
                    C:\*.*
     AUTOEXEC.BAT          402  03-04-91
     AUTOEXEC.OLD          286  01-28-91
     COMMAND  .COM      46,246  03-03-91
     CONFIG   .OLD         260  01-28-91
     CONFIG   .SYS         263  03-04-91
```

Filename and extension

Let's look at the filename and extension first. Notice that a period always separates the filename and extension. Remember, the name of the file is to the left of the period and can have a maximum of eight letters. Obviously, there are also shorter filenames, but the MS-DOS Shell pads the name with spaces, so the periods are always lined up underneath each other.

After the period is the file extension, consisting of three letters. The extension often provides more information about a file. You can't do very much with the extensions you see here, such as .COM, .BAT, and .SYS. You will soon create your own documents, to which you could give the .DOC extension.

Again, a filename consists of a name with up to eight characters, a period, and a three character extension that provides information about the file. However, you don't have to use an extension. You could simply use a filename with eight characters.

The following filenames are examples:

LETTINS.DOC   A letter to an insurance company.

LETTINS.BAK   A backup (duplicate) of LETTINS.DOC.

LETTINS1.DOC   Updated version of LETTINS.DOC.

2. A journey through your PC

LETTINS1.BAK   A backup (duplicate) of LETTINS1.DOC.

Here are a few examples of the files that are included with DOS:

DOSSHELL.VID   Special file for video screen display

DOSSHELL.COM   Command file part 1

DOSSHELL.EXE   Command file part 2

DOSSHELL.GRB   Supplement for screen driver

DOSSHELL.HLP   HELP file with help texts

DOSSHELL.INI   Initialization data for the MS-DOS Shell

More about files

The next column shows the size of the file. The numbers are listed in bytes. The illustration on the previous page shows that our AUTOEXEC.BAT file is 402 bytes long. Therefore, the file must have 402 characters. The size of your AUTOEXEC.BAT file might look slightly different.

The final column displays the date the file was last saved. Before you save a file, DOS notes the date it was last edited. The illustration on the previous page shows that our AUTOEXEC.BAT file has 03-04-91 for the date it was last saved. Your file will probably look slightly different. You will find files that you have created in the File List area, with the creation dates of each file.

MS-DOS also saves the time as well as the date of a file. The MS-DOS Shell doesn't display this in the file list area. However, there is a way to display the time (more on this later).

What's in the AUTOEXEC. BAT file

Now that we have taken a closer look at the information displayed about the AUTOEXEC.BAT file, let's view the contents of the file. To do this, you must activate the file list area.

If you activated the root directory in the Directory List area, press the [Tab] key once. This activates the file list area. The AUTOEXEC.BAT file should be selected. Otherwise use the [↑] and [↓] keys to move the selection cursor.

To display the contents of the file on the screen, you must choose from the Menu Bar. First press [Alt] to activate the menu. Next, press [Enter] or [F] to open the **File** menu. Six lines down you'll see a command

2.5 Room contents

called **View File Contents**. Use the ⬇ arrow key to move to this line and press ⟨Enter⟩ to activate it.

```
               MS-DOS Shell - AUTOEXEC.BAT
Display   View   Help
   To view file's content use PgUp or PgDn or ↑ or ↓.

@ECHO OFF
PATH=C:\DOS;C:\WINDOWS;C:\APPS\WORD5;C:\WINWORD;
PROMPT $p$g
SET TEMP=C:\DOS




  ↲=PageDown   Esc=Cancel   F9=Hex/ASCII                  5:09p
```

An AUTOEXEC.BAT file

A new screen appears with the heading, "MS-DOS Shell - AUTOEXEC.BAT". Underneath is a menu bar listing the **Display**, **View**, and **Help** titles. These new menu entries apply only to the new display (**View File Contents**).

Under the menu bar there is another line with notes about keys. If the file contains more information than the screen can display, you can use these keys to move the screen contents. Use ↑ and ⬇ to move the screen one line up or down, Use ⟨PgUp⟩ and ⟨PgDn⟩ to move the screen one page up or down.

Now, its more important that the AUTOEXEC.BAT file not only has a name, size, and date of creation, but also contents. In this case, the contents are not a letter, list of addresses or total payments. Instead, the file contains important tasks that the PC has to accomplish after you switch it on.

Summary As a shipping box has a label, stating weight and date of manufacture, a file has a filename, file size, and the date/time the file was created or last changed. A file extension usually provides information about the type of file or the application. For example, the three letters (BAT) in the extension of AUTOEXEC.BAT refer to a *batch file*, and determine that this file contains instructions for the PC (batched, or line by line).

45

2. A journey through your PC

This information only describes the "outside" of a file. However, the contents are also important. Unfortunately, the data about the outside of the file don't provide a lot of information about the contents. For example, you could use a word processor to write a letter to Mr. Meyer named MEYER.DOC and then accidentally name it SCHULTZ.DOC. That wouldn't change the contents at all.

Sometimes it's not easy to determine the contents of files (or do anything with the screen display). If you want, you can try it out for yourself on the COMMAND.COM file. You will quickly discover that the display consists only of numbers and other odd characters.

Furthermore, the display is divided into an area on the left with numbers and an area on the right with characters, text, or both. This holds true for all files with either EXE or COM as their extensions.

```
                        MS-DOS Shell - COMMAND.COM
Display   View   Help
    To view file's content use PgUp or PgDn or ↑ or ↓.

  000000 | E95D1400  78140000  B70E0000  750D0000  | θ]..x...π...u...
  000010 | 85110000  00000000  00000000  00000000  | à...............
  000020 | 00000000  00000000  00000000  00000000  | ................
  000030 | 00000000  00FBE864  001E0E2E  FF2E0401  | .....√Φd........
  000040 | FBE85900  1E0E2EFF  2E0801FB  E84E001E  | √ΦY......√ΦN..
  000050 | 0E2EFF2E  0C01FBE8  43001E0E  2EFF2E10  | ......√ΦC......
  000060 | 01E83900  1E0E2EFF  2E1401E8  2F001E0E  | .Φ9......Φ/...
  000070 | 2EFF2E18  01E82500  1E0E2EFF  2E1C01E8  | ....Φ%......Φ
  000080 | 1B001E0E  2EFF2E20  01E81100  1E0E2EFF  | .......Φ......
  000090 | 2E2401E8  07001E0E  2EFF2E28  019C2E80  | .$.Φ......(.£.Ç
  0000A0 | 3E340100  7408E80C  007303E8  1A009DC3  | >4..t.Φ..s.Φ..¥
  0000B0 | EA350100  005350B4  072EFF1E  30010BC0  | Ω5...SP┤...0..└
  0000C0 | 585B7502  F9C3F8C3  5350B405  2EFF1E30  | X[u.•├°├SP┤...0
  0000D0 | 010BC074  03585BC3  EBFECD21  FA0E17BC  | ..└t.X[├δ■=!•..⌐
  0000E0 | 3E05FB0E  1F9C2EA0  4005A880  7407247F  | >.√..£.á@.Çt.$
  0000F0 | 2EFF1E2C  012E8026  40057F9D  E962FF02  | ...,..Ç&@. ¥θb.
  000100 | 00000105  02410200  00020C02  00000000  | .....A.........
  000110 | 00000000  00021E02  032C0203  2A020000  | ..............*.
  000120 | 00000000  00000000  00000000  00000001  | .............,..
  000130 | 05020200  00013802  20026904  00000000  | ......8..i.....
<┘=PageDown  Esc=Cancel  F9=Hex/ASCII                          4:12p
```

Many files are not legible

"Almost" unique files

In closing, here's an important item about filenames. A file must be unique for MS-DOS. MS-DOS distinguishes files by their names and extensions. Within a directory (a room in the factory) a file can only exist once.

46

2.5 Room contents

The easiest way to understand this is to compare a PC to a place with streets and house numbers. The mailman differentiates the various house numbers, such as 12, 16a, and 16b, as MS-DOS differentiates between the AUTOEXEC.BAT, CONFIG.SYS, and CONFIG.BAK files. Although there cannot be a second house number 12 on one street, there can be another house number 12 on the next street over. The same holds true for MS-DOS. There can only be another AUTOEXEC.BAT file in another directory.

What would happen if you tried to create a second file of the same name in the same directory? MS-DOS replaces the old file with the new one. The contents of the old file are then lost.

Summary   Here is a summary of the most important features:

- The file contents of a PC vary with each system.

- Since the AUTOEXEC.BAT file serves a very special purpose, you should avoid changing it unless absolutely necessary. However, you can't hurt the file by just looking at it.

- You must select a file before you can view its contents. Then use the [Alt] key to go to the menu bar and select **View File Contents** from the **File** menu.

- There are many files whose contents you can view, but you can't do anything with the information contained there because you can't read it, let alone understand it. We used the AUTOEXEC.BAT file in our example because you can at least read it.

- Filenames must be unique—you can only use a certain filename once in a directory. The extension counts as part of the filename.

2. A journey through your PC

2.6 Changing the building directory

Directories and subdirectories

We have already pointed out that the building directory of the company, in its current form, is not the only way it can be displayed. On the contrary, you can adapt it to a more or less detailed display. The more details you display, the more difficult it becomes to keep things in perspective.

Ordinarily the Directory Tree area displays only directories from the first level. Since these directories belong to the root directory, they are also called subdirectories of the root directory. In our comparison of the hard drive to a warehouse and the root directory to the entry or hallway, you only see the doors that lead into the building. It's not clear yet whether there is a room behind this door or another hallway with many new doors.

If you continue this example, the MS-DOS Shell has a distinguishing mark on the doors that lead to more hallways, or in PC language, contain more subdirectories. If this is the case, a plus sign is located in the display in the Directory Tree.

If we look at the Directory Tree area again, the LETTERS directory has this identifying mark, showing there are some subdirectories within that subdirectory:

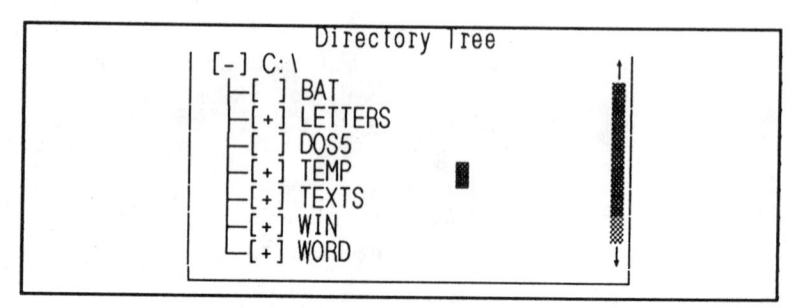

```
                    Directory Tree
    [-] C:\
      ├[ ] BAT
      ├[+] LETTERS
      ├[ ] DOS5
      ├[+] TEMP
      ├[+] TEXTS
      ├[+] WIN
      └[+] WORD
```

Subdirectories indicated by plus signs

Just as you can open each of the doors in the foyer of the big warehouse and find out what their contents are, you can do the same thing with directories that have this plus sign. To do this, use the arrow keys to move the highlight in the Directory Tree to the desired directory and press the [+] key. You could also activate the **Tree** menu (press [Alt] and then press [T]) and use the **Expand One Level** command. In any event, it's easier if you use [+].

48

2.6 Changing the building directory

This procedure only gets results if the directory has a plus sign next to it. If there is no plus sign, it doesn't matter what you do. There's nothing else for the MS-DOS Shell to display.

The MS-DOS Shell now displays the next level on the screen. Here's an example of what the display might look like:

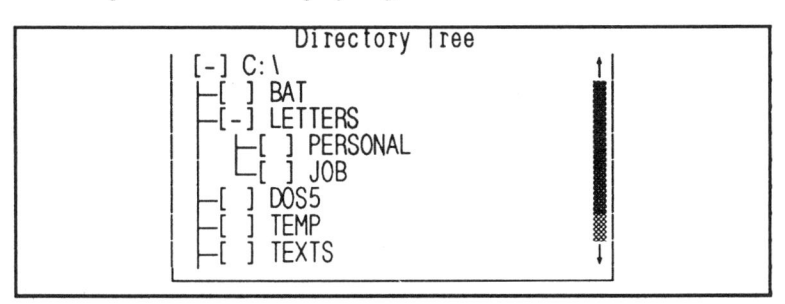

```
                    Directory Tree
        [-] C:\                                    ↑
        ├[ ] BAT
        ├[-] LETTERS
        │   ├[ ] PERSONAL
        │   └[ ] JOB
        ├[ ] DOS5
        ├[ ] TEMP
        ├[ ] TEXTS                                 ↓
```

In the illustration above, the MS-DOS Shell indicates that two more subregions (or subdirectories) are in the LETTERS directory: PERSONAL and JOB. These two directories are indented, and placed below the *parent directory* (in this case, the LETTERS directory), so you can immediately see the allocation.

Open subdirectories with the mouse by pointing the mouse pointer at the plus sign and clicking the left mouse button. In other words, click the plus sign once.

You can also tell that the two subdirectories don't have any subdirectories of their own because they don't have a plus sign. PERSONAL and JOB are not hallways, but rather final rooms.

It's also interesting to note that the plus sign next to LETTERS has changed to a minus sign. The MS-DOS Shell uses the minus sign to indicate that you can close the visible subdirectories with the minus key. Go ahead and try it out. Move the highlight to LETTERS and press the ⊟ key. The original Directory Tree area display reappears.

You could do the same thing with your mouse by clicking the minus sign.

The MS-DOS Shell gives you the option of displaying exactly those elements in the Directory Tree that you want to see. Just imagine what it would be like if the MS-DOS Shell always displayed all the files in a long list. You would have to search through a list of perhaps 1000 elements before you found a series of letters on a particular subject.

2. A journey through your PC

If, on the other hand, you placed the letters in a subdirectory of LETTERS called PERSONAL, all you have to do is open up the "branch" called LETTERS, move the highlight to PERSONAL and the file list area displays all of the files that fit under this subject. If this subdivision is no longer sufficient after a certain period of time, it's no problem to set up a special directory on your hard drive called INSUR, and another one called TAXES. You could subdivide TAXES into TAXES90, TAXES91 etc.

Summary

Let's review what we just read:

- The MS-DOS Shell ordinarily displays only subdirectories in the Directory Tree area. If a subdirectory has any subdirectories of its own, a plus sign next to it brings this to your attention.

- You can make these subdirectories visible and select them by moving the selection to the directory with the plus sign and pressing the [+] key. The MS-DOS Shell then adds some indented lines containing the subdirectories to the display.

- If you move the highlight to one of these subdirectories, the file list area displays the files of that subdirectory.

- To return to the original display of the Directory Tree area, select the minus sign and press the [-] key.

- By dividing the hard drive into directories and subdirectories, you can keep related information together.

2.7 A path to a different building

Changing drives

Up to now we've only been dealing with the hard drive (C:), which corresponds to the warehouse in our example of the PersComp company. However, this one method of storage is not enough. Our company also has some trucks for storing more data. These trucks correspond to diskettes, and the loading dock for loading data from the hard drive onto diskettes is the disk drive.

Obviously, the building directory in the entrance way only shows areas of the factory interior. To display the contents of a truck, you must "switch" the building directory. This is no problem in the age of electronics and computers. The drive icons above the Directory Tree area play a major part in this switch.

Hard drives and diskettes

Before we can try changing drives, we need a diskette that has been prepared. Unlike the hard drive, which is constantly available (provided your computer has one), a disk drive is only a loading dock without a truck. In addition, DOS cannot use new diskettes for data storage until they have been prepared for receiving data. If you have a diskette with data that can be read by DOS, you can insert it in drive A: now.

In case your PC has two disk drives, drive A: is usually the one on top or to the left. If you aren't certain, watch the drive lights when you switch on your computer. Drive A: always lights up first.

To switch to drive A:, you must activate the drive icons by pressing [Tab] until you reach the desired area. When you start out, the highlight is on drive C:. Now press the [←] arrow key to select the icon for drive A: and press the [Spacebar]. The drive light lights up and MS-DOS either shows you the contents of the diskette you inserted in drive A: or else gives you one of the following error messages:

```
┌──────────────── WARNING! ────────────────┐
│ Drive not ready.                         │
│                                          │
│ 1. Try to read diskette again.           │
│ 2. Do not try to read this diskette again.│
│                                          │
│    [ OK ]      [ Cancel ]      [ Help ]  │
└──────────────────────────────────────────┘
```

The "Drive not ready" message means that MS-DOS couldn't get information from drive A:. The drive wasn't ready for data processing.

2. A journey through your PC

This means that either there wasn't any diskette in the drive, or that you didn't pull down the drive lever (5-1/4") or push the diskette all the way in (3-1/2").

It's also possible that you put the diskette in upside down. The 5-1/4" floppy diskettes have the *write protect notch* on the left side while the sturdier 3-1/2" diskettes have either an arrow on the front left pointing in the right direction, or the little write protect notch must be on the left corner closest to you when you insert it.

The following illustration shows the two types of diskettes and how to insert them properly:

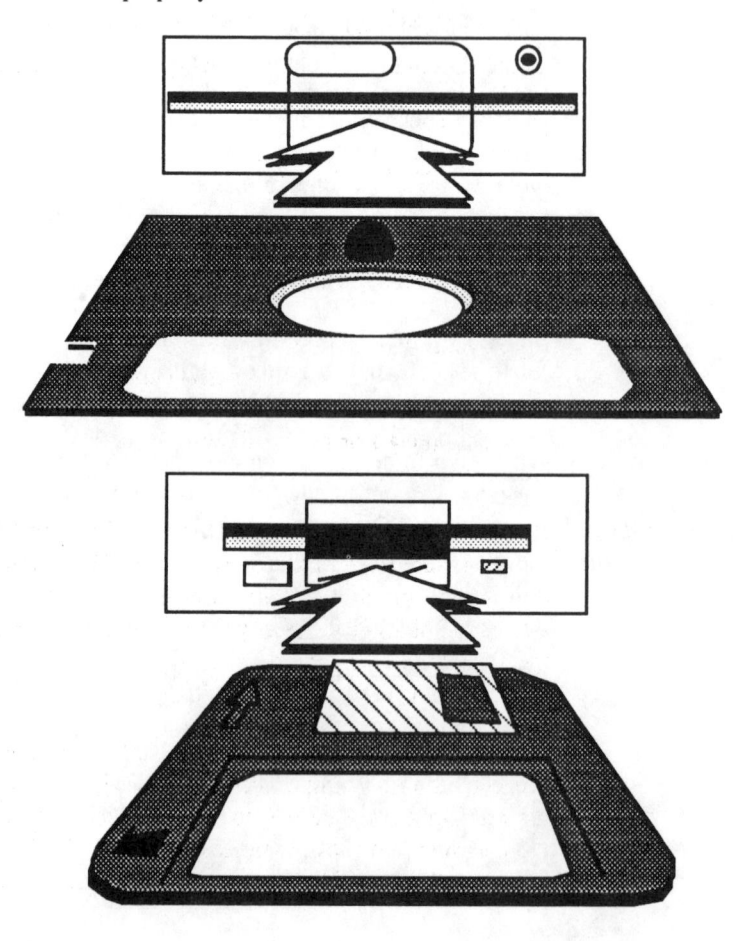

Using different diskette sizes

52

2.7 A path to a different building

The first illustration is that of a 5-1/4" diskette. Be careful not to touch or damage the oval read/write opening. Also, don't bend or break the diskette when inserting it in the drive. When the diskette is all the way in the drive, pull down the lever. At the bottom you see a 3-1/2" diskette, which is sturdier than the 5-1/4" inch diskette. Nevertheless, make certain that the diskette clicks into position and the eject button pops out.

On some PCs the 3-1/2" inch drive is turned 90 degrees to the left, so the top of the drive is to the left.

If an error occurs, make sure the diskette is inserted. Press (Enter) to try again, or press (Esc) to cancel the switch to drive A:

```
─────────────────── WARNING! ───────────────────
 General error.

 1. Try to read diskette again.
 2. Don't try to read diskette again.

        OK            Cancel           Help
```

If you get a "General error" message, the diskette probably hasn't been formatted to receive data or doesn't contain any data that MS-DOS can use. Either insert another diskette (already prepared for data reception) and press (Enter) or cancel the entire process by pressing (Esc). See Chapter 4 for information on *formatting* (preparing) a diskette.

The contents of the diskette in drive A: If everything worked, then the Directory Tree and file list areas display the contents of the diskette in drive A:. What appears in the display depends on the diskette you inserted and what is saved on it. If the diskette is blank (i.e., already formatted but without files saved on it), the Directory Tree should indicate that the diskette in drive A: has a root directory, but no subdirectories.

Subdirectories would have been visible or a plus sign would have preceded the A:\ prompt. The file list area on the right displays the root directory of drive A:. Since no files have been saved there, you only see the message "No files in selected directory." With a blank diskette, the Directory Tree and file list areas will look like the following:

2. A Journey through your PC

```
┌─────────────────────────────────┬──────────────────────────────────┐
│        Directory Tree           │            A:\*.*                │
│  [ ] A:\                        │                                  │
│                              ↑  │  No files in selected directory. ↑
│                              ▓  │                                  ▓
│                              ▓  │                                  ▓
│                              ▓  │                                  ▓
│                              ▓  │                                  ▓
│                              ░  │        ▪                        ░
│                              ↓  │                                  ↓
└─────────────────────────────────┴──────────────────────────────────┘
```

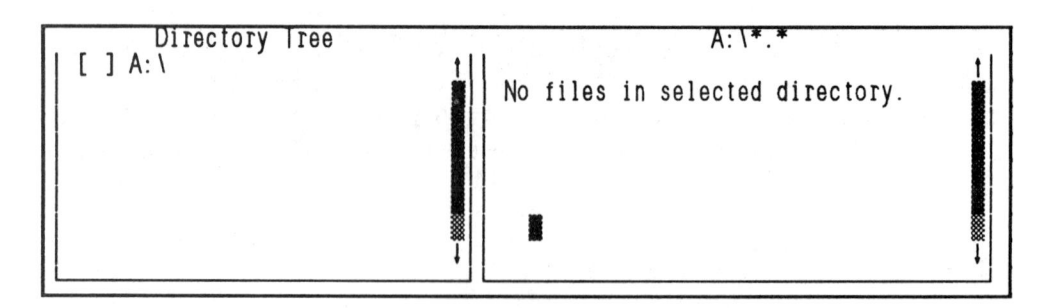

Be careful changing diskettes

Let's say you are finished looking at the contents of one diskette and would now like to look at another one. You're probably wondering how to get the MS-DOS Shell to check out the new diskette. There are two ways of activating drive A: in the MS-DOS Shell. If you select A: and press the (Spacebar) the MS-DOS Shell displays the contents of the diskette in drive A:. If you then switch back to C: and return to A:, the PC remembers the data and displays it again, without checking the disk drive. This saves a great deal of time.

If you changed diskettes, you must get the MS-DOS Shell to retrieve the contents of the new diskette. To do this, select the drive letter and press (Enter).

You can also use the mouse for both of these processes; it's often much faster. To switch to another drive, point the mouse cursor to the drive letter and press the mouse button once. The first time you do this, the MS-DOS Shell retrieves the contents of the drive, while every time after that it only displays the contents that it "remembers."

- To reread the contents of drive A:, for example, after changing diskettes, just *double-click* the drive letter (press the left mouse button twice in rapid succession).

Back to the hard drive

Since we want to continue working with the hard drive (C:), we should know how to switch the screen display back to the contents of the hard drive. For example, move the selection cursor to C: and press the (Spacebar). The directory of the hard drive then reappears. If you press (Enter) instead of the (Spacebar) you will notice that the MS-DOS Shell rereads the contents of the hard drive, which would only waste time in this case.

If you are using a mouse, you can switch back to the hard drive by clicking on the [C:] drive icon.

3. Your first corporate tasks

File handling Up to now we have only looked at the MS-DOS Shell with its different display options and found out what's on the hard drive. In this chapter we'll show you more about working with files and how to change the contents of the hard drive.

3.1 Setting up a workroom

Creating a directory

In the previous chapter we learned that you use directories to create order on the hard drive and make it easy to view. Since we are going to get in a great deal of practice in this chapter, we'll create a special work directory. At the same time, this is also our first exercise in organizing the PC wisely by creating directories (work areas). We will then use only this special work directory for all of the processes that make changes to the contents of the hard drive.

The following process requires you being in the MS-DOS Shell and that your computer have a hard drive. If your computer doesn't have a hard drive, make up a special practice diskette and try everything out on this diskette.

Creating the WORK directory

You must activate the Directory Tree area in order to create a new work directory named WORK. Press the [Tab] key until the Directory Tree is active. Then move the selection cursor to the directory where you are going to create your new subdirectory. In our example, we're going to make the WORK directory in the root directory of the hard drive (C:), so we have to move the selection cursor in the Directory Tree all the way up to "C:\".

After determining the location of the new directory, you are ready to choose the command for creating a new area on the hard drive. Use [Alt] to activate the menu and press [F] for **File**. Now move the selection cursor to **Create Directory...** and press [Enter]. A new window appears, where you can type in the name of the directory:

3. Your first corporate tasks

```
┌─────────────────────────────────────────────┐
│              Create Directory               │
│                                             │
│ Parent name: C:\                            │
│ New directory name. .  ┌──────────────────┐ │
│                        │ _                │ │
│                        └──────────────────┘ │
│                                             │
│                                             │
│                                             │
│       ( OK )      ( Cancel )    ( Help )    │
└─────────────────────────────────────────────┘
```

Creating a work directory

After you type WORK and press [Enter], the new Directory Tree of the new directory appears in the window. Now we can create, change and delete data in this area of the hard drive without causing any harm.

If you want to look at your new directory, simply select the Directory Tree and move the cursor to the new line, WORK. In the file list area you then see "No files in selected directory."

3.2 Sample boxes

Copying files

In this section we want to create some sample files in our directory. We will do this by copying some existing files to the new directory.

Copying files can be useful for many reasons. For one thing, you can copy files that you created on your computer to a diskette, either to have a backup copy of this file or to give it to someone else, who can then copy the file from the diskette to their own computer.

There are several reasons for copying data. For example, all we want to do is use the process to place some practice data in our directory.

Copying files to the new directory

Let's start by copying the AUTOEXEC.BAT file in the root directory of your hard drive to WORK in the directory you just created. We're using this file because we're certain that you have a file by that name. To copy this file, you must first display the files that are in the root directory. Use (Tab) to activate the Directory Tree area and use the (↑) key to select the entry:

```
[-] C:\
```

You have just selected the root directory of the hard drive where the file you want to copy is located. To copy a file from this directory, you must first select it. Use (Tab) to select the file list area. Use the (↑) and (↓) keys to move the selection cursor to the file you want to copy, the AUTOEXEC.BAT file.

If you are in text mode, the file has an arrow to the left of the filename, indicating that it is selected. If you are in graphics mode, switch to text mode using the **Display...** command from the **Options** menu.

Generally, if you want to do something with a file in the MS-DOS Shell, you must specify (select) the file first.

To copy this file, use (Alt) to select the menu bar and press (Enter) to activate the **File** menu. Now use the arrow keys to select **Copy...** and press (Enter) again. The following dialog box appears.

57

3. Your first corporate tasks

```
┌─────────────────────Copy File──────────────────────┐
│                                                    │
│        From:    [AUTOEXEC.BAT ················]    │
│        To:      [C:\··························]    │
│                                                    │
│                                                    │
│                                                    │
│         [  OK  ]      [ Cancel ]    [  Help  ]     │
│                                                    │
└────────────────────────────────────────────────────┘
```

Copy... command dialog box

All you have to do now is enter the target directory. In our example this is the WORK directory in drive C:\. Here's what the entry should look like:

`C:\WORK`

After typing in the target, press (Enter) to copy the file. The screen displays a message that the MS-DOS Shell is copying the file. Then the message disappears and the MS-DOS Shell returns to its normal display screen.

Use (Tab) to change to the Directory List area. Use the arrow keys to select the WORK directory. The file list area then displays the contents of the WORK directory. Notice that a copy of the AUTOEXEC.BAT file is now in the WORK directory. You've just copied a file from the root directory of your hard drive to another directory. When you copy a file, the original copy remains in the original directory.

You can confirm this by pressing (Tab) to switch to the Directory List area, selecting the root directory (C:\) and checking the file list area. The AUTOEXEC.BAT file is still in the root directory.

The following steps describe copying a file using the MS-DOS Shell:

1. Activate the directory containing the file.

2. Select the file you wish to copy.

3. Select **Copy...** from the **File** menu. A dialog box opens where you can enter the target of the copying process. You must enter the complete pathname of the target directory.

3.2 Sample boxes

4. Select OK.

5. To verify the results, activate the target directory and look for the file you copied.

If you are uncertain about the exact pathname of the target directory, activate it before copying and note the name that appears underneath the menu bar.

We want to use this new AUTOEXEC.BAT file in the WORK directory to introduce you to other options of the MS-DOS Shell. We'll use the AUTOEXEC.BAT as a practice file.

Copying more than one file   So we don't have just one file in our practice directory, we're going to copy other files to it, the CONFIG.SYS and COMMAND.COM files from the root directory. In fact, we're going to do it in one process.

To do this, we must first select the files. To select more than one file within a directory, you must press (Shift) + (F8) to switch on *Add mode*. Press both keys simultaneously and the word ADD appears in the bottom line of the MS-DOS Shell.

Now press (Tab) to activate the Directory List, use the arrow keys to select C:\ and press (Tab) to go to the file list area, where you can select the files to be copied. Use the arrow keys to move the selection cursor to the desired file (CONFIG.SYS) and press the (Spacebar) once. The file has an arrow next to it to indicate that it is selected. Then use the arrow keys to move the selection cursor to the next file (COMMAND.COM) and press the (Spacebar) again.

If you are using a mouse, you can select the files by pressing the (Ctrl) key and clicking the desired files, CONFIG.SYS and COMMAND.COM, with the mouse.

Each selected file has an arrow. If you ever accidentally select a file, you can deselect it by using the arrow keys to move the selection cursor to this file and pressing the (Spacebar).

After marking the files you want copied, you are ready to copy them to the WORK directory. Remember to press (Alt) to activate the menu bar and press (Enter) to select the **File** menu. Now use the arrow keys to select **Copy...** and press (Enter) again.

The familiar dialog box appears and you see the files you selected under From:. Specify where you want to copy the files under To:, in our

59

3. Your first corporate tasks

example, the WORK directory. The following is what the entry should look like:

C:\WORK

If you press [Enter], the copying process is displayed in a window. After the MS-DOS Shell is finished copying, you can display the new contents of your directory by pressing [Tab] to activate the Directory List and selecting the WORK directory.

If you change your mind after switching on the ADD mode and want to exit the mode, simply press [Shift] + [F8] again.

3.3 A closer look at the boxes

Filenames Now that we have copied the AUTOEXEC.BAT file to the WORK directory, we would like to take a closer look at this file.

To do this, activate the WORK directory by using [Tab] to switch to the Directory List and using the arrow keys to select the WORK directory. The file list area displays the AUTOEXEC.BAT file that we copied to this directory. Here's what the file entry looks like on our system:

AUTOEXEC.BAT   402   03-04-91

The file icon If you are working in graphics mode, the first thing you see is an icon representing the file type (not visible in text mode). The MS-DOS Shell differentiates between executable and non-executable files. For example, files that you create with a word processor have a different icon than files used for running a program.

The filename To the right of the icon is the filename and its extension. MS-DOS recognizes what kind of file it is by its extension. Just as every box in our factory has a label, each file has a filename and extension.

There are a couple of rules to keep in mind. A filename can't be any longer than eight characters, nor can it have a space in it. The file extension is always separated from the filename by a period and can be no more than three characters long.

MS-DOS can tell by the extension whether a file is a program file or some other kind of file. Programs must have either EXE, COM or BAT as their extension; otherwise MS-DOS doesn't treat them as programs. Therefore, these programs cannot be executed.

Also, for files, MS-DOS doesn't consider the file extension—instead of LETTER.DOC you could also name a text LETTER.000.

File size and creation date Next comes the file size. This corresponds to the weight of the box. This is important, for example if you want to know whether there's enough room on your diskette for a particular file (or whether a box will still fit on a truck without exceeding the legal weight).

Finally comes the date the file was last saved. You could use this date, for example, to determine the last file that you edited. You get all of this information about each file on the computer or a diskette. The information will vary from file to file, since files are always unique.

3. Your first corporate tasks

3.4 Renaming and removing boxes

Deleting and renaming files
Now that we have three files in our practice directory, we'd like to try some more operations in the MS-DOS Shell.

First, delete the CONFIG.SYS file that you copied to the WORK directory.

Deleting a file
If you decide to delete a file from the hard drive, because you no longer need it or because it's an old backup copy, you can use the **Delete...** command from the **File** menu.

Be very careful when you delete files, because once you have deleted a file, it's gone for good and you won't be able to get it back. Before you delete a file, always make certain that you really want to delete it.

To delete a file, you must first mark it. Make the drive containing the file the current drive and select the directory where the file is located. Then use (Tab) to go to the file list area and mark the file.

In our example, you had to use (Tab) to select the directory list and activate the WORK directory. Use (Tab) to switch to the file list area and mark the CONFIG.SYS file.

Now press (Alt) to select the menu bar and press (Enter) in order to activate the **File** menu. Use the arrow keys to select **Delete...** and press (Enter) again. A dialog box appears, asking for confirmation of the deletion. Press (Enter) to continue. Then the file is deleted and you see a message on the screen informing you of this.

If you decide not to delete the file during the dialog box, you can always cancel the process by pressing (Esc).

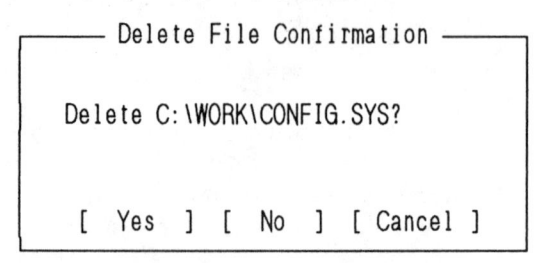

```
┌─────── Delete File Confirmation ───────┐
│                                        │
│   Delete C:\WORK\CONFIG.SYS?           │
│                                        │
│                                        │
│     [ Yes ]   [ No ]   [ Cancel ]      │
└────────────────────────────────────────┘
```

Confirmation before a file is deleted

62

3.4 Renaming and removing boxes

When you delete files, always make the drive and directory containing the file to be deleted current. Then you can mark the file in the file list area and select the command to delete. Before the file is deleted, two security prompts appear that you can confirm by pressing (Enter). Otherwise press (Esc) to cancel the process.

Renaming files

You also have the option of giving a file a new name. To do this, use **Rename...** from the **File** menu.

We'd like to rename the COMMAND.COM file. To do this, press (Tab) again to activate the file list area of the WORK directory and use the arrow keys to select the COMMAND.COM file. Then use (Alt) to select the menu bar and press (Enter) to activate the **File** menu. Use the arrow keys to select **Rename...** and press (Enter) again. A dialog box appears, where you see the current name of the file.

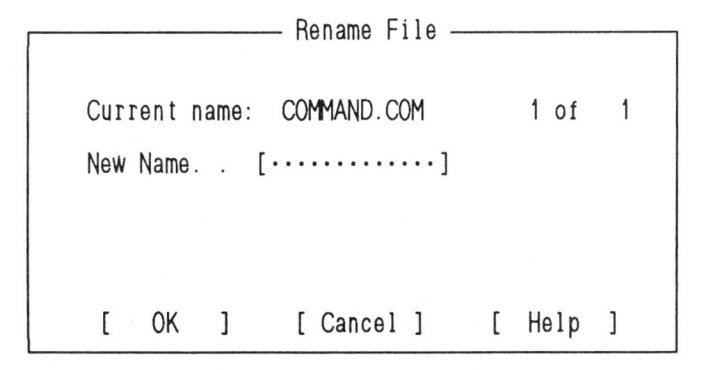

```
┌──────────────── Rename File ────────────────┐
│                                             │
│   Current name:   COMMAND.COM      1 of  1  │
│                                             │
│   New Name. .  [ . . . . . . . . . . . . ]  │
│                                             │
│                                             │
│                                             │
│      [   OK   ]    [ Cancel ]    [ Help ]   │
│                                             │
└─────────────────────────────────────────────┘
```

Rename... command dialog box

You can type in your new name for the file after New Name:. We chose TEST.COM. Now type in the name and press (Enter). When this is done, the MS-DOS Shell displays the file with the changed filename.

3. Your first corporate tasks

3.5 What's in the boxes

File contents   Until now we have read directory contents and showed you how to copy files. Now we'd like to talk more about files and what they contain.

It's not very easy to display the contents of files. Even if you could, there is very little you can do with what appears on the screen. The MS-DOS Shell's **View File Contents** command in the **File** menu displays the contents of files. Earlier we used this command with the AUTOEXEC.BAT file.

However, you cannot use this method to display all files. Make the root directory of the hard drive the current directory. Then use (Tab) to activate the file list area and select the COMMAND.COM file with the arrow keys. Now press (Alt) to select the menu bar, select the **File** menu and press (Enter). Use the arrow keys to select **View File Contents** in the menu.

After you press (Enter), your screen's appearance changes considerably. It looks similar to the following:

```
                    MS-DOS Shell - COMMAND.COM
Display  View  Help
    To view file's content use PgUp or PgDn or ↑ or ↓.

  000000   E95D1400   78140000   B70E0000   750D0000    θ]..x...π....u...
  000010   85110000   00000000   00000000   00000000    à...............
  000020   00000000   00000000   00000000   00000000    ................
  000030   00000000   00FBE864   001E0E2E   FF2E0401    .....√Φd........
  000040   FBE85900   1E0E2EFF   2E0801FB   E84E001E    √ΦY.......√ΦN..
  000050   0E2EFF2E   0C01FBE8   43001E0E   2EFF2E10    ......√ΦC......
  000060   01E83900   1E0E2EFF   2E1401E8   2F001E0E    .Φ9........Φ/...
  000070   2EFF2E18   01E82500   1E0E2EFF   2E1C01E8    ....Φ%........Φ
  000080   1B001E0E   2EFF2E20   01E81100   1E0E2EFF    ........Φ......
  000090   2E2401E8   07001E0E   2EFF2E28   019C2E80    .$.Φ......(.£.C
  0000A0   3E340100   7408E80C   007303E8   1A009DC3    >4..t.Φ...s.Φ..¥
  0000B0   EA350100   005350B4   072EFF1E   30010BC0    Ω5...SP........O.
  0000C0   585B7502   F9C3F8C3   5350B405   2EFF1E30    X[u.•├°-SP....O
  0000D0   010BC074   03585BC3   EBFECD21   FA0E17BC    ..└t.X[├δ•=!..┘
  0000E0   3E05FB0E   1F9C2EA0   4005A880   7407247F    >.√.£.à@.C[t.$
  0000F0   2EFF1E2C   012E8026   40057F9D   E962FF02    ..,..C&@..¥θb .
  000100   00000105   02410200   00020C02   00000000    .....A..........
  000110   00000000   00021E02   032C0203   2A020000    ...........,..*.
  000120   00000000   00000000   00000000   00000001    ................
  000130   05020200   00013802   20026904   00000000    ......8..i.....
  <─┘=PageDown  Esc=Cancel  F9=Hex/ASCII                            4:12p
```

Contents of the COMMAND.COM file

64

3.5 What's in the boxes

You won't be able to do very much with the screen display of this file. Although different numbers and letters are displayed in the left half of the screen, you won't be able to recognize many words in the right half of the screen.

This is either because most files are linked to certain programs or because the files are program files and therefore appear in code. To display these files properly, you need the appropriate program. Press [Esc] to return to the MS-DOS Shell.

There are other files whose contents you can display. One example of this is the AUTOEXEC.BAT file.

First select the AUTOEXEC.BAT file, which is in the root directory of the hard drive. Now use [Alt] to select the menu bar, select **File** and press [Enter]. Use the arrow keys to select **View File Contents** from the **File** menu.

After you press [Enter], the screen changes and you can see the contents of the AUTOEXEC.BAT. In this case, you can also read the contents. To return to the MS-DOS Shell, press [Esc].

3.6 Packing slips

Files and extensions

As we already mentioned in the section on viewing files, file extensions have special meanings in MS-DOS.

MS-DOS actually turns over complete control of the PC to a program when you start it, which is why the program has such a great responsibility. MS-DOS prefers to keep your letters separate from executable programs.

Since almost all programs for PCs used to be commands, they gave them COM for a file extension. Unfortunately, MS-DOS doesn't check whether a program with the .COM extension is really an executable program. So if you named a letter file named IRS.DOC to IRS.COM, you could call it like a command, but your computer would crash (lock up) until you pressed your RESET button or switched the computer off and on.

As a result, they developed another kind of executable file and gave EXE as an extension. If you renamed your IRS.DOC file IRS.EXE and attempted to run it, the system would again crash.

The *batch file* is the only text file you can create that MS-DOS reads as a program. We'll describe batch files in more detail later.

We're telling you this because we believe that this is the best way for you to remember the most important file extensions. You can usually choose any other filenames (at least, as far as MS-DOS is concerned). However, along with the three extensions for command files (.COM, .EXE, and .BAT), a whole series of other extensions have been adopted.

For example, document files usually have the .DOC extension, backups (a kind of copy) usually have the .BAK extension (from BAcKup) and so on (more on this later).

3.7 Access to tools

Starting programs

As we said, in most cases you have to first start the appropriate programs in order to display the contents of files. In the case of a document file, first you have to start the word processing application. If you want to look at a file that contains addresses in the form of data records, then you must first start the appropriate database.

You can use these programs not only to view existing files, but to create new files as well. In a sense, these programs are the actual purpose of a PC, because you use them to make your actual work easier, such as creating documents or managing data.

If you have such a program, but aren't sure how to start it, we'll give you some tips on how to use it.

The user selects certain screen elements with the help of the keyboard or the mouse and calls certain processes. Let's look at what you can do:

- View filenames displayed in the file list area.

- Copy a file by marking it and selecting **Copy...** from the **File** menu.

- View the contents of a single file by marking it and selecting **View File Contents** from the **File** menu.

- Run a program by searching for the file (containing the .EXE, .COM or .BAT extension), marking this file and selecting **Open** from the **File** menu. The operating system (here in the form of the MS-DOS Shell) relinquishes control and you work with the user program. The MS-DOS Shell is no longer visible on the screen.

  Not until you exit the program correctly do you return to the operating system (or MS-DOS Shell).

The following illustration describes the relationship between the MS-DOS Shell and a program:

3. Your first corporate tasks

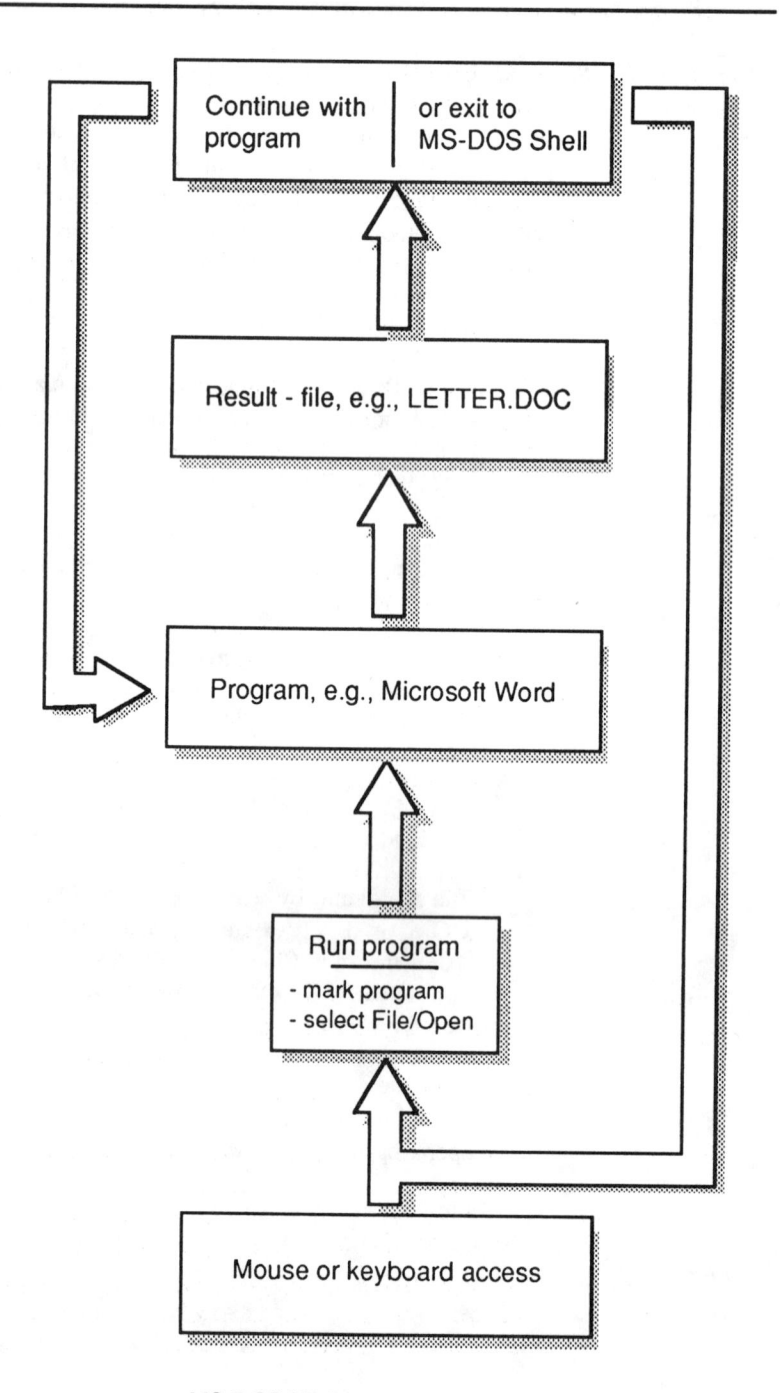

```
┌─────────────────────┬──────────────┐
│ Continue with       │ or exit to   │
│ program             │ MS-DOS Shell │
└─────────────────────┴──────────────┘
              ▲
              │
┌─────────────────────────────────────┐
│ Result - file, e.g., LETTER.DOC     │
└─────────────────────────────────────┘
              ▲
              │
┌─────────────────────────────────────┐
│ Program, e.g., Microsoft Word       │
└─────────────────────────────────────┘
              ▲
              │
┌─────────────────────┐
│ Run program         │
│ - mark program      │
│ - select File/Open  │
└─────────────────────┘
              ▲
              │
┌─────────────────────────┐
│ Mouse or keyboard access│
└─────────────────────────┘
```

MS-DOS Shell/program relationship

3.7 Access to tools

Starting programs

Program files are almost always in their own directories (e.g., DBASE4, WORD5, WORKS). Select the directory containing these files.

To start a program, you must activate the *startup file*. The name of this file is often identical to the name of the program. However, if the filename is longer than eight letters, use either a part of the name or a letter combination which easily identifies the program name. (e.g., MP for Multiplan or WIN for Windows).

To find the name of your program, you must try to find the startup file of your program. You can tell a startup file for a program because it has one of the three following file extensions:

EXE   COM   BAT

To find this file, you must display the contents of the directory where the program is located. First look for files that have EXE as their extensions and the program name (or part of it) as the filenames. If you find such a file, try to start the program by selecting it. Then press (Alt) and (Enter) to select the **File** menu, select **Open**, and press (Enter) again.

If you don't find this file, look for a file with the .COM extension. If you don't find a COM file, look for a file with the .BAT extension. Then try to start the program by marking the name of the file and pressing (Enter).

We'll give you a couple of examples:

Microsoft Word

You will probably find the WORD.EXE file in a directory named WORD. This file has the same name as the application, so it's probably the startup file. If you mark this file and press (Enter), the MS-DOS Shell starts Word.

Microsoft Windows

You will find many files with the .EXE extension in the Windows directory. However, none of these files fulfills the conditions for the name of a startup file. On the other hand, there is a WIN.COM file that fulfills the conditions for a startup file, both in filename (WIN) and file extension (COM). However, you shouldn't start Windows from the MS-DOS Shell, because it may lead to a computer crash. Before you call Windows, make sure you exit the MS-DOS Shell.

3. Your first corporate tasks

Quitting programs

Always quit a program correctly by returning to the MS-DOS Shell. If you simply switch off your computer, you could lose important data. Each program has a special command for exiting.

If you aren't certain how to quit an application or program, here are a few tips. Most applications or programs work with menus and there's usually an item within the menu for exiting.

You can usually select the menu by pressing [Esc] or [Alt]. Use the arrow keys to select the various menus. Then press [Enter] to activate the menu.

Some programs have a special menu for exiting the program. After pressing [Enter], you are prompted to press any key to return to the MS-DOS Shell.

There is a uniform standard that is becoming more and more popular with newer programs. Under this standard, the command for exiting the program is in the **File** menu (usually the last or bottom command). Select the command with the arrow keys and after pressing [Enter] (and pressing any key) you return to the MS-DOS Shell.

The names of menus or commands used in most programs for quitting include: **Exit**, **Quit**, **End** or **System**.

Choose the appropriate command and press [Enter]. Many programs have a security prompt that you must use to confirm that you really want to quit the program.

We'll also give you some examples of quitting programs.

Microsoft Word

To exit Word 5.0, press [Esc], then use the arrow keys to select **Quit** and press [Enter]. If you didn't save the files you were working on, there is a confirmation prompt; otherwise you return to the MS-DOS Shell after pressing any key. To exit Word 5.5, press [Alt], then select the **File** menu and the **Exit Word** command.

Microsoft Windows

Press the [Alt] key and then press [Enter]. In the **File** menu that appears, use the arrow keys to select **Exit Windows...** and press [Enter]. A confirmation prompt follows, asking you whether you really want to exit the program. Press [Enter] a second time, then press any key to return to the MS-DOS Shell.

4. Expanding the company

Working with diskettes It wouldn't be practical to work with just one company. There are other companies with which you can exchange materials. In the PC world, people also rely on data exchange.

4.1 Outfitting a truck

Formatting a diskette When you purchase new diskettes from you must first format them for your computer. If you try to use a diskette that has not been formatted for the computer, your computer will give you an error message. To return to our analogy: You must equip the trucks with shelves, complete the necessary paperwork, etc. before you can load and transport cargo.

To prepare a diskette for your computer, use the **Format** command in the **Disk Utilities** program group. **Disk Utilities** is a group in the program list area of the MS-DOS Shell that provides you with some useful tools for working with your computer. The **Format** command *formats* a diskette (prepares it for receiving data).

To format a diskette, press [Tab] to activate the program list area. The program list area displays various programs supplied with MS-DOS. Use the arrow keys to mark **Disk Utilities** and press [Enter]. The contents and title bar of the area change:

```
 → [Main]
   Disk Copy
   Backup Fixed Disk
   Restore Fixed Disk
   Quick Format
   Format
   Undelete
```

Disk Utilities

Among the commands displayed you will find the **Format** program item. Select this command with the arrow keys and press [Enter]. You are then prompted to specify the drive containing the diskette you want to format. Since the default drive is A:, press [Enter].

The screen of the MS-DOS Shell disappears and a message appears prompting you to insert a diskette in drive A: and press [Enter].

4. Expanding the company

After inserting the diskette and pressing [Enter], the computer begins formatting the diskette. A message on the screen informs you that the MS-DOS Shell is formatting the diskette. The formatting process requires time; exactly how long depends on your computer.

Naming the diskette

After formatting is finished, you are prompted to give the diskette a *volume label* name. Type in the name PRACTICE and press [Enter]. Volume labels can be up to eleven characters in length.

A message appears on the screen informing you of how much memory space is available on the diskette.

The next message asks you whether you want to format another diskette. If this is the case, press [Y] and then [Enter]. If you don't want to format another diskette, press [N] and then [Enter]. The **Format** command is then finished and you are prompted to press any key to return to the MS-DOS Shell. After you have done this, the MS-DOS Shell screen returns.

Follow these steps to format a diskette in the MS-DOS Shell:

1. Select the **Disk Utilities** program group, then select the **Format** program item.

2. In the dialog box that appears, specify the drive or confirm the default drive, A:. The MS-DOS Shell screen disappears and you see a screen that is almost empty, prompting you to insert a diskette.

3. Insert a diskette and press [Enter], to begin the actual formatting process. The MS-DOS Shell displays the progress of the formatting process in percentages. You have the choice of giving your formatted diskette a volume name and are prompted to format another diskette. If you don't want to format another diskette, return to the MS-DOS Shell.

Be careful when formatting diskettes because you can accidentally format diskettes with data on them. Always check whether you have inserted the right diskette before you format it. The best way to do this is to display the contents of a diskette before you format it. If you get an error message, you can be fairly certain that the diskette is unformatted. To cancel the error message, select item 2 with the arrow keys and press [Enter]. You can now begin formatting the diskette.

4.2 Using the loading dock

Copying files to diskette

Copying from hard drive to diskette

After formatting a diskette, you can then copy a file to the diskette.

Let's suppose that you want to copy the AUTOEXEC.BAT file from the root directory of your hard drive to a diskette. First, you must display the files of the root directory in the file list area. Press [Tab] to activate the Directory Tree area and use the [↑] key to select:

```
[-] C:\
```

To copy a file from this directory, you must first select it. Press [Tab] to select the file list area and move the cursor to the file you want to copy (AUTOEXEC.BAT). An arrow to the left of the filename shows that the file is selected.

To copy the selected file, press [Alt] to select the menu bar and press [Enter] to activate the **File** menu. Use the arrow keys to select **Copy...** and press [Enter] again. The following dialog box appears:

```
┌─────────────────Copy File──────────────────┐
│                                            │
│     From:    [AUTOEXEC.BAT ·············]  │
│                                            │
│     To:      [C:\······················]   │
│                                            │
│                                            │
│                                            │
│       [  OK  ]    [ Cancel ]   [ Help ]    │
│                                            │
└────────────────────────────────────────────┘
```

Copy... command dialog box

All you have to do is type in the target of the copying process, drive A:, and the directory. In our example, we want to copy a file from the root directory. Type the following in the To: line:

```
A:\
```

After typing in the target, press [Enter] to copy the file. A message on the screen informs you that the file is being copied.

Change drives by pressing [Tab] to go to the drive icons, select [A:] and press [Enter]. The file list area then displays the contents of the diskette

73

4. Expanding the company

and you can see that the AUTOEXEC.BAT file is actually on the diskette.

Now press [Tab] to activate the drive icons, select [C:] and press [Enter]. You just copied a file from the root directory of the hard drive to a diskette. What if you wanted to copy the TEST.COM file from the WORK directory? Press [Tab] to move the cursor to the Directory Tree area and use the arrow keys to select the WORK directory. The title bar of the file list area then displays WORK as the current directory.

Press [Tab] to go to the file list area, select TEST.COM. Press [Alt] to activate the menu bar, use the arrow keys to select **File** and press [Enter]. In the menu that appears, select the **Copy...** command.

Next, type the target to which you want the file copied:

```
A:\
```

After you press [Enter], the file is copied to the diskette. Once again, a message on the screen informs you of this.

Copying files from diskette to hard drive

Copying a file from a diskette to the hard drive is a similar process. If you wanted to copy the AUTOEXEC.BAT file, which is now on your diskette, back to your hard drive, use the following procedure:

Press [Tab] to activate the drive icons, select [A:] and press [Enter]. The file list area now displays the files in the root directory of the diskette in drive A:. Press [Tab] to activate the file list area and use the arrow keys to mark the AUTOEXEC.BAT file.

Press [Alt] to activate the menu bar, use the arrow keys to select the **File** menu and press [Enter]. Now select the **Copy...** command and press [Enter]. In the dialog box that appears, you must specify the target of your copying process. In our case, the target is the root directory of the hard drive. The following is what the entry should look like:

```
C:\
```

Press [Enter] and a message informs you that the file is being copied.

What if you wanted to copy the TEXT.COM file from the diskette to the WORK directory of the hard drive? First select the TEST.COM file in drive A: (use [Tab] to move to the drive icons, select [A:], and press [Enter]. Then use [Tab] to activate the file list area and select the TEST.COM file with the arrow keys).

4.2 Using the loading dock

Now you can activate the copying command again. Press [Alt] to get to the menu bar, select **File** and press [Enter]. Next, select the **Copy...** command and press [Enter] a second time. Then all you need to do is enter the target of the copying process in the dialog box that appears.

In this case, you must specify the exact target. You must type in the entire path specification of the target in order to copy the file to this directory. The following is what the entry should look like:

```
C:\WORK
```

Press [Enter] to copy the file to the WORK directory.

When you copy files, it's important to make both the drive and directory where the file to be copied is located current. Then you can select the file in the file list area. In the dialog box of the **Copy...** command you must then specify the exact target of the copying process.

Displaying pathnames

If you want to copy a file to a certain directory of the hard drive, you must always specify the exact name of the directory in the dialog box. If you aren't sure about the name of the directory, here's a method for finding it out. As we already explained, the line above the drive icons always contains the exact pathname of whatever directory is current.

To find out the exact name of a directory, you must display the Directory Tree area of the hard drive. Then use [Tab] to move the cursor to the Directory Tree area and select the directory to which you want to copy. In the line above the drive icons you will now see the pathname of the directory. This is exactly what you have to type into the dialog box that will appear when you copy.

If your PC has a mouse, you can use a trick to avoid typing in the path specification for the target. Aim the mouse pointer at the file, press the [Ctrl] key and the left mouse button and drag the file to the target directory in the Directory Tree area.

Release the mouse button. The MS-DOS Shell then asks you whether you want to copy the file to the directory you selected. The Directory Tree must be visible, which means opening up the Directory Tree and moving the mouse (while pressing the mouse button) to the arrows in the scroll bar.

75

4. Expanding the company

4.3 Building the fleet

Disk Copy

Often you must copy entire diskettes. You may need to make copies of program diskettes or you might want to send someone a diskette containing many files but don't want to copy each file separately. We'll make a copy of the PRACTICE diskette containing the AUTOEXEC.BAT and TEST.COM files.

You'll need a blank diskette to copy the files. You also need the **Disk Copy** command in the **Disk Utilities** program group of the **Main** program list area. Use (Tab) to activate the **Main** program list area. Select the **Disk Utilities** entry and press (Enter).

Use the arrow keys to select the **Disk Copy** command and press (Enter). A dialog box appears prompting you to specify the drive containing the diskette to be copied and also the drive with the new diskette. The default entry is A: B:. Change the line to read as follows (even if you have two drives):

```
A: A:
```

The MS-DOS Shell screen disappears and a message appears on the screen, prompting you to insert the source diskette (the one to be copied) in drive A: and press any key. Insert the PRACTICE diskette in drive A: and press (Enter). After that, a message informs you that the diskette is being copied. After a short time, you are prompted to insert the target diskette in drive A:. Remove the source diskette from drive A:. Take the blank diskette, insert it in drive A: and press any key.

If you have high-density diskettes with a memory capacity of 1.2 Meg, you will be prompted to change diskettes a couple of times (your PC can't load much data into its memory at one time).

After the entire diskette has been copied, the computer prompts you to copy another diskette. If you decide to copy another diskette, press (Y) and you will be prompted to insert the diskette you want to copy and the whole process repeats. If you don't want to copy another diskette, press (N). This ends the **Disk Copy** command and you can return to the MS-DOS Shell by pressing any key.

You should also be careful when copying diskettes because if you insert a diskette that already has data as the target diskette, the MS-DOS Shell overwrites the data without giving you any warning.

5. Getting organized

Directories　　This chapter provides more information about using directories, which are extremely important for working with a hard drive. Remember our factory analogy: Directories help ensure organization on the hard drive.

5.1 Creating new directories

We'd like to review the procedure for creating directories. To create a directory, you must activate the directory in which you want to create a new subdirectory.

Earlier we created the WORK directory as a subdirectory of the root directory. Now let's create two new directories, PERSONAL and BUSINESS, as subdirectories of the WORK directory.

Use [Tab] to select the Directory Tree area and use the arrow keys to move the selection cursor to the WORK directory.

Press [Alt] to activate the menu and [Enter] to activate the **File** menu. Select the **Create Directory...** command and press [Enter]. A dialog box appears where you can type in the name of the directory.

Type PERSONAL and press [Enter]. The new directory appears in the Directory Tree area.

If you want to see what's in your new directory, select the Directory Tree area and move the selection cursor to the PERSONAL line. The file list area displays "No files in selected directory."

Now create the BUSINESS directory. Select the WORK directory, select **Create Directory...** from the **File** menu and type BUSINESS. Press [Enter].

The following steps show how to create a new directory:

1.　Select the directory in which you are creating a new subdirectory in the Directory Tree area (e.g., WORK).

2.　Select **Create Directory...** from the **File** menu. Type the name of the new subdirectory (e.g., BUSINESS).

3.　Press [Enter]. The new directory name appears in the Directory Tree area of the MS-DOS Shell.

5. Getting organized

5.2 Removing and renaming directories

Let's look at additional directory options available in the MS-DOS Shell. First, copy the files that are in the WORK directory to your new directory, PERSONAL. You'll need these files in this section.

Activate the WORK directory. Press [Shift] + [F8] to activate the Add mode (the mode for selecting more than one file). Move the selection cursor to each file and press the [Spacebar]. Press [Alt] to activate the menu bar and press [Enter] to select the **File** menu. Select **Copy...** with the arrow keys and press [Enter]. Type the following in the To: line:

C:\WORK\PERSONAL [Enter]

Deleting directories

Now let's delete those directories we've just created. Select BUSINESS in the Directory Tree area. Select the **Delete...** command in the **File** menu and press [Enter]. A dialog box appears with a security prompt. Press [Enter]. The MS-DOS Shell deletes the directory, which you can immediately see from the change in the Directory Tree area.

Select the PERSONAL directory. Use the same procedure we previously described. Select the **File** menu and the **Delete...** command and press [Enter].

A dialog box appears with a message informing you that the selected directory still contains files and that you cannot delete a directory that isn't empty.

Press [Enter] to close the message. You can see the directory still on your hard drive. MS-DOS refuses to delete this directory because it contains files. If you want to delete PERSONAL, you must first delete all the files in the directory. This precaution prevents you from accidentally deleting a directory that still contains important files.

Renaming directories

Let's *rename* (assign another name to) PERSONAL to TEXTS. Use [Tab] to activate the Directory Tree area. Select the PERSONAL directory with the selection cursor. Press [Alt] to select the menu bar and press [Enter] to activate the **File** menu. Select the **Rename...** command and press [Enter].

A dialog box appears with the current name of the file. You can specify the new name of the file after the New Name prompt. Type in TEXTS and press [Enter]. The MS-DOS Shell then displays the directory with its new name.

5.3 Planning for organization

We have already learned how to create subdirectories and move between different levels, but we don't know anything about dividing a hard drive.

The function of subdirectories creates order and help you quickly find files that belong together. You should separate data that you don't use (or seldom use) from data that you work on daily. By doing this, you could avoid the mistake of placing your texts in a directory that also contains the program files.

You can delete certain texts without running into any problems. However, if you delete parts of your word processor or swap them to diskettes, problems can quickly develop, because the program will no longer function.

That's why we recommend that you create a subdirectory, called PROG, for your programs and a subdirectory, called TEXTS, for your texts, in addition to the DOS subdirectory.

When this is done, create a separate subdirectory of PROG for each program that you use. For example, if you used Microsoft Word 5.5, Microsoft Works Version 2.0 and dBASE IV, the following structure might result: When you install WORD5, specify C:\PROG\WORD. A directory for Works 2.0 might be C:\PROG\WORKS2 and a directory for dBASE IV might be C:\PROG\DBASE.

You could break down the TEXTS subdirectory according your needs. For example, you could divide PERSONAL and JOB. This process of changing the current hard drive to subdirectories often reoccurs because certain directories may require to be removed., You could also subdivide other directories by creating more subdirectories.

5. Getting organized

5.4 Moving quickly between rooms

Moving between directories

Moving within a storage medium (and within the Directory Tree area) can be very difficult if you are using a poorly planned structure. Working with different directories can also be very time consuming.

Displaying the Directory Tree correctly

The best way to get to the location in the Directory Tree is to *collapse* it up to the directories that start in the root directory. The quickest way to do this is to place the selection cursor on the root directory (C:\) and press the [-] key once to collapse the directories and then press the plus key to open the first level. With this setting, the complete Directory Tree is usually visible in the area.

If you go to a subdirectory, move the selection cursor to the appropriate directories and open the subdirectories by pressing the [+] key.

Working with two directories

If you use two directories frequently (to copy files or compare files in two directories), it's best if you change the display of the MS-DOS Shell to duplicate the file list area and Directory Tree area. To do this, use the **Dual File Lists** command from the **View** menu. Then the screen displays two Directory Tree areas and two file list areas.

Unlike other utility programs (such as PCTools 6.0), when you copy from one of these directories, the MS-DOS Shell doesn't immediately suggest the other directory. However, you can use a mouse to move files directly from one directory to the other one. To do this, press the mouse button and the [Ctrl] key and move the file to the correct directory in the Directory Tree.

Don't use the mouse to move the file to the second file list area because that would trigger an entirely different function. A program would start with a file as additional information.

The trick with the initial letters

If you frequently move between several different directories, there's a trick for doing this quickly. Open up all the necessary directories. You could also make all of the subdirectories visible by moving the selection cursor to the root directory and pressing the key with an * embossed on it.

Now, whenever you want to activate a certain directory, simply type in the first letter of the directory name and press [Enter]. The selection cursor immediately jumps to the first appropriate directory. If there is a directory in the Directory Tree area with the same first letter, then press

5.4 Moving quickly between rooms

the first letter more than once. This is much faster than using the arrow keys to search.

You can use this method in the other list areas of the MS-DOS Shell, thus saving a great deal of time and work.

Changing directories at the command prompt is even faster. For example, you could create little batch files under the name of the directory that jump to the desired directory. Also, with some utility programs where you only need to specify part of the directory name; the program automatically makes that directory the current directory (check out the TCD program from the book *Batch File Powertools*, published by Abacus).

6. MS-DOS Shell extras

This chapter describes more features that will make your work with the MS-DOS Shell easier in many ways.

6.1 Limiting file display

Frequently it can be to your advantage if the file list area only displays certain files. For example, this is the case when you are looking for files to start a program. It would be better if the screen only displayed files with .EXE, .COM or .BAT extensions.

You can limit the types of files displayed using the **File Display Options...** command from the **Options** menu. Select this command. In the dialog box that appears, enter the name of the file you would like to see after Name. This only makes sense if you just want to see whether the file is in the current directory.

Wildcards If you can't remember the name of the file, you can also use *wildcards*. The two different wildcards in MS-DOS are the question mark "?" and the asterisk "*". You can use the question mark as a wildcard if you aren't certain about single characters in a filename. For example, you might not remember whether a certain file is called MEYER.DOC or MAYER.DOC. In this case, simply use the wildcard, typing M?YER.DOC, and MS-DOS will find the files that fit the filename and display them after you press (Enter).

You can use the asterisk to display whole groups of files. Let's assume you would like to see all files with the ".BAT" extension. Just type "*.BAT" after "Name" and press (Enter). The MS-DOS Shell then lists all files with the ".BAT" extension in the file list area.

You can use the wildcard in several different ways. If you are searching for all files that begin with "A" and end with a .SYS extension, simply type "A*.SYS". If you are only interested in files beginning with "W", you would type "W*.*". If you want to look at all of the files again, type "*.*".

When you select a display option here, it remains in effect until you select a new one. So when you change directories, you won't see all of the files, but only those that fit the setting you made.

83

6. MS-DOS Shell extras

6.2 Rearranging files in a directory

Another option consists of displaying the files sorted. You can sort them according to various criteria. Use [Alt] and the arrow keys to select the **Options** menu and press [Enter]. In the menu use the arrow keys to mark the **File Display Options...** command and press [Enter] to activate it.

The dialog box that appears lets you set the sort sequence for the files in the file list area under Sort by. You can sort by filename, file extension, date of creation or file size. This is called alphanumerical sorting, because it sorts all the letters of the alphabet first before sorting numbers. The numbers are not sorted according to their value. Here is the sequence:

```
        1.DOC    11.DOC    12.DOC    2.DOC
```

To activate one of these options, you must first use [Tab] to place the cursor in this area. Then you can use the arrow keys to select an option. Press [Enter] to confirm your selection.

Let's look at the following sorting options:

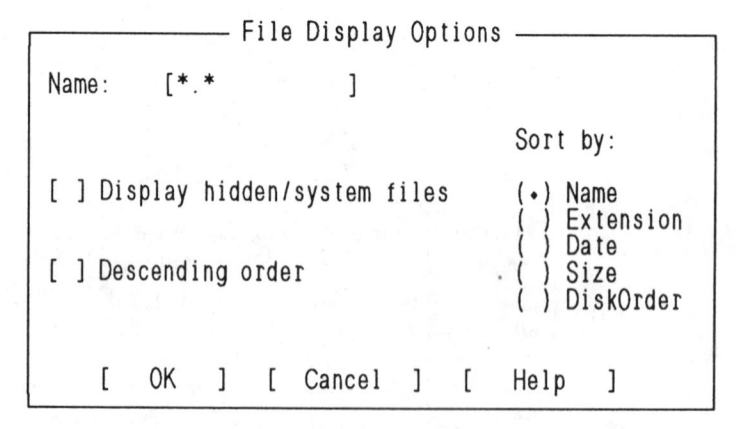

```
┌──────────────── File Display Options ────────────────┐
│                                                      │
│  Name:     [*.*              ]                       │
│                                                      │
│                                          Sort by:    │
│                                                      │
│  [ ] Display hidden/system files       (•) Name      │
│                                        ( ) Extension │
│                                        ( ) Date      │
│  [ ] Descending order                  ( ) Size      │
│                                        ( ) DiskOrder │
│                                                      │
│          [  OK  ]   [ Cancel ]   [ Help ]            │
│                                                      │
└──────────────────────────────────────────────────────┘
```

Notice the *radio buttons* under the Sort by: option. If you activate Name: the files will be sorted alphabetically by name. You could also sort by extension, date of creation, and size. Selecting DiskOrder displays the files in the sequence in which they were found on the diskette or hard drive.

If you activate the Descending order option, the files are displayed in *descending* order (Z, Y, ... B, A and 9, 8, 7). Otherwise, an *ascending* sort sorts files in ascending order (A, B, ... Y, Z and 1, 2, 3, etc.).

6.3 Listing all files

You can also display all the files of a diskette or hard drive, regardless of which directory is current. This option is especially helpful if you can't quite remember the name of a file or program and you want to check through all the files to find it.

This option is also a good way of quickly finding files that are in two or three different places on your hard drive (such as multiple MOUSE.COM files for operating the mouse).

If you select the **All Files** command from the **View** menu, all the files of the current drive will be listed in alphanumerical order. The Directory Tree area is cancelled. The left side of the screen provides additional information about the selected file.

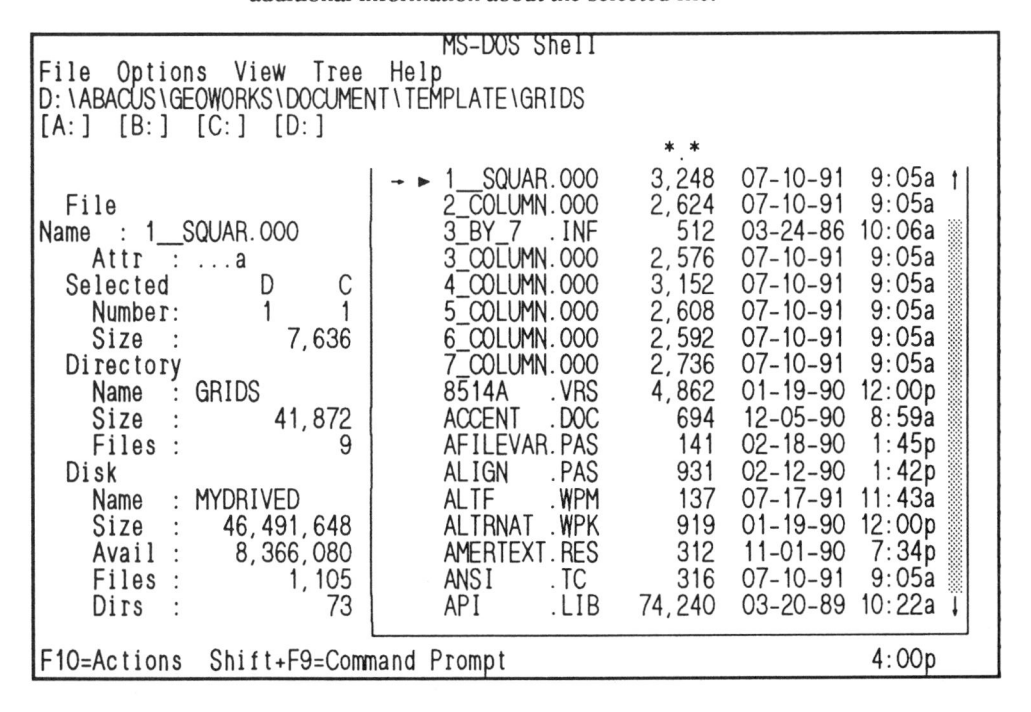

```
                              MS-DOS Shell
File  Options  View  Tree  Help
D:\ABACUS\GEOWORKS\DOCUMENT\TEMPLATE\GRIDS
[A:]  [B:]  [C:]  [D:]
                                             *.*
                              → ► 1__SQUAR.000    3,248   07-10-91   9:05a ↑
   File                           2_COLUMN.000    2,624   07-10-91   9:05a
   Name   : 1__SQUAR.000           3_BY_7  .INF     512   03-24-86  10:06a
     Attr :  ...a                 3_COLUMN.000    2,576   07-10-91   9:05a
   Selected      D      C         4_COLUMN.000    3,152   07-10-91   9:05a
     Number:    1      1          5_COLUMN.000    2,608   07-10-91   9:05a
     Size  :         7,636        6_COLUMN.000    2,592   07-10-91   9:05a
   Directory                      7_COLUMN.000    2,736   07-10-91   9:05a
     Name  : GRIDS                8514A   .VRS    4,862   01-19-90  12:00p
     Size  :        41,872        ACCENT  .DOC      694   12-05-90   8:59a
     Files :             9        AFILEVAR.PAS     141   02-18-90   1:45p
   Disk                           ALIGN   .PAS     931   02-12-90   1:42p
     Name  : MYDRIVED             ALTF    .WPM     137   07-17-91  11:43a
     Size  :    46,491,648        ALTRNAT .WPK     919   01-19-90  12:00p
     Avail :     8,366,080        AMERTEXT.RES     312   11-01-90   7:34p
     Files :         1,105        ANSI    .TC      316   07-10-91   9:05a
     Dirs  :            73        API     .LIB  74,240   03-20-89  10:22a ↓

F10=Actions  Shift+F9=Command Prompt                              4:00p
```

6.4 Searching for files

Select the **All Files** command in the **View** menu to display the files of a diskette or hard drive. You can use that setting with the **File Display Options...** command from the **Options** men to have the MS-DOS Shell search the entire diskette or hard drive for a certain file.

First use [Alt], the arrow keys, and [Enter] to activate the **View** menu. Then use the arrow keys to select the **All Files** command and press [Enter]. The view immediately changes. It takes up the entire screen and the left side of the screen always displays file information about the marked file. If you select the **Options** menu, use the arrow keys to mark **File Display Options...** and press [Enter] to activate. You can enter a filename after Name. For example, if you are looking for the TEST.DOC file, type in this name and press [Enter].

If this file is anywhere on your computer, the file list area will display it. In the file information next to it you can find out which directory it's in by looking under the Directory Name: listing.

7. Keeping things simple

Streamlining with the MS-DOS Shell

You recall how to call programs with the MS-DOS Shell: You had to go to the appropriate directory, find the right startup file and then call it from the menu. This is time consuming if you want to work with the same program(s) on a daily basis.

There's an easier way. With the MS-DOS Shell you can make it easy to start programs that you'll be able to call up immediately later on. You use the program list area, which we have been using up to now to format and copy diskettes. The deciding factor is that you can add programs to the default programs.

7.1 Program items and groups

Use `Tab` or the mouse to move the selection cursor to the program list area.

The program list area displays a list of the available program items, as well as the line **Disk Utilities**. You could combine several program items into a group for easier access. That is, instead of a program name, each line would have the name of a group. When you select a group, the screen contents would change from the **Main** group to the group you selected, just like you did with the **Disk Utilities** group earlier. Selecting a group displays those program items assigned to that group. Each group includes a line called Main. You can select Main at any time to return to the **Main** group of the program list area.

7. Keeping things simple

7.2 Groups

When the MS-DOS Shell is first installed, the program list area has the Main group and the **Disk Utilities** group at its disposal. If you select **Disk Utilities** and press [Enter] to open it, you have your choice of six programs.

You could also add programs and groups to the program list area. This means that you are able to divide your programs and data in a problem oriented manner, creating a separate group for each set of tasks. For example, if you wanted to use your computer to create an advertising brochure, then you probably need a word processor for creating and editing the texts, as well as a graphics program for the graphics. You could then combine both programs into a group called ADSTUFF.

Dividing the **Main** group into groups can be especially useful if more than one person is working on the same PC. Then you could create a group for each person, with all the programs used by this person at his/her disposal. That way you can arrange the interface of the program list area in an easy manner. You can even use the program list area to create finished programs and groups so a beginner can use the PC after a very brief period of time.

Starting programs

It's very easy to start programs. Use the [↑] or [↓] keys to mark the desired program name and press [Enter].

It's even easier with the mouse: Move the mouse pointer to the desired program item name and double-click the name.

Program and group icons

If you are in graphics mode, the MS-DOS Shell displays icons to the left of each name. The program item looks like this:

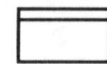

The group icon can be easily discerned from the program icon by the six boxes drawn within it:

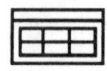

In text mode, groups are indicated by brackets, as you've seen from the Main group and the **Disk Utilities** group.

7.2 Groups

Parameters If after it's loaded, a program requires one or more parameters to start. A dialog box appears on the screen where you can type in the necessary information. Both programs that come supplied with the MS-DOS Shell (the Editor and QBasic) have one of these dialog boxes for entering parameters. The Editor lets you specify which file you want to edit, while in QBasic you can specify which BASIC file you want to open.

Selecting and opening a group is as easy as starting a program. You mark the group line with the [↑] or [↓] keys and press [Enter]. This opens the group.

It's even easier with the mouse: Move the mouse pointer to the desired group name and double-click the name.

After you open a group, the screen displays its contents on the screen. The title bar displays the name of the group instead of Main. Each group has a group line on top with the name of the next highest group. If it's the main group, then it is called Main. You can return to the next highest group by double-clicking this line or by pressing [Esc]. You can also select this line by using [↑] or [PgUp] and then pressing [Enter].

A group can contain an almost unlimited number of lines. The lines within a group can be program lines as well as group lines. This enables you to add as many programs as you want to a group, as well as add subgroups, which can also include programs and groups. The structure is similar to the structure of directories on the hard drive.

7. Keeping things simple

7.3 Existing programs and groups

You will find three program lines and a group line in the Main group of the program list area. By activating the Command Prompt program line you "temporarily" exit the MS-DOS Shell and go to the MS-DOS command interpreter. The second line starts a text editor (small word processor). The third line starts QBasic, a comfortable variant of the BASIC programming language. By activating the fourth line, you open the **Disk Utilities** group. This group contains six programs.

We will explain these program items and the **Disk Utilities** group in the following sections.

System Prompt

When you start this program you temporarily exit the MS-DOS Shell and invoke the MS-DOS system prompt. You can enter all the commands here that the MS-DOS Shell has prevented you from entering so far (more on this in Chapter 8). Go ahead and select this command. You will then see a screen with the system prompt, which will look similar to the following:

```
C:\>
```

☞ The system prompt is called a prompt because it signals the system's readiness to accept commands. You can enter DOS commands after the system prompt.

First, let's return to the MS-DOS Shell with the EXIT command. Type EXIT in lowercase or uppercase letters on the screen and press the [Enter] key.

Pressing [Shift]+[F9] also runs the Command Prompt program.

The MS-DOS Editor

This program line starts the MS-DOS 5.0 Editor. As its name implies, the Editor can be used for simple text entry and editing. After activating this program line, you can specify which text file you want to create or edit in a dialog box. See Chapter 10 for more information about the MS-DOS Editor.

7.3 Existing programs and groups

QBasic

This program line starts QBasic, the BASIC interpreter that comes supplied with MS-DOS 5.0. You can write your own programs with QBasic. It's not as difficult as it may seem (see Chapter 10 for more information about QBasic).

Disk Utilities

This is the only group available in the Main group of the program list area after installation. When you activate this group, the menu bar displays the name **Disk Utilities**. The top line is a group line called Main. You can return to the **Main** group by either selecting this line or pressing [Esc].

In the following sections we give you a detailed description of the six program lines of the **Disk Utilities** group.

Disk Copy You use the Disk Copy program item to copy diskettes. You can specify the source and target drives. The default settings are source drive A: and target drive B:. You can change these settings. After pressing [Enter] to confirm your choices, the MS-DOS Shell executes the DISKCOPY command.

You don't need to know anything about the MS-DOS DISKCOPY command to use Disk Copy from the **Disk Utilities** group.

Backup Fixed Disk The next program, Backup Fixed Disk, is similar. When you *back up* something, you are making a copy of the data stored on a hard drive with the help of an MS-DOS program called BACKUP. Select Backup Fixed Disk to invoke this command. The default setting of our MS-DOS Shell program is a backup of all files and subdirectories of drive C:. Drive A: is set as the target drive. You can also change these settings.

Restore Fixed Disk The Restore Fixed Disk program returns data to the hard drive previously backed up using the Backup Fixed Disk command. The MS-DOS Shell uses the RESTORE command to perform this task. The default setting is a backup of all data from drive A: to drive C:. You can also change the default settings.

91

7. Keeping things simple

Quick Format This program reformats diskettes that have already been formatted. The advantage of Quick Format over Format is that Quick Format is a lot faster. Quick Format deletes the directory areas of the diskette. The only disadvantage to this method is that the command doesn't *verify* (check) the diskette.

Format As you learned earlier, the Format program formats diskettes or hard drives (i.e., prepares them to receive data). This program invokes the MS-DOS FORMAT command, which you'll learn about later. The default setting is drive A:. Here, too, you can change the setting.

Undelete This program can recover most files that you accidentally deleted. Imagine you were a little careless with Delete and now the file is gone. MS-DOS 5.0's Undelete program gives you the option of recovering a deleted file.

After selecting this program line, a dialog box appears where you can display the files deleted most recently. To save one of the files, call the program again and delete /LIST from the dialog box. Now the MS-DOS Shell prompts you to undelete the last files deleted from the current directory. After pressing [Y], you are prompted to type in the first letters of the filename. MS-DOS then tells you whether the file can be undeleted or not.

For example, let's copy the AUTOEXEC.BAT file from the root directory of the hard drive to a diskette. Mark the file in the root directory and call the **Copy...** command from the **File** menu. Enter A:\ as your target.

After copying the file, switch to drive A: to make certain the file was copied. Click the icon for drive A: in drive icons or use [Tab] to move the highlight to drive icons, then to the icon for drive A: and press [Enter].

If the AUTOEXEC.BAT file appears in the file list area (drive A:), mark it and press [Del], or activate the **Delete...** command in the **File** menu. Confirm the security prompt by pressing [Enter] after you are certain that you are really deleting A:\AUTOEXEC.BAT.

Use the [Tab] key to activate the program list area and select the **Disk Utilities** group. Move the selection cursor to the Undelete line and press [Enter]. Enter A:\AUTOEXEC.BAT in the Parameters line and press [Enter]. A new screen appears listing information similar to the following:

7.3 Existing programs and groups

```
?UTOEXEC BAT      690  4-12-91 10:06...A  Recover(Y/N)?
```

The first letter of the filename is missing. To recover the file, first press [Y] to begin recovering it. MS-DOS prompts you for the first letter of the filename, represented by a question mark. This is not a test question, the first letter of the filename is actually lost.

Typing in an A concludes the process and you see a message on the screen, informing you that the process was successful. If you had typed in a B instead of an A, the process also would have worked, only then your recovered file would be BUTOEXEC.BAT instead of AUTOEXEC.BAT.

Here is some very important advice about using Undelete:

- If you accidentally delete a file, call the Undelete program immediately. Do not continue working with the diskette or hard drive. Don't create any files or save data on the disk drive that contained the deleted file. Any kind of change (other than using Undelete) may make it impossible to recover a deleted file.

- After you use Undelete, be sure to read the contents of the directory in the MS-DOS Shell. Double-click the drive letter (in the drive icons line) or select the letter and press [Enter].

- Be very careful when deleting files. There's no guarantee that Undelete will be able to restore deleted files, and sometimes the file may be beyond recovery.

7. Keeping things simple

7.4 Expanding a group

One important feature of the MS-DOS Shell is that you can add your own program lines to a group. This means you can start your existing programs from the program list area. You can also name the program line and specify parameters for the program call.

Adding a program line

Let's suppose that you have your Microsoft Word 5.0 program in the subdirectory C:\PROG\WORD5. You want to add a program to the program list area to call Word with a simple keypress or mouse click.

Select **New...** from the **File** menu to add Word to the Main group. A dialog box appears, prompting you to either add a program group or program item (the default is Program Item). Press (Enter) or click OK. The Add Program dialog box appears:

```
┌─────────────────── Add Program ───────────────────┐
│                                                    │
│  Program Title . . . . [                         ] │
│                                                    │
│  Commands     . . . . [                          ] │
│                                                    │
│  Startup Directory . . [                         ] │
│                                                    │
│  Application Shortcut Key    [                   ] │
│                                                    │
│  [X] Pause after exit        Password . . [      ] │
│                                                    │
│      [  OK  ]  [ Cancel ]  [ Help ]  [ Advanced... ] │
└────────────────────────────────────────────────────┘
```

These prompts request the following information:

Program Title

The Program Title line indicates the name of the title you want assigned to the program item. The title can be up to 25 characters in length. This title can be a more comprehensible name than the program name assigned to the program itself. For example, our example word processor has the name WORD.EXE. The Program Title prompt lets you assign the name "Word Processor" instead. Press (Tab) to move to the next line.

7.4 Expanding a group

Commands The Commands line specifies the name used to call the program, as if you were calling the program from the system prompt (see Chapter 8 for more information). For example, if you have Word stored in C:\PROG\WORD5 and you used PATH (WORD automatically does this when you install it) to set up a search path to this directory, simply type WORD in the Commands line. If you don't have a path to C:\PROG\WORD5, then you must enter the whole command: (C:\PROG\WORD5\WORD).

If you want to execute several commands in a row, you must separate them by semicolons. For example, if you want to format a diskette in drive A: and use CHKDSK to check the diskette, then you must type both commands in the Commands line in the following manner:

FORMAT A: ; CHKDSK A:

See Chapter 8 for more details on MS-DOS commands from the system prompt.

Startup Directory The Startup Directory line specifies which directory you want to be the current directory before the program starts. For example, if you keep all of the documents that you edit with Word in a directory called C:\TEXTS, you could enter that directory here as the startup directory. That makes C:\TEXTS the current directory for Word.

Application Shortcut Key The Application Shortcut Key line lets you assign a key combination with (Ctrl), (Alt), (Shift) and a letter. For example, you could assign (Ctrl) + (W) to Microsoft Word.

Press (Ctrl), (Alt) or (Shift) and a letter, number or function key (avoid using (Shift) + the number keys). The MS-DOS Shell then enters the key combination. The application shortcut key switches between applications when the Task Swapper is active. The Task Swapper lets you *multitask* (run several programs at once) and switch between them at the press of a key.

Pause after exit The Pause after exit option button specifies whether you want the MS-DOS Shell to pause before completely exiting the program. From the keyboard you can use the (Spacebar) to toggle the option button on ([X]) or off ([ ]).

Using the mouse, click on the Pause after exit option button to toggle the option on ([X]) or off ([ ]).

95

7. Keeping things simple

If the option button contains an X, the MS-DOS Shell waits for you to press a key after exiting a program before returning you to the MS-DOS Shell. If the option button is empty, the MS-DOS Shell screen returns immediately after you exit the program.

The reason you should use Pause after exit is because some programs and MS-DOS commands (DIR, CHKDSK, MEM) display information on the screen and then immediately pass a message to the operating system that the program/command has finished. However, you sometimes won't have enough time to read the information. Pause after exit gives you time to read the contents of the screen at any time. Then press a key to return to the MS-DOS Shell screen.

Password If you want to control who can access the program group, enter a password of 1 to 13 characters. Then after you start the program, you're prompted for the password. When you enter the password, the screen displays only asterisks. This is a safety feature so others can't see the password as you enter it.

You can't copy, delete or make any changes to this program line until you enter the password. The MS-DOS Shell is case-sensitive (i.e., it reads both uppercase and lowercase letters when you type your password), so if you enter a password, remember exactly how it was entered.

We recommend that you avoid using a password until you have become more familiar with the MS-DOS Shell.

After you finish with all the entries, press (Enter) to add the program to the program group. Click Cancel or press (Esc) to cancel the process. All the settings you made are then lost.

Adding and changing groups

You can also expand the program list area by adding group lines. Imagine you had several programs that you didn't use very often, but that you wanted to be able to call immediately. You can set up a group called "Miscellaneous Progs" and add the programs that you want to be able to call immediately. It's even easier to set up a new group than it is to create a program line. The Add Group dialog box, as the following describes, appears when you create or change a group. You must type something in Title, while the next two (Help Text, Password) are optional.

7.4 Expanding a group

Adding a group line

To add a new group line, activate **New...** from the **File** menu. You are then prompted to set up a new program group or a program item. Use the ↑ arrow key to select the Program Group radio button and press Enter.

Using the mouse, click on the Program Group radio button and click on the OK button.

The following dialog box appears:

```
┌──────────────── Add Group ────────────────┐
│  Required                                  │
│     Title . . . .    [...................] │
│  Optional                                   │
│     Help Text . .    [...................] │
│     Password  . .    [...................] │
│                                             │
│         [   OK   ]   [ Cancel ]   [ Help ] │
└─────────────────────────────────────────────┘
```

You can enter or change the following entries:

Title
The Title line specifies the group line's title (e.g., "Miscellaneous Progs"). This title can be up to 19 characters in length. After entering the title, press Tab to move to the next line.

Help Text
The Help Text line comprises a 19-character help text (e.g., "Assorted Programs"). Press Tab to move to the next line.

Password
If you enter a password of one to eleven characters here, then after you start the program, you are prompted for the password. When you enter the password, it doesn't appear on the screen. You can't copy, delete or make any changes to this program line until you enter the password. The MS-DOS Shell is case-sensitive (i.e., it reads both uppercase and lowercase letters when you type your password), so if you enter a password, remember exactly how it was entered.

We recommend that you avoid using a password until you have become more advanced in MS-DOS.

7. Keeping things simple

Pressing [Enter] means you accept the settings you made as the correct ones. You have now created a new group.

Changing an existing group line

To change an existing group line, use either the mouse or the arrow keys to mark the group line that you want to change. Next, activate **Properties...** from the **File** menu. This calls the Program Group Properties dialog box. This dialog box has the same settings as the Add Group dialog box, except that each line contains the current values:

```
┌─────────── Program Group Properties ───────────┐
│ Required                                       │
│    Title . . . .    [Miscellaneous Progs.]     │
│ Optional                                       │
│    Help Text . .    [Assorted programs...]     │
│    Password  . .    [swordfish..........]      │
│                                                │
│         [  OK  ]   [ Cancel ]   [ Help ]       │
└────────────────────────────────────────────────┘
```

7.5 Program parameters

If a program requires one or more *parameters* (additional information) when you start it, a dialog box appears on the screen, where you can enter the necessary parameters. Both the MS-DOS Editor and MS-DOS QBasic require such a dialog box for parameters. Specify the file you want to edit in the Editor dialog box, or which Basic file you want to read in the QBasic dialog box.

When you start up a word processor, you can also specify the text you want loaded with the word processor in a dialog box. Many programs can also process other information when you call them, under certain circumstances stopping all further work.

The instruction for starting a program with one or more (up to 9) parameters is called "%1" ("%2", "%3", to "%9"). They chose these special character strings because they are so unusual, hardly ever appearing in command lines or as filenames. The technical term for these is *environmental variables*.

Type in "%1" after the command under the Commands item when you create or change a program line. For example, if you wanted to call Microsoft Word, the word processor, with a parameters dialog box, you would type WORD %1 or C:\PROG\WORD5\WORD %1 in the Commands line. Although this sounds confusing, we'll discuss these parameters in more detail in Chapter 11.

7.6 Renaming and deleting program lines

As you become more experienced in MS-DOS, you'll find that some programs are no longer useful. The MS-DOS Shell also gives you the option of renaming, expanding or completely removing programs.

Renaming a program line

Let's assume you've set up a program called "Word Processor," as we described earlier in this chapter. You use this program line to start WORD.EXE. Now you decide you'd like to change the title of the program so people immediately know that it's Microsoft Word, the word processing program.

Mark the program line with the mouse or the arrow keys. Then select **Properties...** from the **File** menu to change the program line.

Change the Program Title line from "Word Processor" to "Microsoft Word". Press (Enter) or click OK to exit. This implements the change immediately.

Deleting program lines

You can also delete lines from the program list area. You may have already removed the program from the hard drive, or else you use the program so seldom that it's not worth having a program line for it in the MS-DOS Shell.

For example, you have replaced Word 5.0 with Word 5.5. You still haven't deleted the old version of Word from your hard drive, but instead created a new program line for the new version. After a while you notice that you don't even need the "old" version, Word 5.0, any more, so you delete the Word 5.0 directory from the hard drive. Now you must remove the program line from the program list area.

To delete a program from the program list area, select the program line and select the **Delete...** command from the **File** menu. After a confirming prompt, the MS-DOS Shell deletes the marked program.

This process only deletes the program properties needed to start the program from the MS-DOS Shell. To delete the file itself, you must mark the file from the file list area and select **Delete...** from the **File** menu.

7.7 The MS-DOS Shell in practice

The MS-DOS Shell has many practical options that make it safer and easier for any user to work with PCs, especially the beginner.

Unfortunately, first you must *configure* (adjust) the MS-DOS Shell settings. The basic version, as it appears after installation, doesn't have very many options. If you want to make it easier to start programs or combine certain activities into subject groups, you must learn how to create programs and groups, find out the directory paths for programs, type entries in the program definitions and much more.

The situation is a little different if somebody sets up the MS-DOS Shell for a beginner, thus ensuring that the beginner's first access to the computer is also a safe one. That means that the programs available on the hard drive also must be added to the program list area.

If you're adapting the MS-DOS Shell to your own needs, it's important to:

- Make all necessary operations available as programs, so the user doesn't have to access the file list area to view or copy files.

- Make full use of Help Texts. When adding new programs, you must select **New...** from the **File** menu and click on the Advanced... button. Then you can enter a short help text, accessible when you mark the appropriate program line and press the F1 key.

By adding programs you can streamline much of your file management. For example, suppose you wanted to back up all of the document files from a directory called C:\TEXTS to a diskette. You could use the file list area, but you would have to mark all of the document files first. It's much easier if you use the following line:

```
COPY C:\TEXTS\*.DOC A:
```

You could enter this line using the **Run...** command of the **File** menu, but then you would have to remember the exact syntax of the command line and enter it several times. It's easier to select **New...** from the **File** menu, create a program line named "Texts to A:" and type the command in the Commands line.

101

8. The command interpreter

Now that you have become acquainted with many of the options of the MS-DOS Shell, we'd like to introduce you to the command interpreter, which is another way of working with MS-DOS.

We mentioned two different options for working with MS-DOS 5.0. The first option is the MS-DOS Shell, which allows the graphic selection of commands; and the command interpreter, which involves direct keyboard entry of these commands. We mentioned a few of these commands in the previous chapter, where we talked about adding your own MS-DOS Shell programs.

After a certain point, basic knowledge of the command interpreter is to your advantage. You may at a future time use a PC with an earlier version of MS-DOS which doesn't include the MS-DOS Shell—just the command interpreter. Therefore, understanding the command interpreter will help you communicate with these older PCs as needed.

You'll see a lot of information in this chapter that you've already read in earlier chapters. As the MS-DOS Shell and the command interpreter are two methods of performing the same task (communicating with the operating system), some repetition and overlapping will occur.

This chapter features a cross-reference to help you make the connection between the command interpreter and the MS-DOS Shell.

8.1 Hiring an assistant

The command interpreter

We stated earlier that the command interpreter is the non-graphic counterpart of the MS-DOS Shell. As its name suggests, the command interpreter is the program that interprets commands. Your PC understands MS-DOS commands because the command interpreter takes commands and translates them into a language that the PC understands.

The MS-DOS command interpreter is the lower and more traditional level for communicating with MS-DOS. All the tasks that you have performed in the MS-DOS Shell until now can also be done from the command interpreter. Many of these processes, such as copying or deleting, however require very clear instructions given to the PC.

The command interpreter requires that you memorize many items. Also, there are commands that you can only access from the command interpreter and not from the MS-DOS Shell (more on this later).

8. The command interpreter

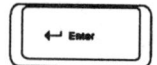

Before starting the command interpreter, first make the root directory of the hard drive the current directory in the MS-DOS Shell.

To do this, use [Tab] to move the selection cursor to the Directory Tree area and select the following entry (this is how the entry will appear in text mode, so your screen may look different if you're in another mode):

[-]-C:\

Press the [Alt] key to select the menu bar and press [Enter] to select the File menu. Select the **Exit** command and press [Enter].

Using the mouse, click on the root directory entry, click on the **File** menu title and click on the **Exit** command.

The MS-DOS Shell disappears. In its place you see a screen that looks similar to the following:

```
C:\>
```

Notice the character string in the upper-left corner of the screen. That's all the command interpreter displays to indicate that the system is ready to accept MS-DOS commands. This string is often called a system prompt or command prompt.

The system prompt usually indicates the letter of the current drive (in this example, C), followed by a colon, the backslash (used for separating directories), and finally the greater than character, pointing to the place where you can type in your commands. The default MS-DOS system prompt consists of the drive letter and a greater than character (e.g., C>).

8.2 How the assistant works

Entering commands and seeing results

Hold down the (Shift) key on the keyboard and type the following text. Release the (Shift) key after entering the text and press the (Enter) key:

```
HELLO (Enter)
```

The disk drive runs for a moment and the PC displays a message similar to the following:

```
Bad command or file name
```

The PC doesn't understand what you just entered. PCs are very dumb machines—they will only accept what they understand. For example, DISKCOPY is a DOS command recognized by the PC. Let's learn a few more DOS commands.

The DATE command

Type the following text and press the (Enter) key. The text can be either in uppercase or lowercase. MS-DOS will accept either in the command interpreter. Throughout this book, we'll print the command words we want you to enter in uppercase:

```
DATE (Enter)
```

The following message or something similar should appear:

```
Current date is Thu 01-13-1992
Enter new date (mm-dd-yy):
```

If another system date should appear, don't worry. Press the (Enter) key and the normal system prompt reappears. Enter the DATE command repeatedly and press (Enter) in response to the Enter new date: prompt. If no system date is entered, the PC retains the original date as "stamped" on the disk.

Pay strict attention to spaces between words. The PC is very particular about the way commands are entered.

Type the following:

```
DATE (Enter)
```

Again, the PC responds with:

8. The command interpreter

```
Current date is Thu 02-13-1986
Enter new date (mm-dd-yy):
```

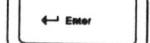

Notice the date structure. It appears in MM-DD-YY format. This means that to assign the current system date, you must enter the month as two digits (e.g., April appears as 04), the day as two digits (e.g., the sixteenth appears as 16) and the year as two or four digits.

Type the following text exactly as it appears here. Separate each number with minus signs:

04-12-89 [Enter]

The computer displays the system prompt. It doesn't look like anything happened. Type the following:

```
DATE [Enter]
Current date is Wed 04-12-1989
Enter new date (mm-dd-yy):
```

Press [Enter].

You can also enter a new date in another way. Type the following text, which makes the new date a parameter of the DATE command:

DATE 1-1-89 [Enter]

The computer displays the system prompt. Now when you enter the DATE command again, the computer responds:

```
Current date is Sun 01-01-1989
Enter new date (mm-dd-yy):
```

Press [Enter].

Notice that months and days numbering less than 10 only require one digit. Also, notice that the year doesn't require the century. We just enter 89 or whatever year, and the PC assumes we're in the 1900s.

The PC generates the day of the week through DATE. Type the following to see what the PC does:

```
DATE 1-1-2000 [Enter]
DATE [Enter]
```

8.2 How the assistant works

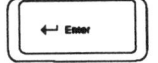

The PC should say that the current date is Saturday, January 1, 2000. The computer will accept any date from 01-01-1980 to 12-31-2099. Any dates outside this range will result in:

```
Invalid date
Enter new date (mm-dd-yy):
```

Why a date? The PC assigns the current system date to any disk data that has been edited, created, or modified. This date stamping helps you keep track of the most recent versions of files.

The TIME command

Now that we've explored the command used for setting the date, let's look at the command used for setting the time. Type the following:

```
TIME [Enter]
```

The screen displays a message similar to the following:

```
Current time is  2:32:58.59p
Enter new time:
```

Enter the current time in HH:MM:SS format. For example, type the following to set the time to 10:00 AM:

```
TIME 10:00:00 [Enter]
```

The time listed above indicates the current time in most modern computers. Newer PCs have real time clocks to keep constant track of the current time. Older PCs without this clock feature display the amount of time elapsed since the computer was switched on. Check your PC manual to find out whether your PC has a real time clock.

You can also enter single digits. Type the following:

```
TIME 7:5:2 [Enter]
```

The PC reads this time entry as:

```
07:05:02
```

If you enter illegal times like 26:00:00, the PC responds with:

```
Invalid time
```

8. The command interpreter

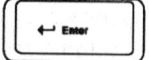

MS-DOS reads time in 24-hour format. For example, typing the following sets the time to 5:32 in the evening:

TIME 17:32:00 [Enter]

Again, you must remember to press the [Enter] key at the end of the input. This instructs MS-DOS to execute the command.

Summary   The DATE and TIME commands let the user set or change the current system date and time at any time. System date and time are stored on disk with any files that are currently updated in any way.

The DATE command accepts input in MM-DD-YY format:

DATE [Enter]
DATE MM-DD-YY [Enter]

DATE [Enter] alone displays the current date.

The TIME command accepts input in HH:MM:SS format:

TIME [Enter]
TIME 13:57:00 [Enter]

TIME [Enter] alone displays the current time.

The PROMPT command

You've seen the system prompt many times so far. It indicates the letter of the current disk drive and normally ends with a greater than character. The prompt we've seen so far looks similar to one of these (yours may look different):

C:\>   [or]   C>

You already know about drive C:. The next hard drive letter is D: and so on. Many PCs have one disk drive specifically for diskettes, and sometimes two drives. The first is drive A: and the second is drive B:. We'll refer mostly to hard drive C: and disk drive A:.

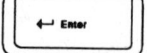

Back to the system prompt. The C:\> acts as a visual indicator from the computer to let you know the current cursor location.

8.2 How the assistant works

You can change the prompt's appearance to suit your own needs. For example, type the following. Be sure that a space follows the PROMPT command word or the command won't work:

```
PROMPT I'm waiting for input...
```
[Enter]

Now every time the prompt appears, it displays the following instead of C:\> or C>:

```
I'm waiting for input...
```

Type the following to create the default prompt (C>):

```
PROMPT
```
[Enter]

The original C> reappears. Type the following:

```
PROMPT Hello
```
[Enter]

Press the [Enter] key several times. The PC displays the word Hello.

The system prompt can serve other purposes. Type the following (remember the space between the command word and the $D):

```
PROMPT $D
```
[Enter]

The new prompt displays the current system date. You can also have the prompt display the current system time. Type the following:

```
PROMPT $T
```
[Enter]

Notice that the system time in the new prompt doesn't change on the screen. However, the time changes whenever you redisplay the prompt.

Type the following to return the system prompt to its default setting:

```
PROMPT
```
[Enter]

If your system prompt looked like this at the beginning of this chapter:

```
C:\>
```

type the following to restore the system prompt to this status:

```
PROMPT $P$G
```
[Enter]

8. The command interpreter

☞ At this point the prompt change is only temporary. In a later chapter we'll describe how to make a new system prompt available permanently. For now you'll have to change the prompt by hand, if you change it at all.

Summary PROMPT specifies the appearance of the system prompt, which prompts the PC user for input. The *default* (normal) appearance of the system prompt is as follows on most systems:

```
C>
```

Entering the command word PROMPT followed by a space and text changes the C> to the text. For example, this:

```
PROMPT By your command:
```

creates a prompt that looks like this:

```
By your command:
```

Additional parameters assign different groups of characters to PROMPT. For example, the $D parameter displays the current date, and the $T parameter displays the current time. Entering PROMPT without other parameters returns to the default system prompt C>.

Command repetition with DOSKEY

Working with the command interpreter can sometimes feel like an endless bout of typing commands. We have a suggestion that will help you cut down on retyping frequently used commands. DOSKEY is an especially powerful extension to the command interpreter, making it possible for you to repeat and edit command lines.

To call DOSKEY, type DOSKEY and and press [Enter]. You should see a message that says "DOSKEY installed". Type in a couple of commands (maybe a few PROMPT commands). Make certain to press [Enter] after each command.

DOSKEY lets you use the cursor keys to recall, edit, or re-execute commands stored in a buffer. For example, press the [↑] key to display previously entered commands. Use the [↓] key to move to the next command.

8.2 How the assistant works

If you've just started DOSKEY and haven't yet entered any commands, nothing will happen when you press the [↑] key. Use the [←], [→], [Backspace], and [Del] keys to edit commands.

The CLS command

The CLS command (short for CLear Screen) clears the screen of data. Type the following to clear the screen:

CLS [Enter]

CLS (CLear Screen) clears any text on the screen and displays the system prompt at the upper left corner of the screen.

The DIR command

Let's look at the names of the programs and other data on a disk. You can't tell a disk's contents by simply looking at it. However, disks contain listings of their contents called *directories*.

The DIR command (the abbreviation for DIRectory) displays the directory of the disk as listed in the system prompt. Type the following to display the disk directory in drive C:

DIR C: [Enter]

The data moves by so quickly that you may not be able to read most of it, at least until the directory stops displaying data. This movement is called *scrolling*, because the information moves past as if you were rolling information past on a scroll.

Your directory may look similar to the following illustration. Each program or set of data appears in the listing as follows:

- The leftmost column displays the eight-character *filename* (the name of the program/data file).

- The three-letter code following represents the *file extension*, indicating the type of file. BAT, COM and EXE files are *executable* (running) programs, while DOC (DOCument) and TXT (TeXT) files are usually readable text files.

- The numbers represent the size of each file in bytes.

111

8. The command interpreter

- The last two entries in each line display the date and time that the file was last saved. Notice that the time uses "a" to represent AM (morning) and "p" to represent PM (afternoon-evening).

- The <DIR> characters indicate a directory.

The end of the directory lists the total number of files, the amount of space these files occupy, and the space remaining on the disk in bytes.

```
Volume in drive C is DOS500409
Volume Serial Number is 1690-5914
Directory of  C:\

ANSI     SYS        9029  03-22-91    5:10p
COMMAND  COM       48475  03-22-91   12:00p
CONFIG   SYS         305  07-24-91    5:00p
DOS         <DIR>         07-24-91    3:22p
        4 File(s)    57809 bytes
                    551289 bytes free
```

Number of files and memory space

The last lines of the directory provide information about how many files and directories are in the displayed directory. The display includes the amount of memory the files occupy in this directory and how much memory is available on the entire diskette or hard drive. The system prompt indicates that MS-DOS is finished processing your command.

Displaying a directory page by page

Now we come to a problem that doesn't exist in the MS-DOS Shell. Sometimes a directory can have several files. If you call the DIR command, the directory listing may move so fast that you cannot read it all.

To get a good look at a long directory, you must enter the DIR with a *switch* (an additional item of information, preceded by a slash [/]) that tells MS-DOS to output the directory on the screen page by page. Use the following command to do this:

```
DIR /P
```

The /P switch stands for "page". Now, when you press [Enter], MS-DOS stops displaying the directory as soon as the screen is full. You will then see the following message on the bottom of the screen:

```
Press any key to continue . . .
```

This message means press a key when you are finished looking at this page of the directory, to display the next page of the directory. This

8.2 How the assistant works

continues until you have viewed all of the files. The system prompt reappears on the screen when the directory display is finished.

Viewing a diskette directory

Before we look at any other directories, we should talk about the contents of diskettes. Up to now, we have only been using the command interpreter to view directories on the hard drive. To display the directory of a diskette, you must first insert a formatted diskette in the disk drive and then make this drive the current drive.

Changing drives

We mentioned earlier in this chapter that different drives have different drive letters assigned to them. The hard drive often has the letter C, which you see in the system prompt. The disk drive usually has the letter A. If you have two disk drives, the second drive, usually the lower one, has the letter B. We assume that you have only one disk drive so we will always use the letter A. To make the disk drive the current drive, you must type the drive letter followed by a colon.

Insert the PRACTICE diskette you created in Chapter 4. Type the following line after the system prompt:

```
A: Enter
```

The system prompt changes to this or a similar prompt:

```
A:\>
```

Now you can type either DIR or DIR /P after the new system prompt. The screen then displays the directory of that diskette. The information means the same as previously described for hard drives.

To return to the hard drive, use the same procedure previously described. After the system prompt, type C followed by a colon and press Enter. The system prompt then indicates that you are back on the hard drive.

Changing directories

Directories appear in the listing as well as files. These directories also contain files. However, the only thing you see in the display is the name of the directory, not its contents.

Define the system prompt as follows to check the directory levels:

```
PROMPT $P$G Enter
```

In Chapter 4, you created a directory called WORK. To display the contents of this directory, you must first make this directory the current directory. Type the following command line:

8. The command interpreter

CD WORK [Enter]

Notice that the system prompt has changed. Now it looks like:

C:\WORK>

So the system prompt not only displays the current drive, but also the current directory.

The CD command means Change Directory. You use this command to change to the directory named in the command. Once in this directory, you can type in the command for displaying the contents of the directory after the system prompt.

DIR [Enter]

The same screen display previously described appears; only the files and the directories are different.

☞ If you notice that the directory you are displaying has another directory, you can also display the contents of this directory. Let's suppose the directory is called TEXTS, such as the one we created in Chapter 4. To look at the contents of this directory, use the following procedure:

CD TEXTS [Enter]

After you press [Enter], the system prompt changes again:

C:\WORK\TEXTS>

The screen displays which directory you are in along with the directory's location in the structure. The TEXTS directory is a subdirectory of WORK. Here too, you can use DIR to display the contents on the screen.

To display the contents of the WORK directory, you must go up one level higher in the directory level. You can't do this by giving the name of the directory after the CD command, because that would only take you one level deeper in the directory tree. To go one level higher, type the following command:

CD .. [Enter]

114

8.2 How the assistant works

The system prompt tells you you're back in the WORK directory. The two periods following the CD command always instruct CD to move to the next highest directory.

Type the following:

CD .. [Enter]

When you press [Enter], you will see the system prompt you had at the beginning:

C:\>

If the system prompt consists of only the drive letter and a backslash (\), then you are in the root directory of the current diskette or hard drive.

Perhaps you're just searching for a filename. The DIR /W command displays the directory in a wide (multiple column) format. Type:

DIR /W [Enter]

Your directory will appear in a format similar to the following:

```
Volume in drive C is DOS500409
 Volume Serial Number is 1690-5914
Directory of  C:\

[DOS]        [VENTURA]      ANSI.SYS       COMMAND.COM     AUTOEXEC.BAT
CONFIG.SYS
        5 File(s)    57910 bytes
                    551289 bytes free
```

It will look completely different. The files are displayed in groups of five on a line, to allow you to read filenames more easily.

8. The command interpreter

8.3 The assistant is quicker

File maintenance

Let's go on to another group of tasks, such as copying, renaming and deleting files. You have already used the MS-DOS Shell for these operations. You'll soon discover that the assistant can be quicker and easier in many cases. As you already know, it can be rather difficult to find, select and copy certain files with the MS-DOS Shell. The command interpreter can do the same thing much more quickly if you use wildcards.

For example, you could use the asterisk "*" as a wildcard for any character string. To process all text files beginning with LETTER, you would use the filename LETTER*.DOC. We'll go into more detail about this option later. Right now, we'd like to go over the basics.

Copying files

First we want to show you how to copy files with the command interpreter. The command for copying is called COPY. You can use this command to copy files from the hard drive to a diskette or vice versa. You can also use it to copy files on a disk to different directories on a disk.

There are different reasons for copying files. You can copy files that you created on your computer to a diskette, either as a backup file or to give to someone else, who then copies the file from the diskette to their computer.

Copying from the hard drive to a diskette

To copy a file from your hard drive to a diskette, you first must know the name of the file. You can use the DIR command to determine the filename. It's important to know the entire filename, both the filename and its extension.

A version of the COPY command could appear similar to the following:

COPY SOURCE.EXT d:TARGET.EXT

Let's look at each part of the above line:

- COPY instructs the command interpreter that you want to copy something.

- The SOURCE.EXT file represents the file you want to copy.

- The d: represents a drive letter. This instructs the command interpreter to copy SOURCE.EXT to a different drive.

8.3 The assistant is quicker

- The TARGET.EXT file represents the resulting file. This can be a blank space, a set of wildcards or a different filename altogether from SOURCE.EXT.

Copying AUTOEXEC.BAT

Let's suppose you want to copy the AUTOEXEC.BAT file, which is in the root directory of your hard drive, to a diskette. You already have the name of the file. Now you must type this name after the COPY command and tell MS-DOS where you want to copy this file to. In our case, it's a diskette in drive A:.

The following is what the command should look like (before entering this, make sure you have inserted a formatted diskette in drive A:):

```
COPY AUTOEXEC.BAT A: Enter
```

After pressing Enter, you can tell by the drive light that your computer is busy. After a few moments, the following message appears on your screen:

```
1 file(s) copied
```

MS-DOS tells you that the file has been copied. You can tell that the computer is finished because the system prompt reappears. Change drives by typing:

```
A: Enter
```

You can use DIR to display the contents of the directory on the diskette. As you can see, the AUTOEXEC.BAT file is on the diskette.

Now type the following to return to the hard drive:

```
C: Enter
```

You have just copied a file from the hard drive to a diskette. What if you wanted to copy TEST.COM, which is in the WORK directory? Make WORK the current directory by typing:

```
CD WORK Enter
```

After pressing Enter you can immediately tell which directory is current by the system prompt:

```
C:\WORK>
```

117

8. The command interpreter

Now you can copy the file, as previously described, by specifying the name of the file and the target drive after COPY. The following is what the command line looks like:

```
COPY TEST.COM A: [Enter]
```

When you copy, it's important that you always make the directory with the file to be copied the current directory. Only then can you use the COPY command. Specify the exact filename, including the extension and then the target drive, followed by a colon.

If the file is not in the current directory, MS-DOS displays the following message to let you know that it didn't find the file:

```
File not found - TEST.COM
        0 file(s) copied
```

Copying from a diskette to the hard drive

Copying a file from a diskette to your hard drive works much the same way. To copy the AUTOEXEC.BAT file, which is on your diskette, back to your hard drive, use the following procedure. First, make certain that the root directory of the hard drive is the current directory. (If not, use CD.. to go back to the root directory). Here's what the system prompt should look like:

```
C:\>
```

Now change to drive A: by typing:

```
A: [Enter]
```

Now you can use COPY again. Specify the name of the file and the target drive after the command. In our example, C is the target drive. Here's what the command line should look like:

```
COPY AUTOEXEC.BAT C: [Enter]
```

Here, too, MS-DOS lets you know that a file has been copied before it displays the system prompt.

Remember that in this process, the AUTOEXEC.BAT file from the diskette is overwriting the AUTOEXEC.BAT file on your hard drive. Do not make any changes to the AUTOEXEC.BAT file during this example.

8.3 The assistant is quicker

How would you go about copying the TEST.COM file from the diskette to the TEXTS directory on the hard drive? First, you must make TEXTS the current directory on the hard drive. Change drives by typing:

C: [Enter]

Then change to the TEXTS directory. To get there, you must change to the WORK directory first. Type:

CD WORK [Enter]

Then type:

CD TEXTS [Enter]

You can tell by the system prompt that TEXTS is the current directory. Now you can change drives by typing:

A: [Enter]

Now you can use the COPY command to copy the file. Here's what the command line should look like:

COPY TEST.COM C:

Remember: When copying from a diskette to the hard drive you must make the directory on the hard drive to where you want to copy the file the current directory before you copy. However, you can also add the entire path specification in the command line (make sure you know the MS-DOS commands and directory paths):

COPY A:\TEST.COM C:\WORK\TEXTS

You can use this command line from any directory on your hard drive or a diskette. However, this method requires remembering the directory paths needed.

Copying files on the hard drive under a new name

You are probably asking yourself whether you can only copy from the hard drive to a diskette or from one diskette to another diskette. You certainly don't want to use a different diskette for each file. Let's quickly create more files on the hard drive with a new name.

The AUTOEXEC.BAT file should still be in the WORK directory. Change to this directory by typing:

8. The command interpreter

```
CD WORK [Enter]
```

Now use DIR to display the contents of the directory.

If you deleted the AUTOEXEC.BAT file, use the following to recopy the file to the WORK directory:

```
COPY C:\AUTOEXEC.BAT C:\WORK [Enter]
```

We'll make multiple copies of this file to allow some experimentation.

If you tried to enter the following incorrect command:

```
COPY AUTOEXEC.BAT
```

you would get the following error message:

```
File cannot be copied onto itself
        0 file(s) copied
```

It makes good sense that you cannot copy files onto themselves. Otherwise, how would you keep order on your hard drive if you had several files with the same name? Type the following:

```
COPY AUTOEXEC.BAT TEST1.BAT [Enter]
```

The following message appears on the screen:

```
1 file(s) copied
```

A file named TEST1.BAT is located in the directory with the AUTOEXEC.BAT file.

If you like, you can try it out now and make as many copies as you want out of TEST1.BAT. Three files should be enough for our work. Type in the following commands:

```
COPY TEST1.BAT TEST2.BAT [Enter]
COPY TEST1.BAT TEST3.BAT [Enter]
COPY TEST1.BAT TEST4.BAT [Enter]
```

Copying files to another disk under a new name

At some point you may need to combine both processes (i.e., transfer a file to a diskette and give it a different name simultaneously). Before proceeding, make certain the PRACTICE diskette is in drive A: and the WORK directory on the hard drive is the current directory, Now, use the following command:

8.3 The assistant is quicker

```
COPY TEST1.BAT A:TEST5.BAT [Enter]
```

Do not include spaces between the drive letter and the colon, or between the colon and the filename.

It does work, as you will quickly discover by checking the directories of the diskette and the hard drive.

Renaming files

Next, we would like to perform another process with the command interpreter that we have already done with the MS-DOS Shell, which is renaming files. We decide to change the name of TEST1.BAT to TRIAL.BAT by using the RENAME command.

Type the following:

```
RENAME TEST1.BAT TRIAL.BAT [Enter]
```

After a moment the ready prompt reappears. If we use DIR to read the directory, we notice that TEST1.BAT has actually become TRIAL.BAT.

Here, too, you can experiment on your own. Just remember that you will run into difficulties if you try to use a filename that already exists for your new filename.

Try the following command:

```
RENAME TRIAL.BAT TEST2.BAT [Enter]
```

If there is already a file named TEST2.BAT in the same directory as TRIAL.BAT, you will see the following error message:

```
Duplicate filename or file not found
```

MS-DOS protects you from unintentionally destroying the other file.

Deleting files

We have learned how to copy and rename files with the command interpreter. Now there's a new problem: How do you delete files?

You use the DEL command. To use this command, first copy the files you have created to the PRACTICE diskette, if you haven't already done so. Then make drive A: the current drive by typing:

```
A: [Enter]
```

8. The command interpreter

Now you can try the DEL command without having to worry about what might happen. We assume that you have the PRACTICE diskette in drive A:, where we transferred the TEST5.BAT. A: should be the current drive. Type:

`DEL TEST5.BAT` [Enter]

If you read the directory (DIR), you will see that the file no longer exists. This doesn't affect you, but imagine that you have been working on an important letter for hours and then you save the letter. Then, instead of typing DIR IMPORT you type DEL IMPORT. By now, you should realize what a powerful, dangerous command DEL is.

Be very careful when you delete files, because once you delete a file, it's lost for good, and you may not be able to recover it using the UNDELETE command described earlier. Always make certain you really don't need a file before deleting it.

8.4 Changing corporate structure

Creating and deleting directories

In this section we'll describe additional commands that you can use to perform tasks you are already familiar with from the MS-DOS Shell. Let's learn about creating and deleting directories.

Creating subdirectories

Creating subdirectories is also easy with the command interpreter by using the MD command.

Change to drive C: using the following:

`C:` [Enter]

Change to the TEXTS directory using the following:

`CD \WORK\TEXTS` [Enter]

Now type the following three lines:

`MD PERSONAL` [Enter]
`MD BUSINESS` [Enter]
`MD OFFICES` [Enter]

Now use DIR to see what your PC has done to your hard drive.

```
.             <DIR>          07-25-91    1:32p
..            <DIR>          07-25-91    1:32p
AUTOEXEC BAT          303    07-11-91   11:58a
TEST     COM        48745    03-22-91    5:10a
PERSONAL      <DIR>          07-30-91    9:36a
BUSINESS      <DIR>          07-30-91    9:36a
OFFICES       <DIR>          07-30-91    9:36a
       7 file(s)        48148 bytes
                       551289 bytes free
```

The new directory tree

At first, it looks as though the PC has used these three commands to create three files. Take a look at the size of the files, though. There is no size listed. Instead, you see a <DIR> in the place where the number of bytes are normally displayed, and you know that this is how directories are labelled. Now let's have a closer look at these three strange entries. Type:

`DIR PERSONAL` [Enter]

8. The command interpreter

If this were a file named PERSONAL, your PC would ordinarily list only this file with the number of bytes and the date. Instead, the computer displays two lines with one and two periods as filenames and this mysterious <DIR> again.

```
.            <DIR>      07-30-91   9:36a
..           <DIR>      07-30-91   9:36a
        2 file(s)            0 bytes
                       551289 bytes free
```

Contents of PERSONAL

You know that <DIR> comes from directory. Apparently, MS-DOS created two new directories with one and two periods as their names. Since both directories were automatically created by MS-DOS, we can't directly work with them.

Changing between directories

In the meantime, you have realized that the three command lines with MD on the hard drive created these directories. Let's check this with the following test. Type:

CD PERSONAL [Enter]
DIR [Enter]

Again, the PC shows the two files with the periods although there aren't any other files yet. We haven't created any files in this directory or copied any files to it. All we did was display the contents of the directory after using CD to change to it.

A little while ago we learned how to get to a higher directory. You can use this knowledge here as well. To return to the TEXTS directory, type:

CD .. [Enter]

Using DIR proves that all three are displayed again. Now it's just a question of explaining these processes and learning how to use them.

1. The MD command creates a subdirectory in the current directory with the name you specified. MD is the abbreviation for "Make Directory."

2. CD is the abbreviation for "Change Directory." You use CD to change to the directory you specify. This is like switching between different drives by entering "A:" "B:" or "C:". However,

8.4 Changing corporate structure

there are a few differences which we'll describe in more detail next.

In the previous listing, Item 2 sounds relatively easy: "You use CD to change to the directory you specify." However, it's not that easy. How do you specify the directory? In our example it still seems easy. At the beginning you just specify the name of the directory (in our example, PERSONAL). At the end, to get out of the directory, you type CD.. and press [Enter].

As we know, however, MS-DOS doesn't just create one level of directories. In each of these directories you can place files, or create new subdirectories. You can imagine how quickly you could lose track with all those directories and subdirectories. That's why we want to go through a case of "directories within directories":

The directory tree

To give you a better illustration of the directory tree of the hard drive, we would like to show you a graphic display of one:

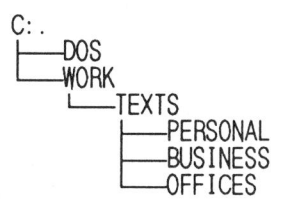

```
C:.
├───DOS
└───WORK
    └───TEXTS
        ├───PERSONAL
        ├───BUSINESS
        └───OFFICES
```

We'll assume that you are currently in the root directory. If not, you can return to the root directory in one step, no matter which level you are in. Just type the following command:

```
CD \ [Enter]
```

Now we'll change to the TEXTS directory and show you the problems you can have with CD. First, type this:

```
CD TEXTS [Enter]
```

The following message appears:

```
Invalid directory
```

This message tells us that the PC cannot find a TEXTS directory. The message occurred because there is no subdirectory called TEXTS in the root directory. There are two methods of changing to TEXTS:

125

8. The command interpreter

1. We can move back to this directory, step by step. First we use CD WORK to go to the WORK directory, which contains the TEXTS subdirectory that we want. We can use CD TEXTS to make it the current directory.

   As you can well imagine, this step by step business can be troublesome. You could have been in an entirely different directory and been forced to use CD.. to return to the root directory first. Then you could select the directory you wanted, step by step.

2. That's why there's a second way to select any directory. To use this method, you must specify the complete location of the directory, called the *pathname*.

The big jump to a directory

To do this, select the root directory by either typing CD.. twice or else CD \, the shortcut. Now type the following line:

```
CD C:\WORK\TEXTS [Enter]
```

Many keyboards have a separate key for the backslash. Otherwise you can get the backslash by pressing the [Alt] key, to the left of the [Spacebar], and then pressing [9] and [2] on the numeric keypad, to the right of the regular keyboard. As soon as you release [Alt] the backslash appears.

The PC immediately makes the TEXTS directory the current directory.

Let's take a closer look at this line so you understand its parts. The drive letter is specified by the C: characters, which instruct the PC to look on drive C:. The first backslash (\) instructs the PC to look in the root directory. The PC then moves to the WORK and TEXTS directories respectively. The backslash separating WORK and TEXTS indicates two directory levels.

Perhaps you're already familiar with C:\WORK from the beginning of the directory display when we were displaying a subdirectory:

```
Directory of C:\WORK
```

After you change to C:\WORK, this name appears in the system prompt:

8.4 Changing corporate structure

```
C:\WORK>
```

To try this, return to the root directory using the following:

```
CD \ [Enter]
```

From there, we're going to select the BUSINESS directory. To do this, type the following line:

```
CD C:\WORK\TEXTS\BUSINESS [Enter]
```

Here's what the command line means for the PC: Look in drive C: in the WORK subdirectory (\WORK), from there in the TEXTS subdirectory (\TEXTS) for the BUSINESS subdirectory (\BUSINESS) and make BUSINESS the current directory.

When you select a directory, you can leave out the drive as long as the directory is on the current drive. For our example, you could also use:

```
CD \WORK\TEXTS\BUSINESS [Enter]
```

We will always include the drive letter because it will protect us from mistakes and misunderstandings later when we work with files in subdirectories.

Copying a file between directories

Now let's do some work with the subdirectories. We need a file for this; we'll take TEST.COM, which is in the WORK directory. You can use the DIR command to make sure the TEST.COM file is in that directory. If not, use the COPY command to copy TEST.COM to that directory.

Although there are some other files displayed on the screen, we're not interested in them at this time.

Although we've located the file, we realize it's in the wrong directory. Instead of this directory, we'd like to have the file in the BUSINESS directory. So we'll just copy it there now. When copying files the complete pathname must be specified . Here's the command line:

```
COPY C:\WORK\TEST.COM C:\WORK\TEXTS\BUSINESS [Enter]
```

8. The command interpreter

The previous line tells the PC to copy the TEST.COM file from the WORK directory on drive C: to the BUSINESS subdirectory on drive C:. If the WORK directory is the current directory, we would type:

```
COPY TEST.COM C:\WORK\TEXTS\BUSINESS [Enter]
```

since the PC will find the TEST.COM file in the current directory. Now let's see whether the file was copied to the right place. To do this, make BUSINESS the current directory:

```
CD C:\WORK\TEXTS\BUSINESS [Enter]
```

Use DIR to see whether the TEST.COM file is now in the once empty directory.

Next we'd like to finish this by copying the TEST.COM file to the PERSONAL subdirectory. There are two ways of doing this. Either we specify the complete pathname for the original file and the target file (in the following line, press [Enter] only when instructed):

```
COPY C:\WORK\TEXTS\BUSINESS\TEST.COM
     C:\WORK\TEXTS\PERSONAL [Enter]
```

or we remember that we are already in the BUSINESS directory so we can specify the original file—which is in this directory—without the path:

```
COPY TEST.COM C:\WORK\TEXTS\PERSONAL [Enter]
```

These command lines are long and awkward. We only used them to give you an illustration of working with directory and path specifications.

Now we'd like to quickly check whether the copying process was successful. To do this, we can either move to:

```
CD.. [Enter]           (TEXTS is current directory)
CD PERSONAL [Enter]    (Subdirectory PERSONAL is active)
```

from our current position (the BUSINESS subdirectory) and then use DIR to look at the results.

We also could have specified the complete path of the desired directory.

```
CD C:\WORK\TEXTS\PERSONAL [Enter]
```

8.4 Changing corporate structure

We could have used DIR then and achieved the same results. Another method would be to read the contents of the PERSONAL directory without changing directories by typing:

```
DIR C:\WORK\TEXTS\PERSONAL [Enter]
```

Deleting data from a subdirectory

That was quite a workout with subdirectories. Before we discuss some special features that could cause trouble for you, we'd still like to show you how to remove subdirectories that you no longer need.

You may think of using the DEL command for this. Go ahead and try it. Make TEXTS the current directory, type the following:

```
DEL PERSONAL [Enter]
```

Suddenly you see a strange message:

```
All files in directory will be deleted!
Are you sure (Y/N)?
```

You might be wondering why MS-DOS asks us whether we want to delete "all files". We're only deleting the PERSONAL directory. Go ahead and type [Y] [Enter], then invoke the DIR command.

The subdirectory is still there, but the <u>contents</u> of the subdirectory no longer exist (i.e., the TEST.COM file you copied to PERSONAL earlier in this chapter).

When you use DEL on a directory, it deletes the files from that directory, without removing the directory itself.

In addition, the developers of MS-DOS added that security prompt as a last chance to exit. Suppose that you are in the root directory of a hard drive containing many subdirectories, among others the DOS directory, where the MS-DOS files are located. You accidentally type DEL DOS [Enter]. This is where the security prompt helps you since you certainly don't want to delete all the files. Therefore, you type [N] and press [Enter].

So how do you delete subdirectories?

- DEL *.* deletes all the files in the current directory. If we used this command in our example in the WORK directory, only the files in the WORK directory would be deleted. The TEXTS

129

8. The command interpreter

subdirectory and all the other subdirectories would remain untouched.

- You could change to the next highest directory using CD, type DEL followed by the name of the subdirectory and press [Enter].

For example, to delete all the files in the WORK directory, type:

```
CD C:\WORK [Enter]
DEL *.* [Enter]
```

Or move to the next highest directory and perform the deletion on the desired directory:

```
CD C:\ [Enter]
DEL WORK [Enter]
```

This deletes all the files in WORK only, and not the contents of any other subdirectories.

Removing directories

Use the RD (Remove Directory) command to remove a directory. This command only works on empty directories. In our example, if you typed the following from the root directory and pressed [Enter]:

```
RD WORK [Enter]
```

you would get the following error message:

```
Invalid path, not directory,
or directory not empty
```

This error message tells us that either the path was wrong, the name wasn't a subdirectory, or the subdirectory wasn't empty. To delete and remove the entire WORK directory, you must first delete all the files in the lower directories, then remove those directories. This would empty the next highest directory, which you could then remove, etc.

We'll show you the necessary commands with some short comments, using the TEXTS directory as our example. Use the following procedure to delete the TEXTS directory:

```
CD C:\WORK\TEXTS [Enter]   Change to TEXTS subdirectory
DEL PERSONAL [Enter]       Delete files in PERSONAL directory
DEL BUSINESS [Enter]       Delete files in BUSINESS directory
DEL OFFICES [Enter]        Delete files in OFFICES directory
```

8.4 Changing corporate structure

RD PERSONAL [Enter]	Remove PERSONAL directory
RD BUSINESS [Enter]	Remove BUSINESS directory
RD OFFICES [Enter]	Remove OFFICES directory
CD.. [Enter]	Change to WORK directory
DEL TEXTS [Enter]	Delete files in TEXTS directory
RD TEXTS [Enter]	Remove TEXTS directory

This requires more steps than using DEL TEXTS from the WORK directory. We also would have been relatively protected from the danger of deleting large amounts of data. Nevertheless, you should always make sure that you are in the right directory and that you only delete the data you really want to delete.

We'll need the TEXTS directory again and the TEST.COM file placed in that directory. Type the following to do this:

CD \WORK [Enter]	Change to WORK directory
MD TEXTS [Enter]	Make TEXTS directory
COPY TEST.COM TEXTS [Enter]	Copy TEST.COM to TEXTS directory

File copying tips

As we finish our work with subdirectories, here's the advice we promised about potential error sources and special features:

- When you copy, always pay attention to the screen message DOS displays indicating how many files have been copied. If you specify the wrong source file or path, MS-DOS displays the message "File not found". On the other hand, if you specify the wrong target path, the only warning you get is "0 file(s) copied". This can be bad, for example, if you want to make backup copies of important files on a diskette, and after losing the original, you discover that there aren't any files at all on the backup copy.

- Simply specify the path of the subdirectory where you want to copy the file. However, if you want to place the file under a different name, you must type a backslash \ followed by the new name. The following example copies the TEST.COM file to the WORK subdirectory under the same name:

COPY C:TEST.COM C:\WORK

The following example copies the TEST.COM file to the WORK subdirectory under the name NEWTEST.COM:

COPY C:TEST.COM C:\WORK\NEWTEST.COM

8. The command interpreter

The computer can remember several directories

MS-DOS remembers the current directory for each drive. You can access this directory by specifying the drive (letter and colon). This saves you the work of typing the complete pathname. So if you have both a hard drive and a disk drive and the disk drive has a diskette with the same subdirectories that we created on the hard drive, here's what it could look like:

```
A:                  Select drive A:
MD WORK             Make a WORK directory in drive A:
CD A:\WORK          Make WORK directory in drive A: current
C:                  Change to drive C:
CD C:\WORK\TEXTS    Make TEXTS current directory
```

By looking at the system prompt, you can see that MS-DOS uses the previously specified directory for every change. Now we'll copy the TEST.COM file from the TEXTS directory of drive C: to the WORK directory of drive A:. Instead of typing this:

`COPY C:\WORK\TEXTS\TEST.COM A:\WORK`

We can achieve the same effect by typing this:

`COPY C:TEST.COM A:`

At first this seems strange. You might get the idea that you are copying TEST.COM from the root directory of C: to the root directory of A:. Soon, however, you will get used to this method and save yourself a lot of work.

However, there's still a potential error source. If you had selected the directories for both drives, and wanted to copy a file from the root directory of C: to the root directory of A:, you would get an error message. In such a case, use PROMPT or CD to check the names of the set directories. Although you could specify the new directory for each drive, it's easier if you use:

`COPY C:\AUTOEXEC.BAT A:\`

The backslashes after the drive labels instruct DOS to copy to and from root directories rather than current directories.

8.5 Formatting and copying diskettes

Now that you know how to work with files and directories in the command interpreter, we'd like to show you how to format and copy diskettes.

Formatting diskettes

You already know from your experience with the MS-DOS Shell that a PC can't do anything with blank diskettes straight from the box. Inserting a brand new (unformatted) diskette in drive A: (don't forget to pull down the lever), and type:

```
DIR A: Enter
```

After a moment, the computer displays the following message:

```
General failure reading drive A
Abort, Retry, Fail?
```

You are better off pressing the [A] key (for abort). Then your PC returns with the normal system prompt.

You must prepare a diskette before using to store data. This process of preparing a diskette is called *formatting*.

At the beginning of this book we said that each room had to be prepared for receiving goods. You must set up shelves, create a layout plan, etc. This is also what happens when you format a diskette.

We're not really interested in a detailed account of what happens during formatting. However, we would like to say that all IBM compatible PCs use the same formats. That is, a diskette formatted on your equipment should be readable by any other IBM compatible computer of similar type (it doesn't have to be the same brand name, as IBM compatibility is the deciding factor). Exceptions to this rule are "high density" AT diskettes, which can only be read by ATs (286 machines, 386s, 486s, etc.) and 3-1/2" diskettes, which won't fit in a 5-1/4" PC drive.

Insert a diskette in drive A: and type the following command:

```
FORMAT A: Enter
```

The FORMAT command instructs your computer that you want it to format the diskette in drive A:. After you press Enter, you are prompted to place a diskette in drive A: and press Enter again to

133

8. The command interpreter

confirm your choice. The computer starts formatting the diskette. Formatting takes time—how much time depends on your computer.

After the computer is finished formatting, it prompts you to give the diskette a *volume label*. Type a name up to eleven characters in length and press [Enter]. If you don't want to give the diskette a volume label name, all you need do is press [Enter].

Next, some lines appear on the screen, informing you of the amount of space available on the diskette and other data.

Another message appears asking whether you want to format another diskette. If you do, press [Y] then [Enter]. The computer then prompts you to insert a new diskette and repeat the whole process. If you don't want to format another diskette, press [N] then [Enter]. The system prompt reappears.

Be very careful when you format diskettes. You could also format a used diskette that already has data on it. If you format such a diskette, you'll lose all the data that was on it. Always check to make sure you have inserted the right diskette before formatting it. Use the DIR command to check the diskette contents before formatting:

```
DIR A: [Enter]
```

If an error message appears on the screen, you can be fairly certain that you are using an unformatted diskette. You must format this diskette before you can use it. Press [A] to cancel the error message. The system prompt returns to the screen where you can type the command to format the diskette.

Volume labels If you didn't give your diskette a name after formatting it and you decide later that you want to give it a name, insert the diskette in drive A: and type the following command:

```
LABEL A: [Enter]
```

A message appears on the screen, displaying the current name of the diskette. Now you can give the diskette a new name up to eleven characters in length. Press [Enter] to accept the volume label name.

You can also assign a volume label name to your hard drive. Simply use LABEL C: to invoke the LABEL command.

134

8.5 Formatting and copying diskettes

The quick format

Ordinarily, a diskette is magnetically "subdivided" the first time you format it. After that, whenever you format a diskette, MS-DOS merely checks it. If you are certain that it's not necessary to perform a complete format (e.g., because you just checked the diskette recently), you can speed up the formatting process considerably. To do this, add the /Q switch to the FORMAT command. To *quick format* a diskette in drive A:, use the following command:

```
FORMAT A: /Q Enter
```

Copying diskettes

You may want to make backup copies of program diskettes or you may want to send someone a disk containing several files. The DISKCOPY command performs this task.

When you copy a diskette with DISKCOPY, it copies the entire diskette, including any unused disk media. You'll need a second diskette before you can make a copy of the PRACTICE diskette. Type the following command:

```
DISKCOPY A: A: Enter
```

After you press Enter, you are prompted to insert the source diskette (the diskette you want to copy) in drive A: and press any key. Insert the PRACTICE diskette in drive A: and press a key. When you have done this, a message appears on the screen telling you that MS-DOS is copying the diskette. After a short time, you are prompted to insert the target diskette in drive A:.

Remove the PRACTICE diskette and insert the second diskette. Press any key. If your diskettes have a memory capacity of 1.2 Meg, you will have to switch from the source diskette to the target diskette a few times (a message on the screen will tell you when to insert each diskette).

After the entire diskette has been copied, MS-DOS asks whether you want to copy another diskette. If you do, press Y. You are then prompted to insert a new diskette, and the whole process repeats itself. If you don't want to copy any more diskettes, press N. The system prompt reappears.

Be careful when you copy diskettes. If you insert a diskette, that already has data on it, as your target diskette, DISKCOPY overwrites that data without any warning.

135

8. The command interpreter

8.6 The assistant calls his friends

Running applications

If you want to display the contents of different files, you must first start the appropriate application that uses these files. For example, if you wanted to look at a text file, you would have to run the word processor used to create the file. To look at a file containing different data records, you must start the appropriate database.

Applications let you view existing files as well as create new ones. In many respects, these application are the actual purpose for owning a PC. Applications often simplify the work you put into creating texts or managing data. For example, to be able to write at all, you need a word processor. You can't do it with MS-DOS.

If you have one of these applications, but don't know how to start it, we'll provide some tips.

The user types in different commands on the keyboard. For example:

- The user changes system settings by specifying the exact date or the time (DATE/TIME).

- The user displays the contents of a diskette (DIR).

- The user views the contents of a file (TYPE).

- The user calls a certain program by typing its name (i.e., PROGRAM). If the program was the word processor Microsoft Word, then the user would type WORD and press [Enter].

After that, the operating system passes control to the application and you work with the application. The application sets the rules and operations that apply here—MS-DOS commands no longer have any effect.

You'll return to the operating system level when you exit the application.

The following illustration shows the general relationship between the command interpreter and a program:

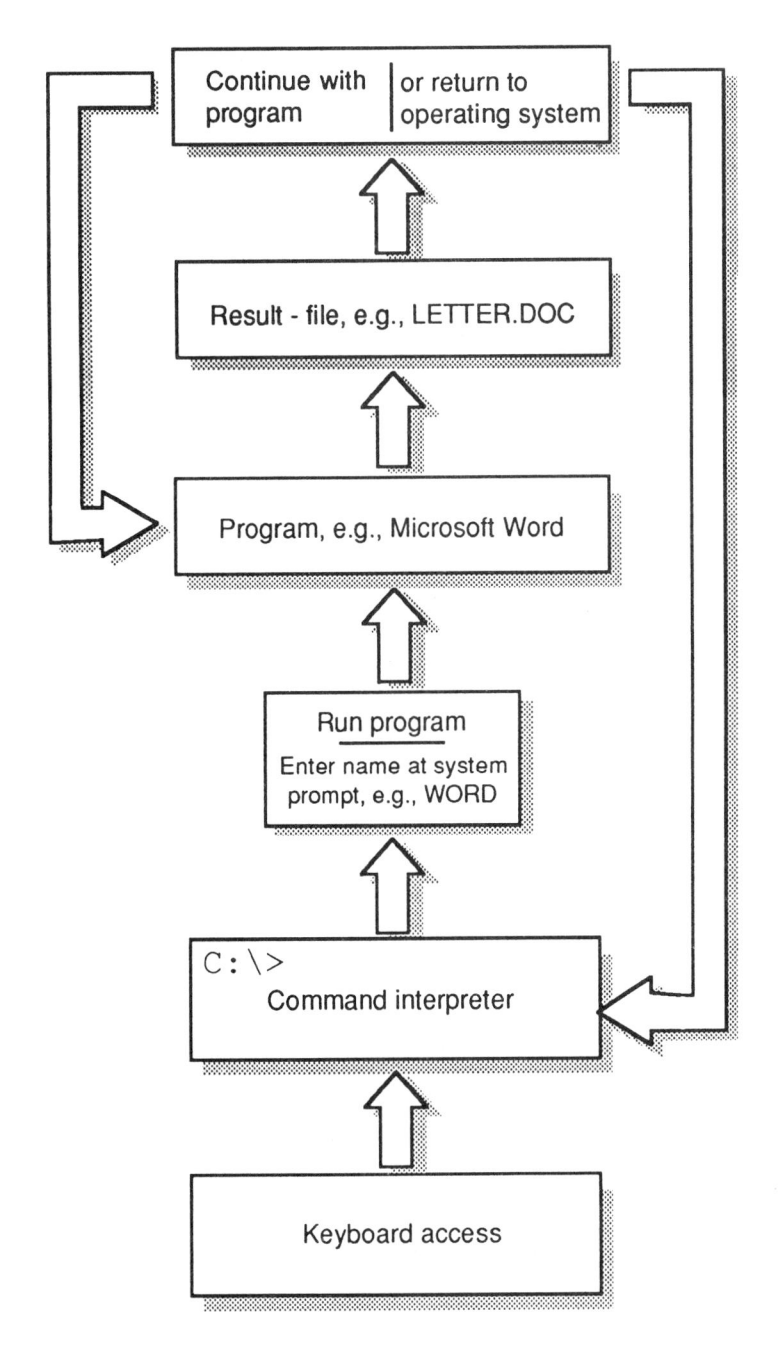

8.6 The assistant calls his friends

The relationship between command interpreter and a program

8. The command interpreter

Starting applications

The application files are almost always located in their own directories. Change to the directory containing these files using the CD command.

To start an application, you must type a certain name and press (Enter). This name is often the same as the name of the application. If the name of the application is longer than eight letters, however, start it by typing either a part of the name or an abbreviation. For example, the abbreviation could consist of the beginning letters of the syllables in the application name.

You can start most programs this way. To find out which of the options applies, you must find the startup file of the program. You can tell which one is the startup file for a program because it has one of the three following extensions:

> COM   EXE   BAT

To find this file, use DIR to display the contents of the program directory. Once you are reading the directory, look first for files with the .EXE extension that also fulfill the other criteria for being a startup file. If you find such a file, try to start the program by typing the name of the file without the extension and press (Enter). If you don't find an EXE file, look for a file with the .COM extension. If you can't find a file with a .COM extension, look for a file with the .BAT extension.

You can make your search for files with the appropriate extension easier with wildcards. For example, to display all files with the .EXE extension on drive A:, use the following command line:

DIR A:*.EXE (Enter)

For the other two extensions, use DIR A:*.COM and DIR A:*.BAT.

The following are additional examples for you:

Microsoft Word

The directory of the Microsoft Word contains a file named WORD.EXE. This file has the same name as the application, so it's probably the startup file. Type:

WORD (Enter)

After you press (Enter), the application is executed.

8.6 The assistant calls his friends

Microsoft Windows

You will find many files with the .EXE extension in the Windows directory. However, none of these files meet the requirements for the name of a startup file. On the other hand, there is a WIN.COM file. This file meets the conditions for a startup file, both in name and extension. If you type this name after the system prompt and press [Enter], the application is executed.

Exiting applications

You should always exit a program properly. That is, you should return to the command interpreter of MS-DOS. If you simply switch off your computer, you could lose important data. Each program has its own command for exiting.

If you aren't sure how to exit an application, we'll provide you some tips. Most programs work with *menus*, containing different commands for operating the program. These menus usually have an item for exiting the program as well.

Ordinarily, you can select the menu by pressing [Esc] or [Alt]. Then use the arrow keys to choose the different menus. You activate the menus by pressing [Enter].

Some programs have a separate menu for exiting the program. After selecting this menu with the arrow keys and pressing [Enter], you return to the command interpreter of MS-DOS.

Often the menu command for exiting from a program is in the **File** menu of the program. This command can have names such as **Exit**, **Quit**, **End**, or **System**. Select the appropriate command and press [Enter] to return to the command interpreter.

Many applications have security prompts where you have to confirm that you really want to exit the application.

The following are examples of exiting applications:

Microsoft Word 5.0

To exit Microsoft Word 5.0, press [Esc], use the arrow keys to select Quit and press [Enter]. A security prompt appears If you didn't save the file you were working on. Otherwise you'll return to MS-DOS.

Microsoft Word 5.5

To exit Microsoft Word 5.5, press the [Alt] key, press [F] then [X]. If you didn't save the file you were working on, a security prompt appears, otherwise you return to MS-DOS.

8. The command interpreter

Microsoft Windows   Press the [Alt] key, press [F] then [X]. A security prompt follows, asking you whether you really want to exit. Press [Enter], and you're back in the command interpreter of MS-DOS.

Search paths

Suppose that your certain that a certain program is stored on your hard drive, but when you try to start it you keep getting the error message "Bad command or filename".

The cause of this problem is that MS-DOS always looks for a program name in the current directory on the current drive. If MS-DOS always searched all the drives and directories for a program, you would have to wait several minutes for the results of the search. Also, you would need diskettes in every disk drive all the time.

The developers of MS-DOS provided two different options for starting programs from different directories without changing the directories. The first method is time consuming and you can't use the second method on as many directories as you want:

1. To start a program from any directory, you can place the complete path specification in front of the name. For instance, if C:\DOS is the current directory and WORD.EXE is in the C:\WORD directory, you can always use the following command line to start WORD:

   C:\WORD\WORD [Enter]

   The disadvantage is that it's requires always work to specify the directory path. Also, some programs can't find important auxiliary files, such as a help file or a spelling checker.

2. You could define a search path for MS-DOS. Along with the current directory, MS-DOS also searches all of the directories defined in the search path for a program before the error message "Bad command or filename" appears.

   For example, if you want MS-DOS to always search C:\DOS and C:\WORD and the current directory, you could define the search path with the following command line:

   PATH C:\DOS;C:\WORD [Enter]

8.6 The assistant calls his friends

Each directory is separated by a semicolon. You can display the existing search path by typing the following command:

```
PATH Enter
```

For our previous example, the display would look like this:

```
PATH=C:\DOS;C:\WORD
```

The disadvantage is that MS-DOS searches all the directories in the search path every time you type a command. This can result in a significant delay if you have a long search path. Also, the search path is limited in length to 127 characters (about one and a half screen lines). You just can't specify all the directories of the hard drive in your search path.

Make certain you include the directory with the MS-DOS commands in the search path. If you do not, your PC may suddenly "forget" many of the MS-DOS commands.

Ordinarily you define the search path once, but not every time you start up the PC. Enter the appropriate command line in the AUTOEXEC.BAT file. You can find out more about this in Chapter 11 of this book.

9. Theft and disasters

Data security with MS-DOS Data security is important to everyone who works with computers. The directories, programs, and files that you have created and saved on your hard drive or on diskettes are subject to the danger of being accidentally deleted or destroyed through carelessness.

This is certainly one of the disadvantages of a paperless office, because data on a diskette or hard drive can be destroyed much more quickly than paper stored in a binder or filing cabinet. However, you can protect yourself—and your computer data will be easier to protect than paper.

If you don't believe that your data is in any danger, the following section describes what could go wrong.

9.1 What can go wrong

Why back up your data? Perhaps you're just reading this chapter by coincidence and are ready to skip to the next chapter because you're not interested in backing up data right now. Wait and take a couple of minutes of your time to skim over this chapter, because a loss of important data often means many hours of work lost as well.

To illustrate that your data is vulnerable to great dangers, we'll describe a couple of examples.

1. Someone you know is having trouble with their hard drive. Apparently the hard drive controller has a defect and can read data, but no longer write data. Since the data is desperately needed, he/she calls their dealer, who promises immediately to help. In all the confusion, the hard drive doesn't get parked (prepared for shipping) before it is transported to the dealer. At the dealership, the PC refuses to work with the hard drive, the read/write head hits the disk and destroys irreplaceable system information. The data is lost forever.

2. A word processor "crashes" while the user is saving a document file (i.e., refuses to work). At first this doesn't seem to be a problem because the word processor automatically creates backup copies of the file. However, when you reboot, MS-DOS displays some error messages. When you run the CHKDSK command, CHKDSK reports over 2000 "damaged sectors". Most of the

143

9. Theft and disasters

files on the hard drive are empty or unusable, including the BAK file of the word processor. There is no data backup.

3. Someone accidentally deleted a file on the hard drive and vaguely remembers that a file can be recovered. The manual for MS-DOS is not available, but the user notices the RECOVER command while checking the MS-DOS commands. The screen message displayed by RECOVER C:

```
To recover files on drive C:, press a key
```

gives the final confirmation that RECOVER is taking care of the problem for you. Unfortunately, RECOVER did exactly the opposite of what the user thought was intended, and all the files are lost. The message:

```
329 file(s) recovered
```

already sounded suspicious—after all, only one file was accidentally deleted—and a look at the contents of the directory shows that all the files of the hard drive were neatly numbered in order from FILE0001.REC to FILE0329.REC in the root directory. There weren't any more subdirectories.

Perhaps these three random examples have convinced you that your data on the hard drive is not as secure and safe as you once thought.

Another possibility is to press (Enter) at the wrong time. Fortunately MS-DOS asks whether you really want to run "dangerous" commands and won't continue processing until you respond. However, there's also danger here. Because when you have to answer a question with (Y) or (N), you might wind up pressing (Y) without checking whether the command is correct. The damage (to your data) could be severe.

Protection from deletion

It's relatively easy to protect data on diskettes from being deleted. You can put a write protect tab over the notch to protect your floppy (5-1/4") diskette from being deleted or overwritten. If you have a 3-1/2" drive, you can use the sliding write protect to open the square hole on your 3-1/2" diskette.

9.2 Backing up data to diskettes

You can't write protect your hard drive, because it's built right into the case of your computer. That means there's no absolutely effective means of protecting your hard drive from being deleted.

It's not very difficult to destroy all or part of the hard drive. Recovering files is time consuming, if not impossible. In an emergency, it means that you would have to start your PC with the DOS system diskette in order to remove the destroyed data from the hard drive. In a worse case situation, you would be forced to reformat the disk. This could cause you to lose files that you did not copy to a backup diskette.

Backing up the entire hard drive
You do have the option of making a backup copy of your hard drive to diskettes at regular intervals. It would only be natural to think of using the COPY command, with which we are already familiar. However, it would be very difficult to back up all the files and programs, one by one, to diskette.

Besides, COPY cannot copy your directories, or their underlying subdirectory structure. You would have to make a list of them on paper and then manually restore the structure if you ever did lose all the data on your hard drive.

The developers of MS-DOS created a special program to solve this problem, which saves all the directories and their contents (or a selected portion of them) in compressed form on diskettes.

The BACKUP command

You can use the BACKUP command to make backup copies of the entire hard drive, certain directories with their subdirectories or just certain files on diskettes.

The advantage of BACKUP is that you only have to provide a little information about the data you want to back up, BACKUP does the rest for you. All you have to do is specify what you want to back up and where you want to back it up to. That is, you don't have to list every single file, simply give the drive, for example the hard drive (C:), or a directory (C:\DOS) or the files (*.TXT) you want to back up and the target drive (A:) where you just have to insert the diskettes. BACKUP takes care of the rest. The only other thing you must do is change diskettes.

9. Theft and disasters

To back up the entire hard drive, you will need time, plenty of diskettes, and the following command:

```
BACKUP C: A: /S
```

You need to allow sufficient time because it takes some time to write all the contents of the hard drive to diskettes. It takes about 3 to 4 minutes for a 1.2 Meg diskette, and about 2 to 3 minutes for a 360K diskette. However, to back up an entire hard drive, you can estimate that it will take a half an hour to forty-five minutes.

Since the hard drive stores much more data than a diskette, you'll need several diskettes to perform the backup. There's an easy way to find out how many diskettes you will need. Type C: and press [Enter] to make your hard drive the current drive, then type:

```
DIR [Enter]
```

At the end of the directory, you will see:

```
xxxxxxx bytes free
```

The "xxxxxxx" represents the amount of free memory area. Now the amount of memory space being used in your computer is are simple arithmetic steps.

For example, if you have a 20 Meg hard drive, subtract the number of free bytes from 20,000,000. This gives you the number of bytes that your programs and files take up on the hard drive.

The next step is to divide this value by the capacity of your diskettes. For example, if you're using 360K diskettes, divide the value by 360,000; if you're using 1.2 Meg diskettes, divide the value by 1,200,000. This gives you the approximate number of diskettes that you will need.

If your diskettes are new and therefore unformatted, BACKUP can automatically format diskettes when backing up your data.

Specify the drive whose data you want to back up after BACKUP. In our example, specify the hard drive C:. Then type a space and specify the drive to where you want to back up the data (A:). The /S switch tells DOS to back up all the drives and subdirectories of C:.

9.2 Backing up data to diskettes

The following line is the command to do a complete backup of your hard drive (C:) to diskettes in drive A:.

BACKUP C: A: /S [Enter]

Follow the instructions on the screen.

The message that follows tells you that BACKUP is deleting the entire contents of the root directory of the diskette you placed in drive A:. Check again to make certain you didn't insert an important diskette in drive A:. If necessary, remove the diskette and insert another diskette in its place. Now press any key. BACKUP tells you that the backup is beginning.

The names of the files that are being backed up are displayed on the left margin of the screen, preceded by the directory names. A backslash separates the directory name and filenames.

When the first diskette is full, you're prompted to insert a second diskette. When the second diskette is full, you will be prompted to insert a third diskette, etc. until the backup is finished.

As soon as you remove a diskette, make certain to label, number, and date the diskette. Use specific titles on your labels, such as "BACKUP 01". It's important to number the diskettes in the correct sequence because you must follow this same sequence later if you restore the data.

Note that 5-1/4" diskettes are very sensitive to pressure. Therefore, under no circumstances should you write on the diskette with a ball point pen. If you're using 5-1/4" diskettes, use a felt marker or a soft pencil. It's best to write on the label before placing it on the diskette.

You don't have to be so careful with 3-1/2" diskettes because they come in a very sturdy case. Writing on them with a ball point pen will not result in damage.

Now if data are destroyed or damaged on your hard drive, you can use another MS-DOS command (RESTORE) to copy the destroyed or damaged data from these backup copies to the hard drive. We'll describe RESTORE in the next section.

Incidentally, when DOS saves the data to a BACKUP diskette, it compresses them, so you won't be able to recognize your files. You can use the DIR command to get an idea of what we mean. DOS

9. Theft and disasters

condenses all the files to BACKUP files and gives each file a consecutive number.

Note for AT owners:

If your diskettes aren't formatted, BACKUP automatically formats them in 1.2 Meg format. If you have DD (double density) diskettes, which aren't suitable for this format, you may experience problems. You must format your DD diskettes with FORMAT /4 (i.e., in 360K format). This is also important if you want to restore data on a 360K drive of another computer (XT). A 360K drive can't read 1.2 Meg diskettes.

Backing up data from a directory

Now that you successfully performed a total backup of your hard drive, you may realize that it took a certain amount of time and several diskettes. Fortunately, you don't have to perform this procedure daily or weekly, only when you have installed new programs or made significant changes to your directory structure.

That's why we recommend doing a smaller backup for directories or files where you often make changes. That way you only back up the data that has changed or that is important. Therefore, you'll save time and diskettes.

Let's assume you have a directory called TEXTS on your hard drive (C:) with a subdirectory called LETTERS. To make a backup of the LETTERS directory, your command line would have to look like this:

```
BACKUP C:\TEXTS\LETTERS A:
```

In this case, the command only backs up the data from the LETTERS subdirectory. Although the backup takes place in the same manner as previously described; you won't need as many diskettes and it is faster.

You could also back up a certain directory along with its subdirectories. To do this, add the /S switch.

When you back up directories, write the name of the directory, backup diskette number, and the current date on the diskette label. You can only use RESTORE to copy data back to the directory from which you backed them up. However, the directories don't necessarily have to be existing directories, because RESTORE creates missing subdirectories.

Backing up with the MS-DOS Shell

You can also back up your entire hard drive or only certain directories with the MS-DOS Shell.

9.2 Backing up data to diskettes

Press [Tab] to activate the program list area. Once there, use the arrow keys and [Enter] to activate the **Disk Utilities** group. Now use the arrow keys to move the highlight to the Backup Fixed Disk program and press [Enter] again.

This program also allows you to back up either the entire contents of the hard drive or just certain directories to diskettes.

After you select this program a dialog box appears on the screen where you can type in the source drive (the hard drive that you want to back up) and the target drive, where you will insert the backup diskettes. The dialog box contains the defaults for the source and target drives. You can change the defaults with the arrow keys. You can overwrite all of the characters. You can make the same specifications here that you would after the BACKUP command in the system prompt. Type in any switches or parameters you want after Parameter.

First you type in the drive whose data you want to back up, then you type the drive to where you want to back them up, and finally, you type in any parameters or switches. After pressing [Enter] to confirm your selections, the MS-DOS Shell prompts you to insert a diskette in the proper drive. Everything else happens as it would with the BACKUP command in the system prompt. For more information, see the previous paragraphs about BACKUP.

The XCOPY command

Instead of using BACKUP, you could also use XCOPY to back up directories in MS-DOS.

XCOPY is a combination of COPY and BACKUP. You can use XCOPY to copy directories and their subdirectories with all their files to diskettes or add them to other directories. That is, when you copy, the tree structure of the directories is preserved.

A big advantage of this program lies in the fact that unlike a backup, where you have to use RESTORE to copy back the data, with XCOPY you can read, copy etc., the data at any time. XCOPY also keeps the names of the directories.

The disadvantage of this command is that you can only use it to copy as much data as will go on a diskette. When the diskette is full, the command is aborted. Before using XCOPY, make sure that the data you want to copy will actually fit on one diskette.

9. Theft and disasters

Specify the name of the drive and directory where you want to start copying from after XCOPY. Type a space, then the target of XCOPY. The target consists of the drive specification and often a directory to where you want to add or copy.

In the previous example, if you wanted to make a copy of the entire TEXTS directory on diskette, and you wanted to include the LETTERS and ESSAYS subdirectories, your command line should look like this:

```
XCOPY C:\TEXTS A: /S
```

In this example, XCOPY creates a directory named TEXTS on the diskette in drive A:. All the files from the C:\TEXTS directory are copied to A:\TEXTS. After that, XCOPY creates the LETTERS and ESSAYS subdirectories on the diskette and copies the files from C:\TEXTS\LETTERS to A:\TEXTS\LETTERS and the files from C:\TEXTS\ESSAYS to A:\TEXTS\ESSAYS.

We also specified the /S switch. As with BACKUP, this switch causes XCOPY to copy all of the subdirectories of TEXTS. Without this switch, only the TEXTS directory and all of its files would have been copied.

If you ever lose any files from this directory on your hard drive, you can use the COPY command to restore them. You can also use XCOPY to restore entire directories. Follow the same procedure you used to back up the hard drive to diskette, only this time from the diskette to the hard drive.

9.3 In case of emergency

What to do after you lose data

Suppose you have been creating and storing important files for weeks or even months on your hard drive. These files may be tax assessments and important telephone numbers. You've spent time designing an optimum directory structure completely suited to your needs.

Then, one hard jolt to your computer case makes it impossible to read your hard drive. Beside the expenses for repairing the hard drive or buying a new one, you'll lose time in creating a workable system from several copies on diskette. This will also take some time, and maybe you urgently need certain data. Quite possibly, you've lost some entire files.

You won't have this problem if you use BACKUP to back up your hard drive at regular intervals. The only question is how to get your data back on to the hard drive. As we said earlier in this chapter, you cannot read the data on the backup diskettes. On the other hand, the DOS RESTORE command will take care of this for us as BACKUP saved the data for us.

The RESTORE command

Use only the RESTORE command to copy the data from your backup copies back to your hard drive. It lets you restore the entire hard drive, with all its files, exactly as it was when you backed it up.

Restoring the hard drive

To restore the entire hard drive with your backup diskettes, use the following command line:

```
RESTORE A: C: /S
```

After RESTORE, specify the name of the drive where you will insert the backup diskettes (A:). Follow this with a space and the target hard drive (C:). The command recopies all the data from the diskettes to the hard drive as they were at the time of the backup. By using the /S switch, you cause the command to restore all directories, subdirectories, and files of drive C:.

Copying back parts of the hard drive

You can also restore parts of the hard drive (selected directories). Specify the drive where you will insert the backup diskettes followed by the drive, path, and filename of the target. For instance, if you accidentally deleted all the files in the C:\DOS directory, type the following command line to restore it:

151

9. Theft and disasters

```
RESTORE A: C:\DOS
```

Restoring a directory with subdirectories

To restore a directory with one or more subdirectories, you must specify the /S switch. An example might be C:\TEXTS with its LETTERS and ESSAYS subdirectories. The /S switch means that all subdirectories of TEXTS (including their files) are copied along with TEXTS. The following is how the command line should appear:

```
RESTORE A: C:\TEXTS /S
```

You don't have to specify the names of the subdirectories in the command line. RESTORE does this automatically with /S. If you left out /S, the command would only restore the files in the TEXTS directory. The subdirectories would be unaffected.

Restoring files

You can also restore files with RESTORE. Specify the filename along with the directory to where you want to restore the file. We'll assume that you have destroyed the QBASIC.EXE file in the DOS directory. The following is what the command for restoring it would look like:

```
RESTORE A: C:\DOS\QBASIC.EXE
```

If you accidentally deleted all files with the .EXE extension from the DOS directory, then you could also use wildcards with RESTORE:

```
RESTORE A: C:\DOS\*.EXE
```

The command restores all files with the .EXE extension in the DOS directory.

How RESTORE works

After you type the command and press [Enter], RESTORE prompts you to insert the first backup diskette. Follow the instructions as they appear on the screen.

Now you know how important it is to number the diskettes in the right sequence. If you labelled a diskette with the wrong number or inserted the wrong diskette, RESTORE immediately prompts you to insert the right diskette. RESTORE even tells you when you've inserted a diskette that is not a backup diskette and the screen will then display the MS-DOS system prompt. However, let's assume you have done everything correctly and after you insert the first backup diskette, RESTORE tells you that the data is being recopied.

Here's where the procedure may become complicated if you're only copying back single directories or files. You must insert the first, then

9.3 In case of emergency

the second, then the third diskette, until RESTORE finds the diskette containing the directory or file you want to restore.

It's less complicated when you restore the entire hard drive because you must insert every diskette anyway.

Now you finally know all the available resources for protecting yourself from data loss.

Retrieving data with the MS-DOS Shell

Of course, you can also use the MS-DOS Shell to back up an entire hard drive. Here's the procedure for restoring data with the MS-DOS Shell:

First, use (Tab) to activate the program list area. Now use the arrow keys and (Enter) to activate the **Disk Utilities** group. Use the arrow keys to move the selection cursor to Restore Fixed Disk and press (Enter) again.

You can use this **Disk Utilities** program to restore the entire contents of the hard drive or certain directories.

After selecting this program, a new screen appears. You can specify all the options here that you would use after the RESTORE command. Type in any switches or parameters after Parameters.

Next, type in information concerning the drive where you inserted the diskettes with the backup data. Then type information about the data that you want to restore. After confirming your information with (Enter), the MS-DOS Shell prompts you to insert a diskette in the appropriate drive. Everything else happens as it does in the MS-DOS system prompt with the RESTORE command. For more information, read the earlier sections of this chapter.

When you use RESTORE to copy back data to your hard drive, the command overwrites all the data already on your hard drive. Therefore, be careful when you use RESTORE.

153

9. Theft and disasters

9.4 A much quicker way

Users often avoid backing up their data because it sounds so difficult. That's why you should also find other options for backing up that are quick and easy.

In practice, the following procedure is very useful and effective:

- First, you create an entire backup of the hard drive. Fortunately, you don't have to do this often. Applications require most of the room on your hard drive and they don't change once they're installed. You only have to do this kind of a general backup about twice a year.

- Back up at regular intervals the directories where you do most of your data processing. For example, you could back up your text directory with the letters you've created, the subdirectory with your new graphics, and so on. It's to your advantage to keep all the files with changes in a single large data directory. Use subdirectories if necessary. Then you can use one single command line to back up all the files.

- Use the COPY command to back up your current data to a diskette. For example, if you're using a word processor to create a document, copy the document onto a diskette daily. Since it is only one file, you can back it up quickly.

Then, if the data you are now working on is destroyed, you don't have to go through an entire backup. Instead, just use COPY to retrieve the data from the backup diskette. If it's a question of data that you have already processed, simply copy back the data directories that you back up at regular intervals.

Here are the three most important methods of backing up data, depending on time and space:

1. Back up all the data on the hard drive at regular intervals. You should always do this when you significantly change the directory structure of your hard drive (for example, by adding several new programs or data directories). This type of backup takes the longest time and requires the largest amount of diskettes.

2. At regular intervals, perhaps weekly, back up a special data directory containing all the subdirectories with data that you often change. This backup is considerably faster.

3. At shorter intervals, back up your files to special backup diskettes.

We would also like to bring two other options to your attention:

- There are some other backup options in MS-DOS. However, these options require a better knowledge of how MS-DOS works with files and diskettes, so we refer you to *DOS 5.0 Complete*. For example, you can read *DOS 5.0 Complete* to find out how to back up only data on the hard drive to which you have made changes.

- There are special backup programs on the market that work much faster and more comfortably than the DOS BACKUP and RESTORE commands. If you are using data that is very important, you should consider one of these programs.

10. MS-DOS Editor: More than a notepad

The Editor

MS-DOS 5.0 also includes the MS-DOS Editor (EDIT.COM). As its name implies, the MS-DOS Editor is a *text editor* used to create text files. These simple text files consist of character strings without any formatting, as you might find in a text file generated by a word processor program.

We mentioned earlier in the book that MS-DOS 5.0 recognizes three file extensions which indicate executable program code: EXE, COM and BAT. *Batch files* (those with a .BAT extension) are text files containing DOS commands. The files AUTOEXEC.BAT and CONFIG.SYS, vital to MS-DOS when you switch on your computer, are text files. The MS-DOS Editor allows you to view and edit these files to suit your own needs (more on this later).

The MS-DOS Editor places the entire screen at your disposal for creating text files. This is a major advantage over the *line editors* provided with earlier versions of DOS, which only allowed editing one line at a time. Like the MS-DOS Shell, the MS-DOS Editor has menus which can be accessed from the keyboard or the mouse, and has an easy to use help system.

10.1 A paperless office

The MS-DOS Editor resides in the DOS directory of your hard drive under the name EDIT.COM. Since there is probably a search path defined by PATH for your DOS directory, you can start the MS-DOS Editor from any directory.

If your computer doesn't have a hard drive, you must insert the diskette with the EDIT.COM program in the current drive.

How you start the MS-DOS Editor depends on whether you are working with the MS-DOS Shell or the command interpreter.

MS-DOS Shell

If you are in the MS-DOS Shell, press [Tab] to activate the program list area. Then use the arrow keys to move the selection cursor to the Editor line and press [Enter]. A dialog box appears where you can type in the name of a file that you want to open. Since we are going to create a file from scratch, simply press [Enter].

10. MS-DOS Editor: More than a notepad

The startup screen appears (we'll go into more detail about this later in this chapter).

Command interpreter
To start the MS-DOS Editor from the command interpreter, type the following line from any directory:

EDIT [Enter]

After you press [Enter], the startup screen appears.

The startup screen
After you start the program, the MS-DOS Editor displays a dialog box in the middle of the screen. Pressing [Enter] activates the "Survival Guide" (a general help system), while pressing [Esc] takes you directly to the main screen of the MS-DOS Editor. Press [Esc].

```
 File  Edit  Search  Options                                      Help
─────────────────────────── Untitled ───────────────────────────




              ┌─────────────────────────────────────────┐
              │       Welcome to the MS-DOS Editor      │
              │                                         │
              │  Copyright (C) Microsoft Corporation, 1987-1991. │
              │            All rights reserved.         │
              │                                         │
              │─< Press Enter to see the Survival Guide >─│
              │                                         │
              │─< Press ESC to clear this dialog box >──│
              └─────────────────────────────────────────┘




  F1=Help   Enter=Execute   Esc=Cancel   Tab=Next Field   Arrow=Next Item
```

The MS-DOS Editor startup screen

The menu bar
If you know your way around the MS-DOS Shell, then working with the MS-DOS Editor shouldn't be any problem at all for you, because the menus work according to the same principle. This is a great advance over the old days, when separate programs sometimes had a style of operation that was all their own.

158

10.1 A paperless office

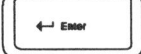

You activate the menu bar, located in the top screen line, by pressing [Alt], just like the MS-DOS Shell. To activate the menus, either press the letter highlighted in the name of the menu or use the arrow keys to select a menu and press [Enter]. The commands for each of the menus also have highlighted letters. Menu commands that you select with the letter keys are executed immediately. You can also select the commands with the arrow keys and press [Enter].

If you are using a mouse, click the desired menu title in the menu bar and the menu opens up. You can also activate the commands by clicking on them.

The scroll bars

At the right screen border is a vertical grey bar with an arrow at the top and the bottom. This is the scroll bar. You can see a black rectangle within this bar. This is the scroll slider. On the basis of its position within the scroll bar, the scroll slider displays which section of the contents of a file are on the screen. That is, if the slider is at the top, you are looking at the beginning of the text. If the slider is in the middle of the scroll bar, then you are looking at the middle of the text. If the slider is at the bottom, you see the end of the text.

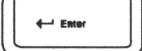

Press the [↑] and [↓] arrow keys, or [PgUp] and [PgDn] to move the contents of the screen up or down. You will see the scroll slider moving along with the text.

You can click both scroll arrows of the scroll bar with the mouse to scroll (move) the text up or down. You can even use the mouse to move the slider directly. Place the mouse pointer on the slider, press the left mouse button and move the mouse pointer in the desired direction. The slider moves along with the mouse pointer, displaying the appropriate area of data on the screen.

You can also use [Ctrl] + [PgDn] and [Ctrl] + [PgUp] for scrolling horizontally. This kind of scrolling is necessary if the lines are too long and cannot be fully displayed on the screen. Many files won't let you end a line prematurely and continue in the next line (e.g., the special AUTOEXEC.BAT file).

159

10. MS-DOS Editor: More than a notepad

10.2 Better than a typewriter

Entering and changing text

They call the MS-DOS Editor a *full page editor* because you can move anywhere on the screen with the cursor. The full page editor makes entering new texts and editing existing texts very easy. There are line editors that only allow you to change one line at a time, making certain processes quite awkward and complicated.

Entering text

You can enter text from the keyboard exactly as you would on a typewriter. Unlike word processors, the MS-DOS Editor scrolls the displayed area to the right when your text moves beyond the right border of the screen.

Most word processors automatically wrap around (start a new line) when you reach the end of a screen line (usually 78 characters). If you haven't opened any text, the length of a line of text is limited to 256 characters. Otherwise, the MS-DOS Editor adapts to the longest line of the text in case it's longer than 256 characters.

You will hear a beep if you reach the end of a line (character 256) when typing text. Press [Enter] to move to the beginning of the next line.

If you don't want to scroll the screen horizontally (for example, to preserve the readability of the text), you must remember to press [Enter] to move to a new line. However, you can't do this with files containing command lines. You can only press [Enter] to end these lines once all command information has been entered.

Now that we've given you some background, we're ready for some practice. Type a short message on the screen:

```
Hello, [Enter]
```

When you press [Enter], the cursor goes to the next line. Next type the following:

```
I went to the city and will be back sometime tonight.
```

Now press [Enter] to move to a new line, the way you would on a typewriter, and type:

```
See you later
```

You've just created a text file.

10.2 Better than a typewriter

Insert and overstrike

The MS-DOS Editor makes different options available for correcting text. Let's take a look at these options.

You can make simple text corrections by deleting the current word and inserting the new one (in *insert mode*) or by overtyping the old word with the new one (*overstrike mode*). You can switch between the two modes by pressing [Ins] (or [Ctrl] + [V]). The cursor shows the current mode. If the cursor appears as a line underneath the letter, the MS-DOS Editor is in insert mode. If the cursor appears as a rectangle the same size as a screen character, then you are in overstrike mode.

Making changes in insert mode

To make changes when in insert mode, use the [Del] key to delete the unwanted word. Then type in the new word. You could also use [Shift] and the [←] or [→] keys to mark the portion of text that you want to delete first and then use [Del] to delete the text you just marked.

In our example, let's replace "sometime tonight" with "at 8 o'clock P.M". To do this, move the cursor to the beginning of "sometime tonight", press the [Shift] key and press [→] until you have marked all three words. Then press [Del]. Now you can type in the new text.

Making changes in overstrike mode

In overstrike mode, the character covered by the flashing rectangle is always overtyped by the character you type. After each overtyped character, the cursor moves one character to the right. When you use this method, make sure you don't overstrike any text you don't want to eliminate with your new text. If the new text is longer than the original text, press [Ins] to switch off overstrike mode before it's too late.

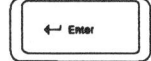

To practice this, you can replace "at 8 o'clock P.M" with "sometime tonight" again. Move the cursor to the beginning of the text. Now press [Ins] and type "sometime tonight".

Deleting text

There are different methods for deleting small text passages. Which method is best depends on whether you want to delete single characters, one or more words, whole lines or even entire paragraphs of text.

Deleting characters left of cursor

You can always use either the [Backspace] key or [Ctrl] + [H] to delete a character to the left of the cursor. It doesn't matter whether insert mode or overstrike mode is active.

Deleting current characters

Use the [Del] key (or [Ctrl] + [G]) to remove the character above the cursor (insert mode) or the character covered by the cursor (overstrike mode).

161

10. MS-DOS Editor: More than a notepad

Deleting words Use [Ctrl] + [T] to delete words. The key combination deletes from the current position of the cursor to the right, with all of the connected letters considered as one word. Special characters such as spaces and punctuation marks are treated as separate words. The key combination deletes from the position of the cursor to the next space or punctuation mark. If the cursor is in the middle of a word, the word is deleted from the character marked by the cursor to the end of the word.

Deleting lines the MS-DOS Editor can also delete an entire line. Press [Ctrl] + [Y] to delete the line where the cursor is currently positioned. No matter where the cursor was positioned in the line you just deleted, it is always at the beginning of the next line.

Deleting marked text One method for deleting almost anything is to mark the part of the text you want to delete and then press [Del]. Marking the text portions is very easy. Press the [Shift] key and press the [→], [←], [↑] or [↓] arrow keys. The MS-DOS Editor displays marked text in inverse video. Now you are ready to use [Del] to delete the text area you have just marked.

Tabs In the MS-DOS Editor, you can also work with *tabs*. Tabs are invisible vertical lines on the screen. You can jump directly to one of these lines by pressing [Tab]. You can use this option to place columns of numbers underneath each other or create tables.

The MS-DOS Editor inserts the number of spaces corresponding to a tab. No tab characters are inserted.

Before you open a text with tabs from a diskette or the hard drive, you can define the desired distances of the single tabs in the **Options** menu under the **Display...** command. In the Display dialog box you can define the distance between tabs at Tab Stops. You can set values from 1 to 99, the default setting is always 8.

Working with blocks of text Like many word processors, the MS-DOS Editor also gives you the option of working with *blocks* of text. A block of text is a continuous area of marked text.

Working with blocks of text in the MS-DOS Editor is easy. The MS-DOS Editor has a buffer for moving, deleting, and inserting marked areas of text. We'll refer to this buffer as a *clipboard*. The **Edit** menu provides commands for controlling this buffer.

Since most of the MS-DOS Editor commands can be invoked from both key combinations and menus, there are also key combinations for

10.2 Better than a typewriter

working with the clipboard, some of which may have already become an industry standard. They are identical to the key combinations for working with blocks of text in many word processors and programming language editors.

Marking a block of text

If you want to edit a block of text, you must mark the desired text area. You can do this easily by pressing the [Shift] key and pressing the [→], [←], [↑] or [↓] arrow keys. The MS-DOS Editor displays marked text in inverse video. There can only be one block of text marked at a time. That is, if you mark one passage of text while another passage is already marked, the first marked passage is cancelled.

Cancelling marked text

Before we turn to the various block commands, we would like to show you how to cancel marked text. All you need to do is press any arrow key to unmark the text.

Moving blocks of text

To move a block of text, you must first delete it to the clipboard. To do this, press [Shift] + [Del] or select **Cut** from the **Edit** menu. The marked block of text is removed from the text, so you no longer see it on the screen. To insert this text at a different location, move the cursor to the desired location. Then either press [Shift] + [Ins] or select **Paste** from the **Edit** menu. The block of text is then inserted back into the text.

Copying blocks of text

If you don't want to move a block of text, but rather copy it, you also use the clipboard. This time, though, you don't delete to the clipboard, instead, you copy to it. To do this, press [Ctrl] +[Ins] or select **Copy** from the **Edit** menu. That way, the block of text you copy remains in its original place in the text. To insert this text somewhere else, move the cursor to the place in the text where you want to insert it and either press [Shift] + [Ins] or select **Paste** from the **Edit** menu and the block of text is inserted into the text from the clipboard.

Deleting blocks of text

We've already explained how to delete a block of text elsewhere without using the term "block of text". You delete a block of text by pressing the [Del] key. Make certain you want to delete the text because deleted text does not go to the clipboard. Therefore you cannot paste or insert it at a different location.

Saving a block of text as a file

If you want to save a block of text as a file on a diskette, you can also use the clipboard. You must copy the desired block of text to the clipboard, save the text you were editing and quit. Now copy the contents of the clipboard back to the screen and save them as a file. Here's how to do it:

10. MS-DOS Editor: More than a notepad

Mark the block of text and press [Shift] + [Del] or select **Cut** from the **Edit** menu to place the text in the clipboard. Select **Save** from the **File** menu to save the original file. Then select **New** from the **File** menu to clear the screen.

Now press [Shift] + [Ins] or select **Paste** from the **Edit** menu to copy the contents of the clipboard onto the blank screen. Select **Save As...** from the **File** menu to give this block of text a filename and save it to a diskette or your hard drive.

Inserting files into text

Just as you can save a block of text separately from the rest of the text, you can also insert the contents of a text file into an existing text. The procedure is the same as described above - only the other way around.

Select the **File** menu and the **Open...** command to open on the screen the file that you want to insert into another text. Mark the passage (or the whole text) as a block of text. Next, press [Shift] + [Del] or select **Cut** from the **Edit** menu to copy the block of text to the clipboard.

Then select **New** from the **File** menu to clear the screen. Now open the file to where you want to insert the contents of the clipboard on the screen by selecting **File/Open...**.

Place the cursor in the position where you want to insert the block of text and either press [Shift] + [Ins] or select **Paste** from the **Edit** menu to insert the block of text from the clipboard into the text.

10.3 Opening and saving finished texts

The MS-DOS Editor has the same advantage as any other word processor. Once you've written a text, you'll never have to type it again (unless you've lost data—see Chapter 9). Every text you create is always available—to re-use or revise.

Opening a file We would like to show you how to open a text file, by using the AUTOEXEC.BAT file, which we copied to the WORK directory as an example.

Press (Alt) and (Enter) to activate the menu in the MS-DOS Editor and use the arrow keys to mark the **Open...** command to open a file in the MS-DOS Editor. A dialog box appears on the screen, where you can specify the filename of the file you want to open.

Before we can type in the name, however, we must first change to the appropriate directory. Press (Tab) to move to the Dirs/Drives option box in order to select the WORK directory (move the highlight to the WORK directory and press (Enter)).

Now type the name of the file you want to open in the File Name: line:

```
AUTOEXEC.BAT
```

After you press (Enter), the file is loaded into the MS-DOS Editor.

Remember if you want to open a text file, you must first select the drive or directory containing the file in Dirs/Drives. After that you can either type in the filename or use wildcards to make a preselection, press (Enter), use the arrow keys to select the file you want from the file list displayed under Files. You can also press (Tab) to get to Files. Press (Enter) and the file you selected is opened in the MS-DOS Editor.

10. MS-DOS Editor: More than a notepad

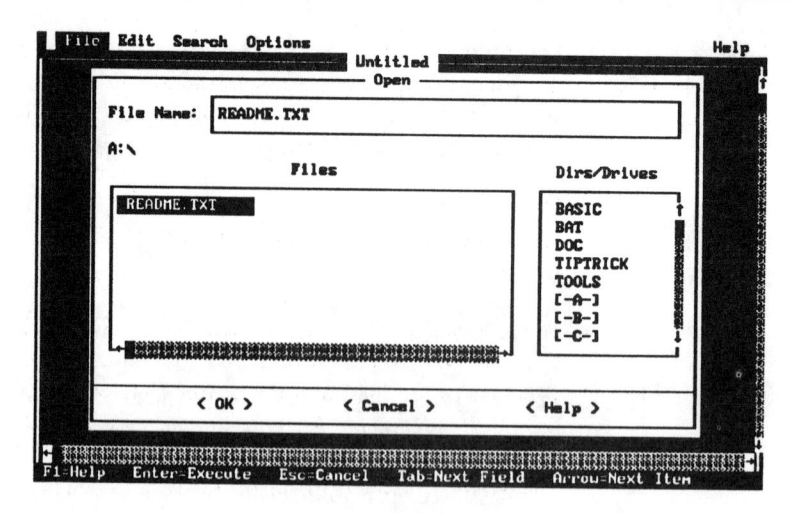

The Open dialog box

Creating new files

It's also easy to create new files in the MS-DOS Editor. You have two options.

The first option is to call the MS-DOS Editor, followed by the filename of your new file, including the extension. For instance, to create a file called TEST.DAT, you would type the MS-DOS Editor TEST.DAT. If there is no file named TEST.DAT in the current directory, the MS-DOS Editor starts with a blank screen. Then you can enter text in the file and store it on a diskette or your hard drive by selecting **Save** from the **File** menu.

If there is already a file by that name in the current directory, the MS-DOS Editor opens and displays it. This lets you know that the filename already exists and that you will have to think of another name for your new file. (You can remove a file that you accidentally opened by selecting **New** from the **File** menu.)

The second option consists of starting the MS-DOS Editor without specifying a filename. You can then be sure that the MS-DOS Editor will appear with a blank screen. After that, you can type in the desired text. To save the file when you are finished, select **Save As...** from the **File** menu and type the filename in the dialog box that appears.

If this filename already exists in the current directory, the MS-DOS Editor brings this to your attention with the message "File already exists. Overwrite?" Press (Enter) to overwrite the file, press (Esc) to exit the message or select Cancel or No.

166

10.3 Opening and saving finished texts

Editing an existing file
To edit an existing file, you must first open it. As we said earlier, you can either do this when you call the MS-DOS Editor, or open the file by selecting **Open...** from the **File** menu. The file you want to edit will then appear on the screen.

Saving a file
The MS-DOS Editor saves files in ASCII format. This makes it possible to edit files created in the MS-DOS Editor with other editors or word processors.

There's one special feature of the MS-DOS Editor that you should keep in mind. When you save a file that already exists in the current directory of the hard drive or diskette under the same name, the MS-DOS Editor doesn't make a backup copy of the "old" file. That is, there is no .BAK file containing the contents of the old file. That means that if you overwrite the contents of the old file, you could lose that data.

Saving a new file
To save a new file that still doesn't have a name, select **Save As...** from the **File** menu. The Save As dialog box appears with File Name and Dirs/Drives areas. In Dirs/Drives select the drive and directory to where you want to save the file. In File Name type in the filename you have chosen for the file. Then press [Enter] or select OK.

Saving an open file
If you open an existing file or call the MS-DOS Editor with a filename, then you already know the filename and its directory. You can save this file any time by selecting **Save** in the **File** menu.

However, you can also change the filename and the directory before you save the file. Open the **File** menu and select **Save As...**. The current filename is displayed in this dialog box next to File Name. The directory from where you opened the file or the active directory is also underneath the filename. Either accept the filename and directory or change them and press [Enter] or OK.

Changing filenames
You can also use **Save As...** to save a file from your hard drive or a diskette under a different name. All you need to do is type in a different name and press [Enter]. The MS-DOS Editor then places the file with its new name on your hard drive or diskette. The old file is also preserved.

10. MS-DOS Editor: More than a notepad

Clearing the memory and the screen

When you save a file, the contents of the file are still in the MS-DOS Editor's memory and on the screen. If you decide to create another file in the MS-DOS Editor, you don't have to remove the old contents with [Del]. Instead, use the **New** command in the **File** menu. When you select **New**, the MS-DOS Editor clears both the memory and the screen.

Quitting without saving

To quit the MS-DOS Editor without saving the file in the memory, select **Exit** in the **File** menu. If you made any changes to the file since the last save, the MS-DOS Editor will ask you whether you want to save. Answer Yes to save the file. If you answer No, the file is not saved, and you exit the MS-DOS Editor.

Printing a file

It's also no problem to see what your text file looks like on paper. Open the **File** menu and select **Print...**.

A dialog box appears, where you are asked which parts of the opened file you want to print. By selecting the Selected Text Only option you can print only the text that is marked. If you select the Complete Document option, the entire document is printed. Press [Enter] to confirm your selection and the MS-DOS Editor begins printing.

10.4 Cursor movement

This section describes how you can move the cursor within the MS-DOS Editor. In most cases, you can choose between two different options. The second option is due to the fact that in the earlier days of the PC, word processors and editors were controlled using the keystrokes listed in the Second option column. Both options for each movement appear in the table below.

Movement	First option	Second option
One character right	→	Ctrl + D
One character left	←	Ctrl + S
One line up	↑	Ctrl + E
One line down	→	Ctrl + X
One word left	Ctrl	Ctrl + A
One word right	Ctrl + →	Ctrl + F
One page up	PgUp	Ctrl + R
One page down	PgDn	Ctrl + C

Other cursor movement keys

Press Ctrl + Home to move the cursor to the beginning of a text. To move to the end of a text, press Ctrl + End.

Horizontal scrolling Unlike ordinary word processors, the MS-DOS Editor doesn't automatically break at the end of a line, so it can easily happen that one or more lines aren't completely visible on the screen. Instead, the rest of the line will be to the left or the right of the screen.

To move completely to the right or the left, press either Ctrl + PgUp or Ctrl + PgDn. This takes the cursor either 78 characters to the left or 78 characters to the right. It doesn't matter whether there are more or less than 78 characters in a line.

Press Home to jump to the beginning of a line and press End to go to the end of a line.

169

10. MS-DOS Editor: More than a notepad

10.5 MS-DOS Editor keys

Key	Description
[Esc]	Cancels commands, closes dialog boxes.
[←]	Moves the cursor one character to the left (also [Ctrl] + [S]).
[→]	Moves the cursor one character to the right (also [Ctrl] + [D]).
[↑]	Moves the cursor one line up (also [Ctrl] + [E]).
[↓]	Moves the cursor one line down (also [Ctrl] + [X]).
[Backspace]	Deletes the character to the left of the cursor (also [Ctrl] + [H]).
[Del]	Deletes the character at the current cursor position (also [Ctrl] + [G]).
[Ins]	Turns insert mode on or off (also [Ctrl] + [V]).
[Home]	Cursor goes to the beginning of the line.
[End]	Cursor goes to the end of the line.
[PgUp]	Cursor moves 14 lines up (also [Ctrl] + [R]).
[PgDn]	Cursor moves 14 lines down (also [Ctrl] + [C]).
[Ctrl] + [A]	Cursor moves to previous word.
[Ctrl] + [F]	Cursor moves to next word.
[Ctrl] + [N]	Rest of the line beginning with cursor is moved to the next line.
[Ctrl] + [PgUp]	Page by page horizontal scrolling (78 characters to the left).
[Ctrl] + [PgDn]	Page by page horizontal scrolling (78 characters to the right).
[Ctrl] + [Q][S]	Cursor jumps to beginning of line.
[Ctrl] + [Q][D]	Cursor jumps to end of line.
[Ctrl] + [W]	Screen scrolls one line down.
[Ctrl] + [Z]	Screen scrolls one line up.
[Ctrl] + [T]	Deletes the next word.
[Ctrl] + [Y]	Deletes the line where the cursor is located.
[Ctrl] + [K] + n	Places a mark: n stands for a number between 0 and 3. Lets you mark passages of text while you are working and place the cursor in these passages. The marks don't appear in the text and are lost when you exit the Editor.
[Ctrl] + [Q] + n	Jumps to mark n. Mark must be set beforehand with [Ctrl] + [K] + n (use appropriate number for n).

10.6 MS-DOS Editor menus

In this section we'll give you a brief course in selecting menus and commands, as well as a short explanation of all the commands.

Selecting with letter keys
Press (Alt) to activate the menu bar. Press the highlighted letters to open the menus. The menu commands of the menus also have highlighted letters. A menu command selected with the letter keys is immediately executed.

Selecting with arrow keys
You can also open a menu with the (↑) and (↓) arrow keys. Use the (→) and (←) arrow keys to select from the various menu titles. Press (Enter) to execute a menu command selected by the arrow keys.

If you are using a mouse, click the desired menu in the menu bar and the menu opens. You can also activate the menu commands by clicking them.

Now we'd like to provide a short overview of the menu structure and what the menu commands do.

The File menu

New
Clears the screen and memory of the MS-DOS Editor.

Open
This command opens an existing file from a diskette or hard drive.

Save
This command saves a file immediately if it has already been saved under a name. If this is not the case, the command corresponds to the **Save As...** command, prompting you for a filename.

Save As
You use this command to save a file. You can also use it to give a new name to the file you are saving or specify a new target.

Print
Use this command to print either the entire file or only the marked text.

Exit
Use this command to quit the Editor.

The Edit menu

Cut
Use this command to delete a marked passage of text (block of text) from the text and save it in the clipboard.

Copy
Use this command to copy a marked passage of text (block of text) from the text to the clipboard.

171

10. MS-DOS Editor: More than a notepad

Paste   With Paste you can insert the contents of the clipboard (block of text) into the text at the position of the cursor.

Delete   Use this command to delete marked passages of text (blocks of text). The deleted text is not copied to the clipboard.

The Search menu

Find...   You can use this command to search for any character string in the entire text. Along with the search word, you can also turn on/off uppercase/lowercase consideration and choose whether to have the search word as a separate word (not part of another word). In the first case, **Find...** would not find the "ox" in flummox, while in the second case it would.

Repeat Last Find
   This command repeats the last search. This allows you to find every place in the text where a search term appears.

Change...   You use this command to exchange any character string in the entire text with any other character string.

The Options menu

Display   Selects the colors of the screen background and the fonts, toggles the scroll bar with the scroll slider and defines the distance between tabs.

Help Path   Specifies the path to the directory containing the EDIT.HLP file.

The Help menu

Getting started   Gives you a help screen that tells you how to work with the Editor.

Keyboard   Displays help with keys and keyboard shortcuts.

About   A small dialog box appears with information about the copyright and version of the Editor.

10.7 Text editing in MS-DOS

We'd like to give you a brief explanation of what you can use the MS-DOS Editor for.

You could use the MS-DOS Editor to create and print short text files. As soon as you started writing more extensive texts or expecting more of the layout, however, you would find that the MS-DOS Editor is no longer helpful, and you would be forced to resort to a proper word processor.

The MS-DOS Editor is intended mainly for editing files that you want to create or change in MS-DOS. Examples of such files would be the AUTOEXEC.BAT and CONFIG.SYS system files, which we'll discuss in Chapter 11.

The Editor is also well suited for creating batch files, which we'll also discuss in Chapter 11.

11. Hiring experts

In this chapter we would like to introduce you to some areas of MS-DOS that allow you to customize your computer and make your computing easier and faster.

11.1 Continuing education

This section introduces two files that are important to your PC. They are responsible for starting your PC without your help, in such a way that you can immediately begin working with it. If you didn't have these two files, many conveniences would not be available. For example, the system prompt would not be configured properly.

Interestingly enough, you can teach your PC some things and it will make notes about the new information in two special files. We'll get you better acquainted with these two files and explain what they do. We'll also tell you how to change these files to fit your own requirements.

The AUTOEXEC.BAT file

The first file we want to talk about is the AUTOEXEC.BAT file. You are already familiar with this file from different exercises. You will find it either in the root directory of your hard drive or on your start diskette.

There are several options for viewing the AUTOEXEC.BAT file:

1. Run the MS-DOS 5.0 Editor and select the **Open...** command from the **File** menu. We explained how the MS-DOS Editor works in Chapter 10.

2. You display the file in the MS-DOS Shell by marking AUTOEXEC.BAT and selecting **View File Contents** from the **File** menu.

3. You can display the command in the command interpreter by making the root directory the current directory, typing the following command and pressing [Enter]:

```
TYPE AUTOEXEC.BAT
```

Then you will see the AUTOEXEC.BAT file on your screen. We will use a sample file to explain the most important elements of the file.

11. Hiring experts

Here's an example of what the AUTOEXEC.BAT file could look like:

```
ECHO OFF
PATH C:\DOS
C:\DOS\KEYB GR,,C:\DOS\KEYBOARD.SYS
SET COMSPEC=C:\DOS\COMMAND.COM
PROMPT $P$G
ECHO ON
```

Now we'll tell you what each line means. The lines consist of MS-DOS commands that are processed in the sequence in which they appear in the file (i.e., one after the other). You could also type each one of these commands in the AUTOEXEC.BAT when you start your PC. You would achieve the same thing, but it would be a lot more trouble. It's much better to start your computer with the certainty that the settings necessary for working with the PC are automatically being made. But now we'd like to explain what each of the MS-DOS commands means.

The ECHO command

As you can see, the ECHO command was used twice in our sample file; what is more, it was used differently both times. One time an OFF was added to the command, while the other time an ON was added to it.

Adding OFF to the ECHO command prevents the rest of the commands in the file from being displayed on the screen before they are executed (like an "echo").

Adding ON to ECHO displays the rest of the commands, if there are any or if a similar file is processed, before they are executed.

The PATH command

If you have a hard drive with all the MS-DOS commands in a certain directory, then the PATH command is extremely important. This command enables MS-DOS to always find all the MS-DOS commands, no matter which directory you are working in. We already mentioned this option in our discussion of different programs in Chapter 8.

In order for MS-DOS to always find the commands, you must specify the directory containing the MS-DOS commands after the PATH command. In our case, it's the DOS directory.

The PATH command creates a path towards the specified directory.

Not only can you specify the path for your MS-DOS commands, but you can also set up paths to other directories. This is practical, for example, if you use a word processor or other programs. By setting up a path to the directory containing the program, you are able to call the program any time, from any current directory or drive.

To set up paths to different directories, you must specify the directory names separated by semicolons. For example, to create a path to your word processor, which is located in the C:\WORD directory, in addition to the directory containing the MS-DOS commands, you would have to add the following line to your AUTOEXEC.BAT file:

```
PATH C:\DOS;C:\WORD
```

You could create a path to all your programs this way. The best way to do it is to specify the directories of the programs in the sequence in which you most frequently use them. MS-DOS searches for the paths in the sequence you specify after PATH.

The SET COMSPEC command

The next command line in the AUTOEXEC.BAT file instructs MS-DOS to find the command interpreter. The command interpreter includes resident commands such as DIR and CLS.

```
SET COMSPEC=C:\DOS\COMMAND.COM
```

The PROMPT command

This command configures the system prompt within the AUTOEXEC.BAT file. The PROMPT command specified in the example displays the name of the current directory and a greater than sign after the drive letter. We covered the importance of this particular form of the system prompt in the introduction to subdirectories.

DATE and TIME

If your computer doesn't have a real time clock, you should type in the current date and time each time you start your PC. You can add the commands for doing this to your AUTOEXEC.BAT so you don't have to do it by hand every time you start the computer. You use the DATE and TIME commands to set or change the date and time. If you add each of these commands to the end of your AUTOEXEC.BAT file (in separate lines) you will be prompted for the current date and time every time you start your computer.

All in all, your PC can learn a great deal from an AUTOEXEC.BAT if you add the right lines.

Be extremely careful when changing the AUTOEXEC.BAT file or the CONFIG.SYS file. Any mistakes that you type in a command line could prevent your PC from working correctly, it might even keep it from working altogether. Your computer isn't "broken", however, just "readjusted".

11. Hiring experts

Before you change the AUTOEXEC.BAT and CONFIG.SYS system files, create a boot diskette. Follow these steps:

- Format a blank diskette with the /S switch, so the PC will be able to start from this diskette:

```
FORMAT A: /S
```

  This copies the COMMAND.COM file to the diskette along with two hidden files.

- Now copy the original AUTOEXEC.BAT and CONFIG.SYS files to your start diskette. It's best if you copy them under different names. If you use the original, reserved names, your PC will try to run these files when you start it from the diskette and you could have problems.

Now, if you get caught in a "hopeless" situation while changing your system files, just insert your boot diskette, switch your computer back on, type PROMPT PG for a useful system prompt and press [Enter]. After that you can copy the system files from the boot diskette back to the root directory of your hard drive.

11.2 Off to the shop

Adapting the PC

Let's talk about the other important file, the CONFIG.SYS file. This file is very important for starting your PC correctly. This file is also located either in your hard drive or on the boot diskette. There are several options for viewing the CONFIG.SYS file:

1. Run the MS-DOS 5.0 Editor and select the **Open...** command from the **File** menu (see Chapter 10).

2. Mark CONFIG.SYS in the MS-DOS Shell and select **View File Contents** from the **File** menu.

3. You can display the command in the command interpreter by making the root directory the current directory and typing:

```
TYPE CONFIG.SYS  Enter
```

The CONFIG.SYS file appears on your screen. We are going to explain some of the elements of the file using the following example:

```
DEVICE=HIMEM.SYS
DEVICE=C:\SYS\DOS\SETVER.EXE
FILES=20
BUFFERS=20
SHELL=C:\COMMAND.COM /P /E:500
COUNTRY=049,,C:\DOS\COUNTRY.SYS
DOS=HIGH
```

Summary

This file configures the PC. CONFIG.SYS settings are accepted before the system runs the AUTOEXEC.BAT file. The CONFIG.SYS file, unlike the AUTOEXEC.BAT, does not get processed. Instead, the system settings are specified according to your wishes. Unlike the commands in the AUTOEXEC.BAT file, you cannot type the lines in the CONFIG.SYS file as commands. CONFIG.SYS contains settings that are read only when you switch on your PC.

Let's look at the commands in the CONFIG.SYS file:

```
DEVICE=HIMEM.SYS
```

11. Hiring experts

The HIMEM command

HIMEM.SYS manages memory above 640K. Years ago, when developers were first working on MS-DOS, there were no plans to manage more than 640K of program memory, so now utility programs perform this management. This command is especially important for using Windows 3.

The SETVER command

This command is used to adapt certain programs to MS-DOS 5.0. We mentioned earlier there are different versions of MS-DOS which you shouldn't mix. Certain programs ask for the exact version of DOS and may not be set up to accept MS-DOS 5.0. The SETVER.EXE program deceives programs into thinking that another version of DOS (such as MS-DOS 4.0) is running. However, using SETVER requires a considerable amount of knowledge about DOS and its different versions, so we won't go into the exact procedure here. We suggest you see *DOS 5.0 Complete* for more information.

The FILES command

You use this command to define the number of files that can be accessed at the same time. In order to work on a file, you must first open it. For many tasks it is necessary to have several files opened at the same time. For instance, if you are working with a word processor, your program files must be opened, in addition to the text file you are working on.

We believe that 20 is a practical value for the number of files opened at the same time. Also, certain programs have requirements for this number which are discussed in the manuals.

The BUFFERS command

MS-DOS places data moved between different drives in a buffer. You use BUFFERS to determine the size of this buffer. This helps speed up your work with MS-DOS.

Do not specify a value that is too large, however; otherwise you will have less memory available for programs. 10 is a good value for PC users who don't have a hard drive and a value of 20 for PC users who do have a hard drive.

The SHELL command

The only time you need this command is when the COMMAND.COM file for loading the command interpreter resides in the same directory as the MS-DOS commands, instead of the root directory. The SHELL command instructs MS-DOS to load the command interpreter when the computer starts. You must specify the directory where the command interpreter is located. In our case, the command interpreter is in the DOS directory.

11.2 Off to the shop

The COUNTRY command

The COUNTRY command configures your version of MS-DOS to a particular country. This configuration includes date, time and currency parameters.

The following sets the PC to the German configuration, while pinpointing the location of the COUNTRY.SYS file:

```
COUNTRY=049,,C:\DOS\COUNTRY.SYS
```

The DOS=HIGH command

If your computer has more than 640K total memory, you can have MS-DOS use part of that memory. This command instructs MS-DOS to use this memory. Sometimes the line reads:

```
DOS=HIGH,UMB
```

However, to influence MS-DOS, you should know exactly how MS-DOS works as well as have a good knowledge of memory management. At any rate, the DEVICE=HIMEM.SYS command line must come before DOS=HIGH, so the extended memory is also available.

Changing these files

Now that we've explained these two files to you, perhaps you'd like to make some changes to them. For example, you might want to add a directory to your path. Just in case your new versions of these files don't work or you decide you'd rather work with the old versions, it's a good idea to back these files up before making any changes to them.

Backing up old files

To back up your old files, you can copy them. We recommend leaving the filenames as they are, but giving them a new file extension. To back up both files, type the following command lines and press [Enter]:

```
COPY AUTOEXEC.BAT AUTOEXEC.OLD
COPY CONFIG.SYS CONFIG.OLD
```

You have backed up the files, which now exist under two different names and you can use the old versions any time by just renaming them and copying them back.

Just to be on the safe side, you should also make a special boot diskette that you can use to start your computer, in cases of emergency. You should always have this boot diskette on hand, because you never know when something might happen to prevent you from starting your computer from the hard drive. A boot diskette comes in handy in such situations because you can use it start up the computer and take care of

11. Hiring experts

the problem on the hard drive or simply to do some work. We already explained how to make a start diskette earlier in this chapter.

Changing the files
To change the files, run the MS-DOS Editor. You can specify the name of the file when you start the MS-DOS Editor:

```
EDIT C:\AUTOEXEC.BAT
```

You could also start the MS-DOS Editor from the MS-DOS Shell and enter the filename in the parameter screen of the MS-DOS Shell.

The new files
If you created a new AUTOEXEC.BAT or CONFIG.SYS file, you can try it out by rebooting (restarting) your computer.

To do this, switch off the computer, wait a few seconds and then switch it back on. A warm boot (start) is gentler on your computer. Simply press the RESET button, which is usually on the front of your PC. There's another way to warm boot your computer if you don't have a RESET button. Pressing [Ctrl] + [Alt] + [Del] also performs a warm boot.

11.3 At no extra charge

Nowadays computers come equipped with more memory than MS-DOS is able to use directly. MS-DOS has a 640K limit. Although MS-DOS 5.0 can use more memory under certain circumstances, a healthy portion of your computer's memory is idle on a computer containing 2 Meg or more, unless you work with user interfaces like Windows 3.

However, you can make some interesting changes with the memory above the 640K limit. For instance, you could create a new drive (pseudo disk drive) or speed up your work on a slow hard drive.

The following examples are for a PC with 2 Meg of memory, that does not use Windows. If your computer has less memory or if you use Windows, find out about the memory division on your computer before you attempt to duplicate these examples. Perhaps one of your friends can help you, or you could get a copy of *DOS 5.0 Complete* and read the chapter on memory management.

A free disk drive: The RAM disk

If you own a computer containing more than 640K of memory, you might be wondering why your computer doesn't use any more memory than a friend's computer that only has a 640K memory.

We're not going to go into a detailed explanation of the facts here. Instead, we'll provide you with an extra drive that's much faster than a disk drive and even faster than a hard drive. Why do you need another drive? As the owner of a computer with a disk drive, you can use an extra drive for copying several files. Also, you can place temporary files there, that can be deleted after a short time. To get this extra drive, you can define part of your memory as a RAM disk, a second or third drive that doesn't cost you a cent.

Look in the directory where your MS-DOS commands are stored—it's probably called the DOS directory. There should be a file in that directory under one of the following names:

VDISK.SYS   RAMDRIVE.SYS   RAMDISK.SYS

The exact name of this file depends on whether you have MS-DOS, IBM-DOS, or some other version.

11. Hiring experts

Change to your MS-DOS directory using CD and type the following command to see all the SYS files in that directory:

```
DIR *.SYS [Enter]
```

The RAMDISK.SYS, RAMDRIVE.SYS and VDISK.SYS files are *device drivers*. Device drivers cannot be run as you would run a standard program. The CONFIG.SYS file calls device drivers to configure different features of your PC.

As soon as you find out the name of the file, call the MS-DOS Editor to open the CONFIG.SYS so you can add a line to it:

```
EDIT C:\CONFIG.SYS [Enter]
```

Don't change any of the existing lines. Just add one of the following lines at the end (which line you use will vary with the name of the SYS file you have):

```
DEVICE=RAMDRIVE.SYS 512 /E
DEVICE=VDISK.SYS 512 /E
DEVICE=RAMDISK.SYS 512 /E
```

If the RAMDRIVE.SYS file is not in the root directory, but in the C:\DOS subdirectory, then you must type a path specification in front of the filename (use the example below that's appropriate for you):

```
DEVICE=C:\DOS\RAMDRIVE.SYS 512 /E
DEVICE=C:\DOS\VDISK.SYS 512 /E
DEVICE=C:\DOS\RAMDISK.SYS 512 /E
```

Save the changed CONFIG.SYS file by pressing [Alt] [F] [S].

If you do a warm boot now (pressing [Ctrl] + [Alt] + [Del]), this or a similar message appears on the screen (we assume you have the RAMDRIVE.SYS file and a PC with a disk drive and a hard drive.):

```
Microsoft RAMDrive Version 3.06 Virtual Drive D:
   Drive size: 512 KB
...Sector size 512 Bytes
   Size of an allocation unit: 1 Sector(s)
   Directory entries: 64
```

This means that your PC has created a *virtual disk drive* (or a *pseudo disk drive*). Your PC acts as though there is an additional drive. It reserves a certain area in its RAM (Random Access Memory). In this

11.3 At no extra charge

case, the reserved area is 512K. If you have a PC with two disk drives and no hard drive, a third disk drive is created and given the label of C.

We assume that you have a PC with a disk drive and a hard drive. If you have a different configuration, please change the drive letter accordingly in the entry you type into CONFIG.SYS.

You can quickly find out that your PC is acting as though it has another drive by displaying the contents of the directory on your new drive (depending on your system, the drive letter for the RAM disk may be different from this example):

```
DIR D:
```

which results in the message:

```
Volume in drive D is MS-RAMDRIVE
Directory of D:\
```

To test the applications of your new drive, first copy the FORMAT command to the new drive. Type:

```
COPY A:FORMAT.COM D:
```

If you then type DIR D:, you get the message:

```
Volume in drive D is MS-RAMDRIVE
Directory of D:\

FORMAT   COM     11474  05.28.86  12.00
       1 file(s)      11747 bytes
                     189440 bytes free
```

However, as soon as you switch off your PC and switch it back on, you will notice that the entire contents of your new drive are lost. This pseudo drive is placed in your PC's RAM—a temporary setup.

A RAM disk may not seem very practical to you, but think about this: If you frequently copy files from one diskette to another and don't have a second disk drive, you can use your RAM disk as a way station and save yourself the trouble of changing diskettes. This is especially applicable if you want to copy several files using wildcards.

For example, let's suppose you want to copy all files with the .TXT extension from one diskette to another one. Simply insert your first diskette and copy it to the RAM disk:

11. Hiring experts

```
COPY A:*.TXT D:
```

Then insert the second diskette in drive A: and copy the texts from the RAM disk to the diskette:

```
COPY D:*.TXT A:
```

Finally, you can use the following command to delete the text files in the RAM disk:

```
DEL D:*.TXT
```

or switch the computer off to remove the information from the RAM disk.

If you had tried to copy all the files from one diskette to another without using the RAM disk, you would have had to insert the source diskette and the target diskette for each file.

An even faster hard drive: Cache programs

Like computers, hard drives have also gotten faster over the years. The last 2 to 3 years have seen a great deal of development in this area. For many users, hard drives still aren't "fast enough", especially when you have to move large amounts of data between the computer and the hard drive. If you have enough memory and you haven't been using a part of your expanded or extended memory up to now, you can use it to "speed up" your hard drive. Strictly speaking, your hard drive doesn't really operate faster—information can be stored temporarily in RAM, so programs can access this data from RAM instead of from the hard drive. The result is an increase in speed.

We are talking about programs that temporarily store data called *cache programs*. The basic premise of a cache program lies in the temporary storage of information. This information is read once by the hard drive and placed in memory. When the PC needs the information, this information is taken from RAM, which is much faster than the hard drive. If there's no more space available in RAM and you want to store some information that has just been read, the cache program has to create room in the cache.

Unlike the RAM disk, the cache program determines the data placed in RAM. This determination is made based on the following principle: What came last and what is used the most frequently stays in RAM for quick access.

MS-DOS 5.0 comes supplied with a cache program named SMARTDRV.SYS. Like the RAM disk driver, SMARTDRV.SYS is

11.3 At no extra charge

a device driver rather than a program, to be called from the CONFIG.SYS file. To start SMARTDRV.SYS, load the MS-DOS Editor and CONFIG.SYS. Add the following command:

```
DEVICE=SMARTDRV.SYS 512
```

If the SMARTDRV.SYS file isn't stored in the root directory, include a path specification in front of the filename. For example, if this file resides in the DOS directory of drive C:, type:

```
DEVICE=C:\DOS\SMARTDRV.SYS 512
```

Now, if you do a warm boot ([Ctrl] + [Alt] + [Del]), a message similar to the following appears on the screen:

```
Microsoft SMARTdrive Hard drive cache Version 3.13
    Cache size 512 KB in expanded memory
...Room for 60 tracks with 17 sectors each
    Minimum cache size is 0 KB
```

This means that your PC is now using 512K of expanded memory for temporary data storage. The rest of the information from the screen is of no interest to us at this time.

You will soon notice that the programs or data you use the most will be available 2 to 3 times faster than they were without the cache program.

187

11.4 The boss goes on vacation

Batch files

We'd like to show you another way to streamline your PC sessions: Batch files. The AUTOEXEC.BAT file is a batch file, and saves you the effort of typing commands by hand. This section gives you some background on batch files, and how to create your own.

Batch file basics

The MS-DOS operating system is sometimes difficult to control from the command interpreter. You reach a point where it's not enough just to type a command on the keyboard and wait for DOS to carry it out. A batch file gives you the option of batching MS-DOS commands together in sequence, and running these commands as a group.

Earlier we mentioned that MS-DOS recognizes three file types as executable files: EXE, COM and BAT. You call a batch file as you would a program, by typing its name (without the .BAT extension) and pressing [Enter].

The AUTOEXEC. BAT file

This file, as its name suggests, automatically executes (runs). The AUTOEXEC.BAT file contains the commands that your computer runs after you switch on your computer, such as DATE or TIME. You can test the fact that this is a batch of MS-DOS files available at any time. Simply call the file from the root directory by typing the following:

AUTOEXEC [Enter]

Depending on what your file looks like, you could get an error message, because the AUTOEXEC program is performing tasks that have already been performed. The principle of the batch file should be clear.

Batch files can be created that will save you time, effort and typing, by streamlining repetitious keyboard entry. Certain MS-DOS commands require quite a bit of typing. These same commands can be written to a batch file, and given a short name by which you can call it.

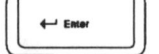

For example, let's suppose you are working with Microsoft Word, which is located in the WORD subdirectory of the APPS directory. If you wanted to run Microsoft Word, you might have to change from another directory to the WORD directory:

CD \APPS\WORD

11.4 The boss goes on vacation

Then run Microsoft Word:

`WORD`

There's an easier way. Run the MS-DOS Editor and type the following:

```
CD \APPS\WORD
WORD
```

After doing that, you could save the file to the root directory under the name W.BAT. The .BAT file extension is important, as it tells MS-DOS that the file in question is a batch file.

After exiting the MS-DOS Editor, typing the following changes directories and calls Microsoft Word:

`W` [Enter]

The following illustration shows what batch files are as well as their basic importance to users of MS-DOS:

```
┌─────────────────┐   ┌────────────────────────────────┐
│ Batch files     │   │ Entered from system prompt     │
│ combine         │   │   C:\>DOS COMMAND 1  [Enter]   │
│ repetitive      │   │                                │
│ command         │   │   C:\>DOS COMMAND 2  [Enter]   │
│ entry into      │   │                                │
│ one file,       │   │   C:\>DOS COMMAND 3  [Enter]   │
│ available       │   │ Each must be entered by hand   │
│ by entering     │   └────────────────────────────────┘
│ the filename    │   ┌────────────────────────────────┐
└─────────────────┘   │   Batch file DOTHIS.BAT        │
                      │      DOS COMMAND 1             │
                      │      DOS COMMAND 2             │
                      │      DOS COMMAND 3             │
                      │   Call from system prompt:     │
                      │      DOTHIS  [Enter]           │
                      └────────────────────────────────┘
```

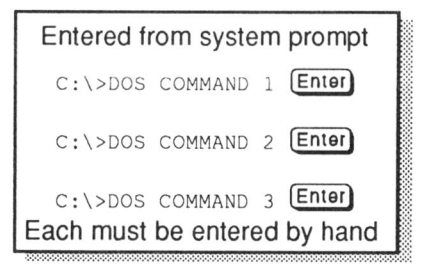

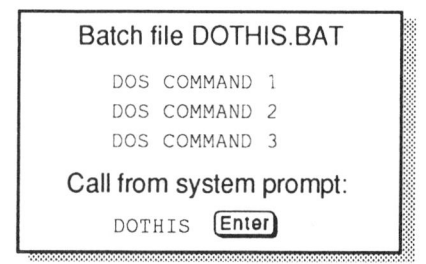

DOS vs. batch files

Using MS-DOS, DOS commands are entered at the system prompt, producing the appropriate results. For example:

11. Hiring experts

DOS COMMAND 1 = FORMAT A: formats a diskette.

DOS COMMAND 2 = COPY *.* A: copies all the files from the current directory to the diskette that has just been formatted.

DOS COMMAND 3 = DIR A: displays the results.

You could also write the same three commands to a batch file using some form of text file generation (the MS-DOS Editor, COPY CON or the EDLIN line editor) and save them using the .BAT extension.

Call the file by entering its name (without the .BAT extension). MS-DOS takes the commands from the file and processes them in sequence. You get the same results you would if you typed them by hand and pressed [Enter].

That's a rather simple way of making your work easier. But now, just imagine you have been working on a project for a long time and you always have to back up the same text files. You could write a BAKCO.BAT file that copies certain files without using wildcards. BAKCO stands for BAcKup COpy. You could create the following file using the MS-DOS Editor:

```
CD C:\PROJECT
COPY CONTENTS.TXT A:
COPY CHAPTER1.TXT A:
COPY CHAPTER2.TXT A:
COPY CHAPTER3.TXT A:
COPY INDEX.TXT A:
COPY PICT*.* A:
DIR A:
```

Save this file under BAKCO.BAT and you can call it any time with BAKCO. After that, MS-DOS will do a great deal of work the way you want it done without your having to lift a finger or touch a key. Let's look at this batch file one step at a time:

- The C:\PROJECT directory becomes the current directory.

- Five TXT files are copied from C:\PROJECT to drive A:.

- All filenames starting with PICT are copied to drive A:.

- MS-DOS displays the directory of drive A:.

Selecting a subdirectory by batch

In this next example we assume that you have a well divided hard drive so you've already reached the fourth directory level:

```
C:\TEXTS\PERSONAL\SPORTS\FOOTBALL
```

It's very irritating to have to select so many directories just to get to the FOOTBALL directory. It's much easier to jump to it right away with the following batch file, FOOTBALL.BAT (or FB.BAT):

```
CD C:\TEXTS\PERSONAL\SPORTS\FOOTBALL
```

All you have to do is enter this line in the MS-DOS Editor and save the file under the name FB.BAT.

By the way, if you want to look at all the files with the .TXT extension, just add this command:

```
DIR *.TXT
```

as another line to your batch file. Once again, you have grouped together several commands into a batch file.

Another backup batch file

Next, we'll create a batch file that also processes several commands in sequence. To be more specific, it's a sequence of commands that can be useful for backing up a subdirectory that is directly under the root directory.

Here's what the batch file does:

1. First, the batch uses the BACKUP command to back up a subdirectory along with any subdirectories it might have. It also uses the /L switch to create a LOG file which contains the names of all the files that have been backed up.

2. Next, the batch copies the LOG file to the backup diskette, renaming it at the same time.

3. The batch also copies the LOG file to a subdirectory of the hard drive—under another new name that reveals its directory.

4. The batch deletes the LOG file in the root directory.

11. Hiring experts

As far as the character strings are concerned, "sd" stands for the subdirectory, so you would change it to the subdirectory in question. DISKLOG is a subdirectory where the backup log files for different backup processes are saved.

If you want to try out this batch, don't forget the SD and DISKLOG directories.

The BSD.BAT program could contain the following program lines:

```
BACKUP C:\SD\*.* A: /S/L
COPY C:\BACKUP.LOG A:BSD.TXT
COPY C:\BACKUP.LOG C:\DISKLOG\BSD.TXT
DEL C:\BACKUP.LOG
```

This is a very practical example of a clever batch file that you can customize to fit your own requirements.

The only problem here is that we would have to create a separate batch file for each subdirectory. You could easily do that in the MS-DOS Editor by replacing SD with the name of the desired subdirectory and saving the new file under an appropriate name.

You could also write a general batch file that passes the name of each object to it. First, let's take another, easier example.

General batch file for deleting subdirectories

Imagine that you wanted to delete an entire directory with all its files after a backup. In MS-DOS, you can only remove a subdirectory when it no longer contains any files or subdirectories. This protects you from accidentally deleting all the files and directories in a "directory branch". However, it also makes deleting a directory with files rather difficult. First you must make the directory current, then use DEL *.* to delete all the files, then use CD.. to move up one directory in the hierarchy so you can finally remove the empty directory with RD.

A batch file can help. You can create a batch file that deletes all the files in a subdirectory, then changes to the parent directory and removes the subdirectory. After that, it displays the contents of the parent directory so you can check to see whether the subdirectory is gone, then select other subdirectories.

11.4 The boss goes on vacation

You can only try the following batch file if the subdirectory that you want to delete really exists. Otherwise there could be problems and errors. Later on we'll show you a variant that is shorter and less obvious, but makes up for it by being a "safer" batch file.

```
CD %1
DEL *.*
CD ..
RD %1
DIR
```

If you saved this program under DS.BAT (for Delete Subdirectory) and wanted to delete a subdirectory named TEST, you could call the program from the appropriate parent directory with:

```
DS TEST  Enter
```

MS-DOS inserts TEST for the %1 *environment variable* everywhere in the batch file.

You still have to answer the security prompt, but it's much less work this way than it would be if you typed everything repeatedly.

Here's another version of the same batch file, which uses fewer lines of code but performs the same task:

```
DEL %1
RD %1
```

Now we can redesign our backup batch program in such a way that we don't have to rewrite it for each subdirectory:

```
BACKUP C:\%1\*.* A: /S/L
COPY C:\BACKUP.LOG A:BA%1.TXT
COPY C:\BACKUP.LOG C:\DISKLOG\BA%1.TXT
DEL C:\BACKUP.LOG
```

We save it under BA.BAT and can call it from the root directory with:

```
BA PROG
```

In this case, the batch backs up the C:\PROG subdirectory along with all of its subdirectories. It also makes LOG files.

193

11. Hiring experts

Summary

Let's sum up our first experiences dealing with batch files:

Batch files are special files characterized by the .BAT extension. These files contain DOS commands that are processed in sequence after you call them. The most frequently used batch file is probably AUTOEXEC.BAT. It automatically executes right after you switch on or reset your computer.

How to create batch files

You can create batch files in different ways, just like texts. They must be saved as pure ASCII (unformatted) text. Also, you must press the [Enter] key at the end of a command, as you do when you type a command yourself.

The MS-DOS Editor provides the easiest method of batch file entry. The Editor lets you write as many MS-DOS commands as you want, one after the other. You can then save the commands under NAME.BAT and call the batch file after you quit the MS-DOS Editor.

The COM/ EXE/ BAT sequence

Batch files have a similar function to MS-DOS programs. They also have the .COM or .EXE extension, which you can also call and execute. Now it's important to have a sequence of priority in directories. Imagine you had a program called TEST.COM and another one called TEXT.EXE in the same directory. If you added a batch file named TEST.BAT to this directory and tried to call it with:

```
TEST
```

the TEST.COM command file is the only file that is executed. If you deleted that file, the TEXT.EXE program file would be next in line. You wouldn't have a chance to call your TEST.BAT batch file until you had removed this file. The easiest way to avoid this problem is not to give batch files names that are already used for command and program files.

However, another way of avoiding this problem is to save all of your batch files in a special directory called BAT.

If you wanted to make all the options of your batch directory available to MS-DOS, you should create a path for this directory. The best way to do this is in the AUTOEXEC.BAT file. You're then certain that this information is noted and available whenever you switch on your computer.

11.4 The boss goes on vacation

You remember how to define a search path for commands and programs: You define a path as a direct command. For example, in the AUTOEXEC.BAT file, you specify the appropriate drive and directory after the PATH command. For example:

```
PATH C:\BAT
```

You can also specify several search paths, separated by semicolons. These search paths are then used in the corresponding sequence. For instance:

```
PATH C:\DOS;C:\BAT;C:\WORD
```

In this case, MS-DOS would first search the current directory, then your DOS directory (for example, for FORMAT.COM), then in your batch directory and finally in the directory of your word processor.

Here's what happens when you enter a command after using PATH to define a search path:

1. MS-DOS looks for a command file or program file in the current directory (in the example: C:\TEXTS\PRIV). MS-DOS searches in the sequence of COM, EXE, and BAT.

2. MS-DOS looks in the first directory defined in the path definition (i.e., C:\DOS). The other directories follow in the sequence in which they are specified in the path. Therefore, the C:\TOOLS directory is the last directory (seventh) in which MS-DOS searches.

The length of the path specification and the number of directories specified in the search path determine the time MS-DOS requires to search for the specified command.

Remember that if your batch files don't work, it might be because MS-DOS cannot find them since they're not in the search path specification.

By the way, you can always use the DOS PATH command to display the current path specifications.

When you add a path, you must retype all the other paths into the path specification. This can be very time consuming.

11. Hiring experts

Fortunately, there are utility programs that solve this problem. For example, our *Batch File Powertools* (available from Abacus) has a special PATH command that you can use to expand or shorten the search path without retyping the complete path.

Also, remember the sequence that MS-DOS follows when executable files have the same name but different extensions. The first is .COM, then .EXE, and then files with the .BAT extension.

Important batch file commands

The following list shows the most important commands used in batch files. If you want to learn more about batch files, read either *DOS 5.0 Complete* or *MS-DOS Tips & Tricks*.

ECHO and @ The ECHO command has two different tasks. If you enter it after a text, the text outputs on the current output device (usually this is the screen). With the ON and OFF parameters you can determine whether the following command lines of the batch file output on the screen or not. ECHO without any parameters simply gives you the present status (on or off).

If you only want to suppress a particular batch command from displaying on the screen, you can place the @ character in front of the command. You can display this character by pressing the [Alt] key and pressing [6][4] on the numeric keypad. After you release the [Alt] key, the @ character appears on the screen.

For example, this option is valuable when you start a batch file with the command ECHO OFF. This prevents all subsequent commands from displaying on the screen. However, the first command (ECHO OFF) still appears on the screen. You can stop the first command from displaying by typing the following line as your first:

```
@ECHO OFF
```

End your batch file with:

```
@ECHO ON
```

REM The REM (short for REMark) lets you add comments to make your programs easier to read and understand. MS-DOS doesn't execute these comments, but just skips them. We'll show a few examples in the following programs.

11.4 The boss goes on vacation

Abort option   You can abort a batch file like any other MS-DOS program by pressing ⌈Ctrl⌉ + ⌈C⌉. MS-DOS then asks you:

```
Terminate batch job (Y/N):
```

Depending on your answer, the batch file terminates or continues.

PAUSE   There's another option for stopping a batch file that you can build into your batch file. Imagine you had a batch file that you could use to delete all the .BAK files in the current directory. Under certain circumstances, it's wise to think it over before you finally execute this file. The following batch file, called DELB.BAT (for DEL BAK files) gives you a chance to do this:

```
@ECHO All files with the BAK extension are deleted.
@ECHO If you don't want that to happen:
@ECHO please press CTRL + C to cancel!
PAUSE
DEL *.BAK
```

The PAUSE command sees to it that MS-DOS waits for the press of a key before continuing to process the batch file.

Avoiding mistakes: illegal characters

Perhaps you've also had this happen to you: You call a batch file that you wrote but the computer displays an unexpected screen. It's possible that you used some illegal special characters.

There are some characters that you either cannot use in batch files or can only use under special circumstances. These characters are:

%   MS-DOS uses this character to show the environment variables %1 to %9. These are statements that you specify after the name of the batch file. To use this character in text and display it with ECHO, you have to enter it twice (%%).

<   This character redirects the input from the keyboard to a new device or file. You cannot use this character in batch files.

>   This character redirects the output to a device other than the screen. You cannot use this character in batch files.

| This character filters (passes) program output to a different program. You cannot use this character in batch files.

197

12. QBasic

This chapter introduces you to another program supplied with MS-DOS 5.0: The programming language QBasic. QBasic is an improved version of GW-BASIC, which was supplied with earlier versions of MS-DOS. However, in many respects QBasic is more convenient to use and more efficient.

What's a programming language?

Throughout this book you've become more familiar with your PC and how it works—MS-DOS is no longer a foreign phrase to you. Now you stand at the crossroads, because the operating system only offers a means of operating the PC, rather than an end. You have two choices to reach that end:

1. You buy programs (*software*) for your PC. These programs let you write texts, find a telephone number, create a bar chart of sales figures, and much more. A wealth of programs exist on the market—you may already have some on your PC.

2. Sometimes commercial programs don't offer a solution to your special problem. It would be preferable if you could tell the PC your problems and get the solution from the PC. You can resolve these situations by your developing your own programs using *programming languages*.

   These languages are a group of instructions that tell your computer exactly what you want done. Programs and applications are created in these languages to solve problems.

The most widespread programming language available is BASIC (the acronym for **B**eginners **A**ll-purpose **S**ymbolic **I**nstruction **C**ode). It was developed in the 1960s by John Kemeny and Thomas Kurtz. Microsoft Corporation marketed BASIC to provide the average user easy access to a computer's capabilities.

Why BASIC?

Although many programming languages are available, we feel you should know BASIC because:

1. QBasic is provided with MS-DOS 5.0.

2. Many users find BASIC easiest to understand of all languages.

3. Some existing BASIC programs run in QBasic with a few changes.

12. QBasic

This chapter lists a few QBasic programs you can type in and run. We'll list the code, then give you explanations of what each program does.

Starting QBasic

After installation, you will find the QBasic program on the hard drive in the DOS directory. It's called QBASIC.EXE. Since you probably have a path for your DOS directory, you can start QBasic from any directory.

If you don't have a hard drive, insert the diskette containing the QBASIC.EXE program in the current drive.

To be able to work with QBasic, you must first start it. There are two different ways to do this.

MS-DOS Shell

If you are in the MS-DOS Shell, use [Tab] to activate the program list area. From there, use the arrow keys to move the highlight to the MS-DOS QBasic program and press [Enter]. A dialog box appears where you can type in the name of a file that you'd like to load. Since we don't want to do this yet, press [Enter].

The startup screen of QBasic appears.

Command interpreter

To start QBasic from the command interpreter, type the following command line from any directory:

```
QBASIC
```

The same startup screen appears that you see when you start QBasic from the MS-DOS Shell.

An operating standard

QBasic follows the SAA (System Application Architecture) standard. This means that you can apply much of what you know about operating the MS-DOS Shell and the MS-DOS Editor to QBasic.

If how QBasic operates is familiar to you, it's because of the SAA standard.

The startup screen

After you start QBasic, you will see a dialog box on the screen. Pressing [Enter] activates the Survival Guide (help system), while pressing [Esc] takes you directly to the screen of QBasic. Press [Esc].

12. QBasic

```
File Edit View Search Run Debug Options                    Help
┌──────────────────────── Untitled ────────────────────────┐
│                                                          │
│         ┌────────────────────────────────────────┐       │
│         │        Welcome to MS-DOS QBasic        │       │
│         │                                        │       │
│         │  Copyright (C) Microsoft Corporation,  │       │
│         │           1987-1991.                   │       │
│         │         All rights reserved.           │       │
│         │                                        │       │
│         │  < Press Enter to see the Survival Guide > │   │
│         │                                        │       │
│         │  < Press ESC to clear this dialog box >│       │
│         └────────────────────────────────────────┘       │
│                                                          │
├──────────────────────── Immediate ───────────────────────┤
│                                                          │
└──────────────────────────────────────────────────────────┘
 F1=Help  Enter=Execute  Esc=Cancel  Tab=Next Field  Arrow=Next Item
```

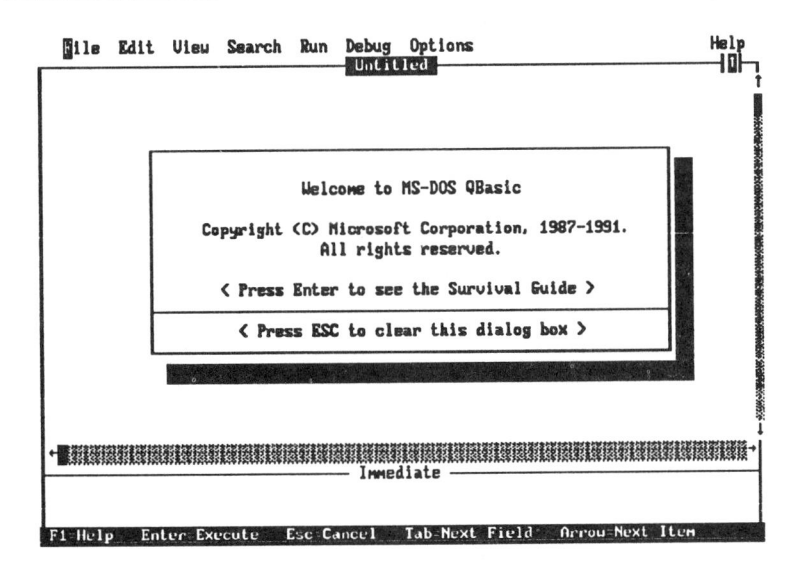

QBasic startup screen

The menu bar   You activate the menu bar, located at the top of the screen, by pressing (Alt). You open the menus by either pressing the highlighted letters or by using the arrow keys to select them and pressing (Enter). The commands of the menus also have highlighted letters. Menu items (commands) selected with the letter keys are immediately executed. You can also select the commands with the arrow keys and press (Enter).

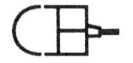

If you're using a mouse, click the desired menu in the menu bar and the menu will open. You also click to activate the commands.

The title bar   In the middle of the next line you see the name of the current BASIC program. If there is no program in the memory, you will see "Untitled" here. You also see "Untitled" whenever you restart QBasic.

The work area   The *work area* takes up the largest part of the screen. The work area is bordered by a scroll bar on the right and bottom (see next page).

Underneath the work area is an area with the heading, "Immediate" where you can type in single command lines. Press (Enter) to immediately execute these command lines.

Press (F6) to get to "Immediate" (or return to the work area).

12. QBasic

The status bar The last line on the screen is the status bar. This provides brief information about the menu currently selected. If there is no active menu, you can click commands in the status bar with the mouse.

The scroll bars (scroll slider) On the right border of the screen is a gray bar which has a scroll arrow at the top and the bottom. This is the scroll bar. The black rectangle within this bar is the scroll slider. Its position within the scroll bar shows you which section of the QBasic program is displayed on the screen.

If the slider is at the top, then you are looking at the beginning of the file. If the slider is in the middle of the scroll bar, you are looking at the middle of the file, and if the slider is at the bottom, then you are looking at the end of the file.

This probably reminds you of the screen structure and operation of the MS-DOS Editor, but this is all part of the SAA standard.

If you use the [↑] and [↓] arrow keys or [PgUp] and [PgDn] to scroll the contents of the screen, you can see how the scroll slider moves along with them.

You can also click the two scroll arrows of the scroll bar with the mouse to scroll up or down. You can even move the slider with the mouse. Place the mouse pointer on the slider and press the left mouse button

Then, while holding the mouse button down, move the mouse pointer in the desired direction. The scroll slider moves along with the mouse pointer, displaying the contents of the section on the screen.

The horizontal scroll bar at the bottom of the screen works exactly like the vertical scroll bar, except it moves horizontally. To scroll horizontally, you can also press [Ctrl] + [PgUp] and [Ctrl] + [PgDn].

12.1 Programs supplied with QBasic

In the next part of our introduction to QBasic, we'd like to describe the programs that are included with QBasic.

Loading the program

To work with these programs, you must load them into QBasic. To do this, press [Alt] to select the menu bar and press [Enter] to select the **File** menu. Now use the arrow keys to move the selection cursor to **Open...** and press [Enter] again.

Next a dialog box appears on the screen. Type the filename (with the path, if necessary) of the program that you want to load in the top line.

There's another way to load a BASIC program. When you first see the Open dialog box, a wildcard appears in the top line where you ordinarily type in the filename of the BASIC program you want to load. This wildcard displays all the QBasic files in the lower part of the screen.

If you don't see any QBasic files displayed on the screen, then you don't have the DOS directory set as the current directory. Set the DOS directory by following the procedure described in the next paragraph. The DOS directory contains the QBasic programs.

Press [Tab] to move to the Files list box. Then use the arrow keys to select the file you want to load. The filename of the file you select is automatically entered in the filename text box. You can even change directories if necessary.

To get to the next highest directory, move the cursor to the two periods ".." and press [Enter]. You can go to a lower directory by moving the cursor to the directory name (always displayed in uppercase) and pressing [Enter].

The QBasic files are also displayed in these directories. Select the file you want to load and press [Enter]. The file is then displayed in the work area.

You can also use this method to search for programs on your hard drive or diskette, since the available QBasic files are always displayed.

First we're going to load the game called NIBBLES. Select the directory where your DOS files are located. The QBasic files are displayed in the file list. Select the file called NIBBLES.BAS and press [Enter].

12. QBasic

QBasic then loads the file and displays the BASIC program in the work area. Now you're ready to start the program.

Starting the program

To start the program, press `Alt` to select the menu bar, use the arrow keys to select the **Run** menu and press `Enter`. After the menu opens, the selection cursor is already on the **Start** command. Press `Enter` to start the program.

The NIBBLES game

The object of this game is to hit the number that appears on the screen with your cursor. As soon as you hit the number, a new number appears, and you have to try to hit the new number with the cursor. The cursor turns into a snake that grows longer every time you hit a number. So what you have is a snake that is supposed to "nibble" numbers.

When the game starts, you'll hear a short melody. This is followed by information about the keyboard actions of the game. Press a key to continue to the next message. You're prompted for the number of players. Type in the number of players and press `Enter`.

Next, you are prompted to set the skill level. This is followed by questions on the game speed and type of monitor. After answering these questions, press the `Spacebar` to begin the game.

A cursor appears on the screen as a mini snake. You can use the arrow keys to control the snake's movements on the screen. The object of the game is to hit the number. At the start, you are better off just trying to avoid running into the edge of the playing area. If you run into the edge or (later when the snake is longer) the snake's tail, the snake loses one of its lives.

To cancel the game, press `Ctrl` + `Pause`.

After quitting the game, you can either play again (press `Y`) or return to QBasic (press `N`).

Once you are back in QBasic, the program is once again displayed on the screen.

You can use this method to try out all the supplied programs. First select **Open...** from the **File** menu to load the program and then select **Start** from the **Run** menu to start it.

12.2 Writing your own programs

If you have a Hercules monitor, you will definitely be disappointed, because most of the QBasic programs included with MS-DOS 5.0 only run on color monitors. However, we're going to show you how to work with finished programs, and give you a glimpse of the QBasic programming language. We'll also guide you through writing your own program.

To do this, you must first remove the last program from the screen and let QBasic know that you want to create a new program. Select the **New** command from the **File** menu.

Entering a simple program

We are going to enter a program for calculating gasoline consumption in the QBasic programming language. This short program will help you calculate your car's gas mileage.

It's extremely easy to enter a program. You can start making entries immediately. You could press (Enter) at the end of a line or you could use the arrow keys to move to the next line.

Here's what our program for calculating gasoline consumption looks like:

```
INPUT "Gallons consumed"; GALLONS
INPUT "Miles driven"; MILES
CONSUMPTION = MILES / GALLONS
PRINT "Gas mileage:"; CONSUMPTION; "miles per gallon"
```

Starting the program

You start this program the same way you started the previous programs. Press (Alt) to activate the menu bar, select the **Run** menu, press (Enter) and then press (Enter) again to activate **Start**.

After starting the program you are first prompted for the number of gallons consumed. Type in 10. After you press (Enter) the program prompts you for the number of miles driven. If you type 320 here and press (Enter) again, the screen displays the following message:

```
Gas mileage: 32 miles per gallon
```

This program works and, as you would expect, produces the correct results.

12. QBasic

How the program works

After seeing that this program works, you probably also want to know why it works. We'll give you a brief explanation of what each command means.

INPUT

The INPUT command allows you to type in input while a program is running. The program stops and doesn't run until after the input is finished and the user presses [Enter].

If you include a text enclosed in quotation marks with the INPUT command, the program displays this text on the screen as extra information for the user. If you omit this information, the screen displays a question mark while the program is running to let you know that QBasic is waiting for input. This explanatory text must always be in quotation marks. QBasic automatically puts the question mark at the end of the text during program execution.

In our example the system prompt is followed by a semicolon, and then the word GALLON. What is GALLON? Here we use the word GALLON as a *variable*.

Variables

Variables are placeholders that allow you to work with any value you like (variable) within a program. Think of it this way: When QBasic encounters a variable, it creates a drawer with the name of the variable. This drawer is empty at the beginning. While the program is running, the INPUT command allocates a value that you type in to this variable. QBasic then places this value in the appropriate drawer. The drawer is no longer empty now, but contains the value you entered. If this variable is addressed again within the program, QBasic finds the appropriate drawer and takes its contents. QBasic then performs the desired operations (e.g., calculations) with these contents.

You can give these variables almost any name you wish. Of course, it is wise to give a variable a name that is both obvious and descriptive. In our sample program, QBasic creates a drawer named GALLONS. While the program is running, QBasic fills this drawer with input from the user. In our example, QBasic first fills it with "10", the first number we typed in.

The next line in our program has the same structure as the previous line, an INPUT command, and brief text describing the input needed. After this comes a semicolon, followed by a variable name. QBasic creates a new drawer named MILES, and fills it with certain contents. In our example, the contents are "320".

12.2 Writing your own programs

The calculation

In the next line, QBasic calculates the consumption. First it defines a new variable, or drawer. This drawer gets the name CONSUMPTION. QBasic divides the contents of the MILES drawer by the contents of the GALLONS drawer and places the product in the CONSUMPTION drawer. The equal sign indicates that this is supposed to be the contents of the CONSUMPTION drawer. In our case, the contents of the consumption drawer amount to: 320/10=32.

PRINT

Now let's take a look at the last line of the program. Here's a new BASIC command: PRINT. This command displays something on the screen. If you type something in quotation marks after the PRINT command, PRINT displays exactly what you typed between the quotation marks on the screen. You could also type variables after the command, but you cannot put them in quotation marks. Then QBasic displays the contents of this variable. You can combine text and variables, as we did in our example.

Saving a program

Save this program so you can use it again. There is also a menu for saving programs. Press [Alt] and [Enter] to select the **File** menu. Use the arrow keys to select **Save As...** and press [Enter].

A screen appears, where you can type in a name for the program. We chose GASOLINE. Press [Enter] to save the program under this name. You can also choose the directory to where you save this program. To save the program in the PROG directory (provided such a directory exists), type in the following (for GASOLINE):

```
C:\PROG\GASOLINE [Enter]
```

Loading and restarting a program

To restart a program later, you must first load it. Use the **Open...** command from the **File** menu, as previously described.

Viewing and editing programs

To view a program, load it as we just described. It is then displayed on the screen. If you find mistakes in this program, move the selection cursor to the first mistake and correct it. By doing this, you can move from mistake to mistake, correcting them.

After correcting all the mistakes, save the program again by selecting **Save** in the **File** menu. The program is automatically saved under its old name. You have just created your first program and learned some commands in QBasic.

12. QBasic

12.3 Dollars and cents

Have you ever been on vacation abroad and wondered how much 750 francs, 3000 schillings or 500 marks are in US dollars?

In this section we would like to show you some more of the possibilities you have with QBasic. We developed a program for converting foreign currency so you might get some use (and even profit) out of our example.

To write this new program, you must first remove the program that is in the memory. Do this by selecting **New** from the **File** menu.

If you have already saved the program in the memory, the screen clears immediately. If you didn't save after making changes, a security prompt appears before the screen clears.

As soon as the screen clears, we can begin entering the new program. Here's what it looks like:

```
Start:¶
INPUT "Convert to which currency"; CURRENCY$¶
INPUT "What is the rate of exchange (1 US Dollar = )"; RATE¶
INPUT "Start conversion at how many US Dollars"; STARTING.NUMBER¶
INPUT "End conversion at how many US Dollars"; ENDING.NUMBER¶
FOR US.DOLLARS = STARTING.NUMBER TO ENDING.NUMBER¶
AMOUNT = US.DOLLARS * RATE¶
PRINT US.DOLLARS; "US Dollars equals"; AMOUNT; CURRENCY$¶
NEXT US.DOLLARS¶
INPUT "Calculate another exchange rate (Y/N)"; ANSWER$¶
IF ANSWER$ = "Y" THEN GOTO Start¶
IF ANSWER$ = "y" THEN GOTO Start¶
END¶
```

Some of the program lines are longer than the lines printed in the book. Each program line ends with a ¶ character. Press (Enter) only when this character occurs.

After entering the program, start it by selecting **Start** from the **Run** menu.

12.3 Dollars and cents

The program asks you some questions first. You must choose the kind of currency, such as marks or gulden. Then you must specify how much of the currency you get for one US Dollar. Be sure to use the decimal point; otherwise you might get an error message. You also must specify a starting value and an end value for the conversion (i.e., the dollar amount you want the conversion to start with and the dollar amount you want the conversion to end with).

After typing in all of this information, you see the different conversions in a table. At the end, the program asks whether you want to convert any more exchange rates. Depending on your answer, you either start answering questions again or the program ends.

After running this program once, save it. Select the **Save As...** command from the **File** menu. In the dialog box that appears, specify a filename. We chose EXCHRATE as our filename.

How the program works

You will recognize the first lines of the program. We used the INPUT command again, so you could type in input while the program is running. This input is allocated to the variables at the end of a line. But now let's talk about a peculiarity of variables. You probably noticed the $ character after the CURRENCY$ variable, and are curious about what it means.

String variables

This variable is a *string variable*, or *text variable*. This is defined by adding the $ character to the variable name, making it possible to assign text to the variable. This wasn't possible with the variables we have learned up to now. If we added text to one of those variables, we got an error message. You were only able to allocate numbers to those variables.

Let's return to our example with the drawers. Up to now, we could only fill these drawers with numbers. With the help of string variables, characterized by the $ character, we can also fill the drawer with text. Of course, you can no longer perform calculations with these text variables, but we don't need to in our example anyway. We use numeric variables for calculating.

That explains the lines beginning with the INPUT command. We type in the necessary input on the kind of currency, rate of exchange and the starting and end values.

12. QBasic

FOR ... NEXT

Let's move on to the next part of the program. This is a block of program lines that belong together. The entire block forms a loop. This loop is made up of the following program lines:

```
FOR US.DOLLARS = STARTING.NUMBER TO ENDING.NUMBER¶
AMOUNT = US.DOLLARS * RATE¶
PRINT US.DOLLARS; "US Dollars equals"; AMOUNT; CURRENCY$¶
NEXT US DOLLARS¶
```

What happens within these program lines? After the FOR command, which we will explain in a moment, we defined a new variable, US.DOLLARS. This variable gets the contents of the STARTING.NUMBER variable.

In the next line the program performs calculations with this new variable. It calculates the newly defined AMOUNT variable, which is the result of multiplying the two variables, US.DOLLARS and RATE.

In the next line, the PRINT command outputs the variables and text in quotation marks that come after it on the screen.

Let's move to the next line, which has a command we haven't seen yet, NEXT. This command is linked with the FOR command to form the structure or frame for the loop. If a program encounters this NEXT command, QBasic is given to understand that it should return to the line with the FOR command. The program runs a check in this line.

The variable US DOLLARS had the contents of STARTING.NUMBER up until now. The program now checks whether these contents match the contents of the ENDING.NUMBER variable, which comes after TO. If the contents do not match, then the contents of the US.DOLLARS variable are automatically increased by 1, and the following program lines are processed with the new contents of the variable until the program reaches the line with the NEXT command.

Then the program jumps back to the program line with the FOR command. The program again runs the check, and increases the contents of the US.DOLLARS variable by one, if necessary. If the program determines that the contents of US.DOLLARS are greater than the contents of ENDING.NUMBER, it does not process the following program lines, but instead jumps to the program line that comes after NEXT.

12.3 Dollars and cents

Such a loop is a very interesting method for processing a part of the program several times, which can save a great deal of work in our case.

IF ... THEN The next program lines are also a block. A prompt follows, which the program uses to determine which course the rest of the program will take. Here's what the lines look like:

```
INPUT "Calculate another exchange rate (Y/N)"; ANSWER$
IF ANSWER$ = "Y" THEN GOTO Start
IF ANSWER$ = "y" THEN GOTO Start
END
```

In the first line you are prompted to type in some input. To be specific, you are to decide whether you want to make any more calculations. Your decision ("Y" or "N") is placed in the ANSWER$ string variable.

The next two lines check the contents of the ANSWER$ variable, and, depending on the contents, the program runs again. The first line of the program is included in these two lines, to be precise:

```
Start:
```

The IF ... THEN command runs this check. IF ... THEN checks whether the contents of the ANSWER$ variable are equal to the contents of the text in quotation marks, in other words, "Y" or "y". If so, the program carries out the THEN instruction; otherwise it continues processing the program in the next line.

If we assume that the contents of the ANSWER$ variable are equal to "Y", then the program carries out the instruction that comes after THEN. After THEN you see GOTO START. This means, GO TO the program line called START and continue processing there. This command line causes the program to run from the first line again.

Labels In QBasic, these branch addresses are called *labels*. A label is a mark in a program that must be defined once, then you can specify it as a branch target at any time.

To define such a mark in QBasic (also refer to this as "setting a label") you must think of a name for the label. In our sample program we called the label START. You must set this label at the place in the program where you want to go later on. Since in our case this is the beginning of the program, the label also comes at the beginning. Labels must be followed by a colon so QBasic can identify them as

211

12. QBasic

labels. When the label is used later in the program, you no longer need to specify the colon.

If you want to jump to this label from somewhere else in the program, you must specify the name of the label. That's why we have the START label after the IF ... THEN prompt in our example.

If the contents of the ANSWER$ variable are not equal to "Y" or "y", the program processes the next line. This line is almost identical to the previous line, except that the contents of the variable are now checked for "Y" or "y". The program does distinguish uppercase from lowercase, and we thought that both an uppercase Y as well as a lowercase y should be permitted. Here too, if the variables match, you return to the beginning of the program.

If the variables don't match here either, the next program line is processed, which contains the END command, and the program ends.

Improving the program

Although this program works well enough, you might not like having to enter a number with several places after the decimal point as the conversion amount. To avoid doing this, all you have to do is change one line in the program and add a new line.

We have already discussed changing lines in QBasic. The following line must be changed:

```
PRINT US.DOLLARS; "US Dollars equals"; AMOUNT; CURRENCY$¶
```

Here's what the line should look like after you change it:

```
PRINT US.DOLLARS; "US Dollars equals"; USING "###.##"; AMOUNT;¶
```

Furthermore, you must add a new line.

Inserting new program lines

Inserting new program lines is very easy in QBasic. Move the cursor to the beginning of the line that comes after the line you want to insert and press [Enter]. Now move the cursor back to the new line you just made and insert the text. In our case, we insert the line:

```
PRINT " "; CURRENCY$
```

Here's what our program looks like after all the changes:

12.3 Dollars and cents

```
Start:
INPUT "Convert to which currency"; CURRENCY$
INPUT "What is the rate of exchange (1 US Dollar = )";
RATE
INPUT "Start conversion at how many US Dollars";
STARTING.NUMBER
INPUT "End conversion at how many US Dollars";
ENDING.NUMBER
FOR US.DOLLARS = STARTING.NUMBER TO ENDING.NUMBER
AMOUNT = US.DOLLARS * RATE
PRINT US.DOLLARS; "US Dollars equals"; USING "###.##";
AMOUNT;
PRINT " "; CURRENCY$
NEXT US.DOLLARS
INPUT "Calculate another exchange rate (Y/N)"; ANSWER$
IF ANSWER$ = "Y" THEN GOTO Start
IF ANSWER$ = "y" THEN GOTO Start
END
```

You should also save this improved version of the program. To do this, select **Save As...** from the **File** menu. Type in a filename of your choice in the dialog box. We called this program EXCHRAT1.

Exiting QBasic

To quit QBasic, select the **File** menu first, then select the **Exit** command. After you press (Enter), you will find yourself either at the MS-DOS system prompt or in the MS-DOS Shell, provided you remembered to save all the files. Otherwise a security prompt appears on the screen, asking whether you want to save any files that haven't yet been saved.

Did you have fun on our little excursion into the world of QBasic? Then you ought to take advantage of the opportunity to practice a game or create programs for home use soon. Actually, programming (with QBasic) is not very difficult and can be a lot of fun.

Appendices

If you read the book from front to back, then you probably have already installed MS-DOS on your computer and the most interesting part of the Appendices is the glossary of important MS-DOS terms.

If you're still at the beginning of the book, however, then you either still haven't installed MS-DOS 5.0 or you are looking for the section on breakdowns. You will find most of the information on both subjects here - let's start with installing MS-DOS 5.0.

A. Non-hard drive systems

Although most computers come equipped with a hard drive these days, some of them still don't. This section covers special features that are related to installing MS-DOS 5.0 on such a computer.

First, have enough diskettes ready for installation. During installation, you must create a start diskette that you use to start the computer. When you start the computer, you have to insert this diskette in drive A: and close the drive lever.

During installation MS-DOS was distributed on several diskettes, depending on the type of drive. To work with MS-DOS you must insert the correct diskette. On a system with 360K diskettes, MS-DOS is divided into seven diskettes with the following labels:

1. STARTUP
2. SUPPORT
3. SHELL
4. HELP
5. BASIC/EDIT
6. UTILITY
7. SUPPLEMENTAL

The STARTUP diskette starts the computer. The STARTUP, SUPPORT, UTILITY and SUPPLEMENTAL diskettes contain other MS-DOS commands. Insert the SHELL diskette to run the MS-DOS Shell. The HELP diskette lists help for the MS-DOS Shell, the MS-DOS Editor and QBasic.

You should also use the FORMAT command to create two work diskettes. Type the following command:

Appendices

FORMAT B: [Enter]

From now on you should always use drive B: as your current drive. To do this, insert a work diskette in drive B: and type:

B: [Enter]

Now you can follow the same procedure described in the book. However, here are some points to remember:

- When we look at the contents of the directory with the DOS commands on the hard drive, you should display the contents of the directory on your DOS diskette. To do this, type DIR A: and press [Enter].

- Whenever we mention drive A: in the book, you should use drive B: so your diskette with the DOS commands can remain in drive A. This saves constant diskette changes.

- One exception here is the COPY command. When you copy files from the hard drive to drive A:, you should also copy to drive A:. To do this, remove the diskette with the DOS commands from drive A: and place the second work diskette in drive A:. This is simple, because you don't have to get the COPY command from the DOS diskette in drive A:. Don't forget to place the diskette with the DOS commands back in drive A: after you finish copying.

- If you ever get the error message "Bad command or file name" when you type in a command, the DOS command you want is probably on a different diskette. You may have to try all the other diskettes before you find the one containing the command.

We suggest you print each diskette directory using this or a similar command (the command may change depending on which port you have connected to your printer):

DIR A: > LPT1:

This printed list helps determine which diskette contains which commands.

- If you want to work with the MS-DOS Shell, you must insert the SHELL diskette. Then call the MS-DOS Shell as described earlier.

B. Troubleshooting

Computers and operating systems tend to be very particular about the way the user enters commands. The computer does exactly what it is told, rather than what the user means. This particularity includes the kind of mistakes that a beginner could make.

We have put together some tips on potential problems and what you can do to solve them.

Booting problems

Problem You have trouble starting your PC.

You switched on your PC, but the messages we described don't appear on the screen. Instead, you get a message similar to the following:

```
Non-System disk or disk error
Replace and press any key when ready
```

Solution Check the following:

1. If you installed MS-DOS 5.0 on your hard drive, is there a diskette in the drive? Remove it and press the RESET button, or press [Ctrl]+[Alt]+[Delete].

2. If you have a diskette only system, check the label on the diskette in the disk drive. If this is not the STARTUP diskette, replace it with the STARTUP diskette.

3. If you have a diskette only system, make sure the drive lever of the disk drive containing the STARTUP diskette is closed.

There may be differences between the way we described the behavior of the PC and the way your PC actually behaves. Read Chapter 3 to find out where DOS resides on your hard drive. Also, check whether the AUTOEXEC.BAT file includes a PATH command pointing to the directory containing the DOS command.

MS-DOS Shell not responding

Problem The MS-DOS Shell doesn't respond properly to your commands, nor are you sure which area of the MS-DOS Shell is currently active.

Appendices

Solution   The [Tab] key moves the selection cursor from one area to the next in the following sequence: Drive icons, Directory Tree area, file list area, program list area. When the selection cursor is in a particular area, the title bar of the currently active area is highlighted. Sometimes a poor choice of colors can make it difficult to see what's active. Press [Tab] to move the selection cursor a couple of times. Usually you will notice which area is active by some small changes. Also, select a different screen display in the **Display...** command of the **Options** menu, or select a different color scheme using the **Colors...** command of the **Options** menu.

Error message occurs after command entry

Problem   You enter a command but the PC responds with the following:

```
Not ready reading drive A
Abort, Retry, Fail?
```

Solution   MS-DOS cannot read the diskette in drive A:. Make sure there is a diskette in drive A:, and that the drive lever is closed. Press [R] to retry the action. If there is a diskette in that drive and the drive lever is closed, the diskette may be unformatted. Replace this diskette with a formatted diskette (e.g., your STARTUP diskette) and press [A] to abort. Check the Index for information on formatting diskettes.

No response to a command

Problem   You entered a command, but the PC doesn't react to it.

Solution   You may have forgotten to press the [Enter] key at the end of the command. Or you may have chosen to enter a batch file using the COPY CON command. Press [Ctrl] + [Z] and the [Enter] key to end COPY CON.

If your PC still doesn't react after you have pressed the [Enter] key several times, you may have accidentally pressed the [Prt Sc] key for printing the output to the printer. Turning on the printer might help. If not, insert a DOS diskette (if you haven't installed MS-DOS 5.0 completely on the hard drive) and reboot your PC by pressing [Ctrl] + [Alt] + [Del].

B. Troubleshooting

Bad command or filename entered

Problem You enter a command printed in the book, but the PC keeps giving you the message:

`Bad command or file name`

Solution Check these are possible sources of the error:

1. If you have a hard drive based system, did you make any changes to the search path with the MS-DOS PATH command? You must reenter the complete search path each time you make a change. If the search path was PATH=C:\DOS;C:\WORD and you now want to include C:\WORKS in the search path, you cannot simply enter:

   `PATH C:\WORKS`

   That makes this directory (along with the current directory) the only directory that MS-DOS will search for commands and programs. You can view the current path by typing:

   `PATH`

   without any parameters or switches and pressing [Enter]. At the very least, the directory of MS-DOS commands should appear in the display.

2. If you have a diskette based system and this command is an external MS-DOS command (a command that has to be loaded from diskette), you may have inserted the wrong diskette. Insert the proper DOS diskette in drive A:, close the drive lever and enter A:. Now try the command again.

   If you installed MS-DOS 5.0 on a PC with two disk drives, then you have several other diskettes along with the STARTUP diskette. Use DIR to check whether the command is on one of these diskettes.

3. If you have the correct diskette inserted, make sure the PC is set to the correct drive. Check your system prompt to see which drive is currently active—A: or B:.

4. You made a mistake typing the command. Compare what you typed with the command as listed in this book. Pay special

219

Appendices

attention to spaces. For example, to display the contents of a directory on the screen, the command line must read:

DIR A:

The following is incorrect:

DIRA:

Accidentally entering a command

Problem You accidentally enter FORMAT A:, but you have the DOS diskette in drive A:, which you don't want to format. You don't have any blank diskettes that you could insert instead of the DOS diskette either.

Solution Remove the diskette from the drive, press the [Ctrl] key and press [C]. A ^C should appear on the screen, and DOS displays the system prompt. Pressing [Ctrl] + [C] cancels the FORMAT command.

This key combination cancels most MS-DOS commands.

This Appendix doesn't help

Problem You have already typed a command from the book several times, but you keep getting the same error message from your PC. You have already read through all the possibilities in this Appendix and checked each breakdown, but the error still exists.

Solution Look in the index in the back of the book. The most important processes are described again. If there is a different command listed there, try it out.

Command won't cancel

Problem You can't cancel DOS commands with [Ctrl] + [C]. Here's an example: You have a long text file you want to view with:

COPY TEXTFILE.DOC CON

It works beautifully, only you can't stop the output of the text on the screen. You know that you can cancel many processes by entering [Ctrl] + [C], but it doesn't seem to work this time. What's more, after a while the PC starts beeping and the screen begins flashing.

Solution Wait for command to finish executing, or press [Ctrl] + [Alt] + [Del] to reboot. After rebooting, type the following:

BREAK ON [Enter]

Now when you TYPE the file, you should be able to stop the output with [Ctrl] + [C]. If necessary, add the BREAK ON command to your AUTOEXEC.BAT.

Files not copied to right location

Problem You have created several subdirectories. You copied a file from drive A: to drive C:, but you cannot find it. Or you discover that the PC always copies the file to a different directory.

Solution Probably you chose a subdirectory as the current directory and you wanted to copy the file to the root directory instead. If you use the following to copy the file, the PC will read from and write to the current directory rather than the root directory:

COPY A:FILENAME.EXT C:

To be sure that it does read from and write to the root directory, you must type the command as follows:

COPY A:\FILENAME.EXT C:\ [Enter]

Check which directories are active for each drive. Use either CD or the PROMPT command in the following form:

PROMPT pg

Now DOS displays the valid directory for the current drive. If you only specify the drive letter (e.g., A:), DOS takes the current directory for this drive.

Program or file not found

Problem You know for a fact that a certain file or program must be on your hard drive, but you simply cannot find it in the directory structure.

Appendices

Solution
(MS-DOS Shell) Select the **Search...** command from the **File** menu. Enter the name of the file or program in the Search for: line. If you aren't sure of the name, or you only know part of it, you can use a wildcard (* or ?) to represent the part you're uncertain about. Make sure that the "Search entire disk" option button is activated. After you press [Enter], the MS-DOS Shell creates a list of all the matching files and displays it with complete path specifications.

(Command interpreter) Type the following to change to the root directory:

```
CD \ [Enter]
```

Use the DIR command with the /S switch to search all directories. To search for the BOOK.TXT file, use the following command:

```
DIR BOOK.TXT /S
```

If you don't know the exact filename, you could also use the * and ? wildcard characters to represent the unknown characters. Each of the following commands searches for similar filenames where wildcard characters can represent any character:

```
DIR BO*.TXT /S
DIR ?OOK.T?T /S
DIR B??K.TXT /S
```

The DIR command then displays each directory containing matching files and lists these files.

File list area refuses to create new directory

Problem
You want to use the **Create Directory...** command from the MS-DOS Shell's **File** menu to create a new directory. MS-DOS won't accept the name you entered and gives you the message:

```
Access denied
```

Solution
You tried to create a directory whose name already exists in another directory. Before you create any new directories, take a good look at the listing of directories you already have. There might even be a file with the same name as the directory you want to create, so look in the file list area as well.

222

B. Troubleshooting

PC won't simulate a second drive

Problem You want to copy the contents of a diskette onto another diskette, but you only have one drive. You selected the **Disk Utilities** group in the program list area and started the Disk Copy program. In the screen that appears, you confirmed "Parameters . . . A: B:" with the (Enter) key and are now at the system prompt.

You are prompted to insert the source diskette in drive "A" and the target diskette in drive "B". You assume that your computer will also simulate a second disk drive, although it can only have one. So you insert the source diskette in the drive first and press the (Enter) key. Up to now, nothing unusual happens, but as soon as you try to write the data copied from the source diskette to the target diskette, you get an error message. Everything seems to indicate that your computer cannot simulate a second drive.

Solution Exit to the MS-DOS Shell, restart the Disk Copy program and change the "Parameters" from "A: B:" to "A: A:". You shouldn't have any more problems.

Program not executable from the MS-DOS Shell

Problem You're in the MS-DOS Shell and you attempt to run a batch file that you created yourself. However, instead of running that batch file, the MS-DOS Shell displays the following:

```
Bad command or file name
```

Solution There are two reasons this might have occurred:

1. You may have made an error entering the command when you created the batch file. Run the MS-DOS Editor and when the File to Edit dialog box appears, enter the name of the batch file you created. Check the commands, basing them on those commands you learned earlier. Save the file, exit the MS-DOS Editor and try the batch file again.

2. If this batch file is assigned to a group (i.e., the program list area), the parameters pointing to this file may be incorrect. Mark your batch file in the program list area and select **Properties...** from the **File** menu. You can change the parameters of this batch file. Check the Commands line to ensure that you have the correct batch filename entered in that line. Also, check the

Appendices

Startup Directory line to ensure that the correct path to the batch file is listed there. You will have to specify the complete path to the batch file, unless you already did this with the MS-DOS PATH command.

Problems with programs run from the MS-DOS Shell

Problem You start programs from the MS-DOS Shell by activating the file list area or through the **File Open** command from the program list area. Some programs crash the computer (i.e., the PC no longer responds to your input).

Solution Certain programs cannot be started from the MS-DOS Shell, because they won't behave the way you expect them to. Practically any programs that remain in memory after you start or exit the MS-DOS Shell (e.g., DOSKEY, APPEND, FASTOPEN or PRINT) will cause this.

Screen clears too quickly

Problem You created a batch file that displays information on the screen while it is running. When you start this batch file as a program from the MS-DOS Shell, the PC clears the screen and returns to the MS-DOS Shell, before you have a chance to read everything that was displayed.

Solution Add PAUSE to your batch file as the last command. This command, which you can only use in batch files, displays the following prompt on the screen:

```
Press any key to continue ...
```

Now the PC will wait until you press a key before returning to the MS-DOS Shell.

When you define new programs in the MS-DOS Shell you can use the Pause after Exit option button to have the MS-DOS Shell wait for you to press a key before clearing the screen.

C. Glossary

The following glossary should be helpful when you need a fast, short reference section. We designed it so that most of your questions will be answered. Cross references help lead you to other information quickly. If you want more detailed information, see *DOS 5.0 Complete*, available from Abacus.

[Alt] This key is one of the special keys on the PC keyboard. The [Alt] key is used with the numeric keypad to create characters not readily available on the PC keyboard. For example, you can print the pound sign (£) on the screen by pressing and holding the [Alt] key, pressing [1] [5] [6], then releasing the [Alt] key. Graphic characters are also available through the [Alt] key and the numeric keypad.

Application see Program

Arrow keys The keys which move the cursor in the four possible directions. These keys are usually arranged in a group on the keyboard. The arrows correspond to the direction of the movement.

ASCII Acronym for American Standard Code for Information Interchange. ASCII is the standard for keyboard character codes, which applies to some extent to keyboards and printers. The ASCII standard covers key codes 0 to 127; individual computer manufacturers assign their own characters to codes 128 to 255 (see Byte).

Asterisk see Wildcard

AT Acronym for Advanced Technology. The AT has a more powerful microprocessor, usually a higher processing speed, and a larger memory capacity, and higher disk storage capacity.

AUTOEXEC.BAT Abbreviation for AUTOEXECute BATch file. This text file contains a series of commands stored in a group. Immediately after you switch on the PC, the computer searches for an AUTOEXEC.BAT file. If one exists, the commands in this file execute automatically.

AUTOEXEC.BAT commands often include the display of the version of DOS in use (VER), the DATE and TIME commands.

The AUTOEXEC.BAT file is a special form of batch file. Like all other batch files, AUTOEXEC.BAT can also be called and executed direct from the system prompt.

Appendices

Backslash (\)   A character found on most PC keyboards. If you don't have a backslash on your keyboard, you can create it by pressing and holding the [Alt] key, and pressing [9] [2]. When you release [Alt] the backslash appears on the screen. The backslash is import with disk directories and subdirectories, because of it influences the disk path (i.e., backslashes separate directories in DOS commands).

[Backspace]   Key used for editing lines; often marked on the keyboard as [Backspace] or as [←]. Pressing [Backspace] deletes characters to the left of the cursor.

Backup copy   Duplicate of an original disk or file. Making backup copies is a good habit to get into, since data on a disk can be accidentally destroyed. See DISKCOPY for information on making backup disks, and COPY for information on making backups of files.

BASIC   Acronym for Beginner's All-purpose Symbolic Instruction Code. BASIC is a programming language. Unlike programs, which usually supply a specific solution to a problem area and cannot be changed, programming languages allow the user to solve almost any problem. Various commands can be used to construct a program to solve a problem. These programs function like batch files and are executed one command after another. BASIC has become popular with users as a computer language because it is easy to learn. MS-DOS 5.0 includes a form of BASIC called QBasic (see QBasic).

Batch file   A file containing a collection of commands (see AUTOEXEC.BAT). MS-DOS executes these commands in sequence when you type the name of the file.

Batch files are created using the COPY CON command (e.g., COPY CON FILE.BAT), the MS-DOS Editor, a word processing program, or the EDLIN line editor. The .BAT extension must be included with any batch filename.

Binary   A number system consisting of only two numbers (0,1), sometimes called bits. The binary number system is the number system most directly understood by the computer (see also Bit).

BIOS   Acronym for Basic Input Output System. The BIOS performs the most basic functions when you switch on a computer. These functions include the internal self test (adding up available memory, testing for peripherals such as disk drives) and the search for an operating system on disk.

C. Glossary

Bit	The smallest unit in the binary number system. It can only assume two states (0,1) and therefore store only two different pieces of information. Eight bits can be combined into a byte.
Boot	The loading process which places the operating system in memory. A disk used for booting a PC must have two "hidden" files available for telling the PC to boot, as well as the COMMAND.COM file.
Bootable	A disk which can be used for booting (see Boot).
BREAK	Interrupt capability. Pressing Ctrl + C stops most programs during execution. For example, the display of the directory on the screen (see DIR) can be interrupted in this manner. In many programs this interrupt capability has been disabled to permit an orderly termination of the program without loss of data. Even MS-DOS does not constantly test if this key combination was activated. If the capability is desired, type BREAK ON. With BREAK OFF the constant testing is disabled, which increases execution speed for some programs.
Byte	A group of eight bits. While a bit can only assume two states, 0 and 1, a byte can store from 0 up to 255 conditions.
CD	Command entered from the system prompt to determine the current directory. The PC searches for files in this directory unless the user provides a complete pathname. For every drive a current directory can be indicated. If during file operations only the drive specifier is indicated, DOS automatically accesses the current directory.
Centronics interface	Also called parallel interface: Standard connection between the PC and a printer. Most printers are connected to the PC through the Centronics (parallel) interface. It has the device designation LPT1: (Line Printer 1).
Change Directory	see CD
Chip	Complicated electronic circuitry built into a small piece of silicon. The most important chip in the PC is the microprocessor, which does most of the basic tasks needed in a computer.
Clear screen	see CLS
Clock frequency	The speed of the processor is measured sometimes with the clock frequency. Unlike people, the processor consistently works internally at the same clock frequency. The IBM PC has a clock frequency of 4.77 mHz (megaHertz). Compatibles sometimes use higher frequencies, but higher speeds may create compatibility problems.

Appendices

Clone	Another word for an IBM compatible computer (see IBM compatible).
CLS	Command entered from the system prompt to clear the screen. After the user enters CLS, the system prompt and the cursor appear on the upper left corner.
Cold start	The complete switching off and switching on of the computer. Since switching the computer off and on puts much stress on the electronic components, use the warm start ([Ctrl] + [Alt] + [Del]) whenever possible (see also Warm start). Use [Ctrl] + [C], [Ctrl] + [PgDn] or [Esc] to stop a program or command during execution, without having to cold start or warm start the computer.
Command interpreter	The COMMAND.COM program, which acts as the mediator between user and PC. The command interpreter can be accessed through the system prompt or the MS-DOS Shell.
Compatibility	Hardware and software that work together. A computer which is fully IBM compatible should be capable of executing all programs which exist for the IBM PC.
Control key	see [Ctrl]
COPY	Instructs the command interpreter to copy files. You can copy files between disks, to the same disk using a new name, and from one disk to another using a new name.
COPY CON	Instructs the command interpreter to copy data from the console (keyboard) to either a printer (COPY CON PRN) or a file (COPY CON FILENAME.EXT). The latter method can be used to create batch files.
Copying disks	Disks can be copied from the MS-DOS Shell using the **Disk Copy** program in the **Disk Utilities** group. You could also use the DISKCOPY command from the system prompt.
Copying files	see COPY
Correction	Corrections during input on the screen can be performed with the [Backspace] key. This deletes the character to the left of the current cursor position. You can also use the [Del] key, which deletes the character at the current cursor position.
CPU	Abbreviation for Central Processing Unit. This is the main microprocessor of the PC; sometimes used to describe the PC's case as well.

C. Glossary

Ctrl	The most important special key on the PC keyboard. It produces important commands in combination with other keys.
Current directory	To access a file or a directory, DOS uses the current directory. You make a directory current by showing the position relative to the current directory using the CD . . command
	A second method is to use the CD NAME command. You must indicate the drive (letter and colon) and then the path through the subdirectories separated by the backslash.
Current drive	The standard drive or current drive is the drive to which all disk commands of the computer apply. Usually, and especially for systems with only one drive, this is drive A:. If two drives are available, the second drive can be selected with B:. This command can be reversed with A:. The hard drive can be selected with C:. The standard drive is displayed in the system prompt (see Prompt).
Cursor	A small, rectangular, blinking spot of light on the screen. It marks the spot where a character can be placed from the keyboard. You normally use the arrow keys to move the cursor (See Arrow keys).
Cursor keys	See Arrow keys
Database	Program which allows fast access to data. Many database programs allow different sets of data to be combined into one package, permitting access to the different data sets simultaneously.
DATE	Sets or displays the current date. This date and time are stored with files during every storage process.
DEL	Deletes files. The command DEL FILENAME deletes the file FILENAME. File extensions must be included in the filename when necessary. Wildcards can be used.
	The command DEL *.BAK deletes all files with .BAK extensions from the current directory.
	Be very careful when using the DEL command.
DIR	Displays the directory of the disk which is in the current drive. First the name of the disk appears, if present (see VOL and LABEL). Then the following information is displayed:

229

Appendices

First, the filename (with up to eight characters allowed), then if available an extension (maximum of three characters). This is followed by the size of the file in bytes.

Finally, the date and time is displayed when the file was stored. The assumption is that the correct time was available when the file was stored (see DATE and TIME).

Directory — Part of a storage medium. Before the hard drive was commonly used, all files were stored in one directory, the root directory. Because of the large capacity of the hard drive, separate directories became necessary.

They're arranged in a tree structure where the root directory can contain files and subdirectories. Every subdirectory in turn can contain files and subdirectories.

DISKCOPY — Permits the complete copying of disks to make identical copies. This command is accessible from the MS-DOS Shell and the system prompt.

Disk drive — Devices which allow the PC to work on the data stored on the disk. Disk drives are available for 5-1/4" diskettes and for 3-1/2" diskettes.

The PC must have at least one built-in disk drive. The usual configuration is two disks drives. When the PC reads in the MS-DOS operating system, it accesses first the upper or left drive. You can see this by looking for LCD on the disk drive. This is the main drive. Its designation is A:. The other drive is then drive B:. If there is a hard drive, it has the designation drive C:.

The drive designation is important because with it commands and files can be assigned. Only one drive can be current. Its letter appears in front of the system prompt on the screen and is constantly displayed (see drive designation).

Disk name — see LABEL and VOL

Diskettes — Removable data storage media. PC systems use two sizes: 5-1/4" diskettes and 3-1/2" diskettes. Each diskette size has two types—double density (capable of holding 360K and 720K of data respectively) and high density (capable of holding 1.2 Meg and 1.44 Meg of data respectively).

DOS — Acronym for Disk Operating System; also used as abbreviation for MS-DOS (see MS-DOS).

C. Glossary

Double density	Double density means that this type of disk has twice as much magnetic material for recording as a single density disk. Use double density disks only for PCs.
Drive change	see Current drive
Drive letter	The drive letter consists of a letter and the colon following. To indicate the standard drive, enter the drive letter that pertains to it.
Editing	Creating a new file or correcting an existing file (see Editor).
Editor	A program which makes it possible to write or edit text. You can use the MS-DOS Editor or EDLIN can be used to edit text.
	An editor (also called text editor) normally has fewer but easier options than a word processor.
EDLIN	Line editor included with MS-DOS. EDLIN is very limited because it is a *line editor*. Therefore, you can only work on text line-by-line. Although EDLIN is suitable for writing batch files or other small files, use a text editor or word processor for larger documents.
Empty directory	A directory containing no files or subdirectories. An empty directory displays entries with one or two periods and a <DIR> identifier instead of filenames if you use the DIR command.
	You can remove empty directories by moving up one directory level using CD .. and typing the RD command.
[Enter]	A very important key on a computer keyboard. The [Enter] key can have different names: [Enter], [Return], or [←]. Pressing [Enter] instructs the computer to execute the MS-DOS command that you typed at the system prompt line.
Extension	Any filename can have a three-character extension separated from the filename by a period. The extensions .COM, .EXE and .BAT have special meanings in MS-DOS, but any other combination of letters can be selected for various files. There are some conventions which are observed, such as TXT for ASCII text.
	The following extensions are commonly used in MS-DOS:

.BAK   Backup copy of file (e.g., generated by programs)
.BAS   Program written in the computer language BASIC
.BAT   Batch file

Appendices

.COM	Executable program file
.DOC	Word processing document file
.EXE	Executable program file
.TXT	ASCII Text file

External — Commands which must be read from the DOS disk before they can be executed. The best known and most often used of these commands are FORMAT and DISKCOPY.

File — Data stored under a name assigned by the user or manufacturer. Data files (for example, programs, text, graphics, etc.) appear in the directory of a diskette or hard drive as an entry containing the name, extension, size and date it was saved.

File management — Working with data. Related information is stored in a data set and these are presented in sorted format. An address file is a simple form of file management.

File structures — The type and method of storing files on a medium (see tree structure). The root directory can contain both files and subdirectories, and any subdirectory can also contain files and subdirectories.

Filename — An unique group of letters and numbers assigned to a file. You assign the filename when you create it.

The length of the filename cannot exceed eight characters. The optional extension can have no more than three characters. The name and extension must be separated by a period.

Note that spaces are not allowed in either the name or extension.

Formatting — Preparing a disk to store data. The MS-DOS Shell uses the **Format** program from the **Disk Utilities** group. You can also use the MS-DOS FORMAT command.

Function keys — A block of ten keys lettered F1 through F10. These keys are assigned different functions, depending on the program or application you are using.

Hard drive — A hermetically sealed disk drive which usually cannot be removed from the PC (a few newer models are removable). Hard drives have a much higher storage capacity than diskettes. Normal storage capacities range from 10 Meg to 140 Meg.

C. Glossary

	Hard drives are usually located inside the PC. They include nonflexible disks, read/write head assembly and electronic parts.
	Since hard drives are very sensitive to shock and vibrations, they must be treated with care.
Hardware	Includes the computer and everything its parts (processor, keyboard, monitor, disk drives, hard drive). The software is responsible in sending instructions to the hardware (see Software).
IBM compatible	A program, hardware, or an adapter that follows IBM standards.
	Many manufacturers sell IBM compatible computers. These computers (also called clones) run virtually all software written for the IBM PC.
	These compatible computers must also accept adapters, peripherals, and other parts designed for the IBM-PC.
Interface	An electronic connection between a PC and different peripherals or other computers.
	Two interfaces of different design are used: Parallel interfaces and serial interfaces. If a device should be attached to the PC and a suitable interface is not available, circuit boards are available which contain an interface.
K	Abbreviation for Kilobyte.
Keyboard	The easiest and most widely used device for data input. The keyboard supports several alphanumeric, punctuation, symbol, and control keys to send coded signals to computer.
Kilobyte	1,024 bytes (see also Byte).
LABEL	This command lets you add an 11-character volume label name to the specified disk. Unlike filenames, volume label names may include spaces.
MD	Abbreviation for Make Directory (sometimes also called MKDIR). You must use this command when you want to create a subdirectory in the current directory.
	The MD command requires a directory name up to eight characters long and an optional three character extension.

Appendices

Meg	Abbreviation for Megabyte: Approximately 1 million (1,048,576) bytes (see also Byte).
Microprocessor	Integrated circuit chip. When used in computer science, the term chip usually refers to the main microprocessor of the computer, which controls the basic functions.
Mouse	Alternate input device. The mouse is a small box with two or three buttons on top and either a ball poking out the bottom, or a series of photoelectric cells. Moving the mouse on a table or special optical pad moves the cursor in the same direction on the screen. The mouse is most important for paint programs and graphic user interfaces such as the MS-DOS Shell.
MS-DOS	The standard operating system for IBM compatible PCs. The first version of MS-DOS was released by the Microsoft Corporation in 1981. MS-DOS is an abbreviation for MicroSoft Disk Operating System.
	Since MS-DOS uses command lines, you must memorize several commands and syntax to operate your PC successfully.
	MS-DOS uses resident and external commands. Resident commands are always available from within memory and include DATE, TIME, PROMPT, CLS and VOL. External commands must be loaded from disk before they can execute and include FORMAT and DISKCOPY.
MS-DOS Editor	Text editor supplied with MS-DOS 5.0. Can be used for writing batch files or unformatted ASCII text files (see also ASCII).
MS-DOS Shell	Graphical user interface which allows the user to communicate with MS-DOS in a friendly manner. Commands and files can be accessed using the keyboard or mouse. Although more limited in capabilities than the system prompt, the MS-DOS Shell offers the beginner an easy start with MS-DOS.
Operating system	The program which makes the computer capable of performing basic memory and disk management tasks. The operating system also lets you communicate with the computer through the keyboard.
	The operating system is loaded either from a disk (MS-DOS) or permanently stored in the computer.
Parallel interface	Centronics interface, usually leading to a printer (see also Centronics interface). Parallel interfaces exchange data 8 bits at a time. LPT1: is

C. Glossary

	the device designation for the first parallel interface. Additional parallel interfaces (if present) can be accessed as LPT2: and LPT3:.
Parameter	Command elements of a DOS command separated from the command name by a space. The command COPY CON FILENAME uses the command name COPY and the two parameters CON and FILENAME.
PATH	Shows the directory where DOS should search for commands and programs. Without such a path, the search is limited to the current directory. PATH without a parameter displays the path currently set.
Pathname	Shows the location of a file or a directory on a disk, consisting of the drive letter, colon and a series of backslashes separating filename and directories.
PC	Abbreviation for Personal Computer, which was originally an IBM product first introduced in 1981. Now refers to all computers which are IBM compatible (able to use programs written for IBM computers).
Power supply	Electrical component of the computer which prepares normal household electrical current for use by the circuitry of the computer, similar to the transformer found on a model train layout. The size and quality of the power supply determines how many peripherals can be added to the computer, since most of them must be connected to the power supply. For example, a small capacity power supply may only be able to handle the computer and two disk drives, but not a hard drive.
Printer	Device which places computer data on paper. An indispensable tool for computing. Everything displayed on the monitor screen is printed on paper and thus made portable. Printer types include daisywheel, dot matrix, and laser. A printer can be addressed through either the serial or Centronics parallel interface of the computer.
Processor	Short for microprocessor. Most references to a microprocessor in computing refer to the main microprocessor of the computer, which controls the computer's essential internal tasks (e.g., math, data movement). In the same way that different engines determine the performance of a car, various processors determine the performance of personal computers, mostly through execution speed.
Program	Products which instruct a computer to perform a specific task or group of tasks (for example, a word processor). Sometimes called applications.

Appendices

`Prt Sc`	A key usually located on the right side of the keyboard. You can send the screen display to the printer by pressing `Shift` + `Prt Sc`.
QBasic	Programming language included with MS-DOS 5.0 (see also BASIC).
Question mark	see Wildcard
RAM	Abbreviation for Random Access Memory. This is your PC's most important area of memory. Data and other instructions are stored in RAM so that the CPU can write to and read from them quickly. The contents of RAM are lost when you switch off your PC.
RAM disk	An area created in RAM by a program to act as a disk drive temporarily. on the DOS disk. Since it is not a mechanical device, the RAM disk allows very fast file access, but loses all data when you switch off your PC. PC users with only one disk drive will find the RAM disk extremely helpful. Anything can be kept in a RAM disk, provided the files do not exceed the memory limits.
RD	Abbreviation for Remove Directory. The RD command removes empty subdirectories from a disk. If the subdirectory is not in the current directory, the complete pathname must be provided.
RENAME	Command used to rename files. You follow the command with a space, then the old filename, another space, and the new filename (RENAME OLDNAME NEWNAME).
Renaming disks	see LABEL
Renaming files	see RENAME
Reset	see Warm start
Resident	Commands loaded as MS-DOS boots into the memory of the PC. Resident commands are always available. Resident commands which we described include: CD, CLS, COPY, DATE, DEL, DIR, ECHO, MD, PATH, PROMPT, RENAME, RD, TIME, TYPE, VER, and VOL.
`Return`	See `Enter`.

C. Glossary

ROM	Abbreviation for Read Only Memory. ROM consists of start-up information and codes on a chip (see Chip). When you switch on your PC, the computer reads the information from this ROM.
	The contents of ROM are not lost when you switch off your PC.
Root directory	The main, or top-level, directory, on either a diskette or a hard drive. Since it's created by MS-DOS when you format the disk, it is given the highest level.
	You can access the root directory by typing the drive letter, colon, and a backslash (for example, A:\ to move to the root directory of drive A:).
RS-232	Standard serial interface. Serial transfer involves the transfer of data one bit at a time.
Scrolling	A process in which the display on the screen moves lines toward the top/bottom or left/right because the screen must make room for new lines. Scrolling can be performed in many programs and the MS-DOS Shell, but not from the system prompt.
Serial interface	see RS-232
[Shift]	Two keys on the keyboard, normally located at the left and right edges of the keyboard. Press either [Shift] to display uppercase letters and punctuation marks.
Single density	A disk type with a very limited amount of magnetic media. Most inexpensive disks are single density. Avoid using single density disks on your PC: Use double density disks only.
Single sided	A disk which is single sided can record on only the "top" side. Most inexpensive disks are single sided. Avoid using single sided disks on your PC: Use double sided disks only.
Slot	Name for a connector inside the PC where additional circuit cards can be inserted to enhance the capabilities of the computer. Recently, some PC compatibles do not have these slots. Therefore, adding cards may be difficult.
Software	Computer programs, including the operating system and any drivers for peripheral devices.
Source disk	The disk which the user wants to copy. When the DISKCOPY command is invoked, a prompt requests the source disk.

Appendices

Startup	see Booting, Cold start, and Warm start
Storage media	The various devices used to store the contents of the PC's memory outside the computer. Generally these include disk drives, hard drives and tape drives.
Subdirectory	Refers to a directory stored within another directory. For example, the following path refers to drive A:, the TEXT directory, the PRIVATE subdirectory contained within the TEXT directory, and the GIFTS subdirectory contained within the PRIVATE subdirectory: `A:\TEXT\PRIVATE\GIFTS`
Switch	Additional information for a command, usually preceded by a slash character. The /W switch, when added to the DIR command, displays a disk directory in wide (multiple-column) format.
System prompt	The character or set of characters that MS-DOS uses to show that the PC is ready to accept a command or other input. The default (normal) prompt in MS-DOS consists of the current disk drive and a greater than character (for example, C>). The PROMPT command lets change the appearance of the prompt.
Target disk	The disk to receive data; sometimes called the destination disk. When copying data from one disk to another, the disk being copied is the source disk, and the target disk is the disk receiving data.
Text editor	see EDLIN, MS-DOS Editor and Word processor
TIME	MS-DOS command for setting or changing the current system time. The directory display shows the user which version of a file or program is the most current through the date and time.
Tree structure	The tree structure is often used to compare how files are stored. Starting at the stem (root directory), there can be branches (subdirectories) and leaves (files). Branches can have other branches (subdirectories can include other subdirectories) or leaves (files).
TYPE	Instructs the command interpreter to display a text file on the screen. The TYPE command cannot be used in conjunction with wildcards.
User interface	The communication point between the user and the PC. MS-DOS 5.0 allows user communication from the MS-DOS Shell or from the command interpreter.

C. Glossary

Utilities	Programs that either help you program more efficiently or act as tools in disk and file management. Some utilities optimize the performance of a hard drive. Other utilities can help you recover deleted or destroyed files.
VOL	Resident command which displays the volume label name of the disk in the current drive as assigned using the LABEL command.
Warm start	The warm start (pressing [Ctrl] + [Alt] + [Del]) restarts the system without reloading the BIOS or switching off the PC.
Wildcard	Characters which can replace one or more characters in filenames, often allowing multiple file access. The question mark (?) can represent single characters, and the asterisk (*) can represent multiple characters. The following typed at the system prompt copies all files from drive C: to drive A:

```
COPY C:*.* A:
```

The following deletes all files with the .TXT file extension:

```
DEL *.TXT
```

The following displays all five-character filenames starting with A and ending with B and with extensions starting and ending with T:

```
DIR A???B.T?T
```

Word processor	A program for creating and editing text files. Most word processors on the market today allow inclusion of graphics, text formatting and more.
Write protect	Protects disks from accidental formatting or file deletion. Disks can be write protected by covering the square slot on the left side with a paper sticker (5-1/4" disks), or by moving the write protect slider (3-1/2" disks). Data can be read from this disk into the memory of the PC, but nothing can be changed on the disk. This disk and its data is protected.
XT	Generic term for a PC with a hard drive, or a PC capable of running a hard drive.

Index

%1 99
.... 203
@ 196

[Alt] 19
Access denied error 222
Add mode 59
Alphanumerical sorting 84
Alt key 19, 225
Appendices 215
Apple Computer Inc. 11
Apple Macintosh 11
Applications 28, 225
Arrow keys 14, 19, 225
Ascending 84
ASCII 225
Asterisk (*) 225, 239
AT 225
AUTOEXEC.BAT 175, 225

Backing up 145
Backslash (\) 226
Backspace key 226
Backup 145
Backup copy 226
Backup Fixed Disk 91
Bad command or file name error 219
BASIC 199, 226
BAT 61
Batch file 45, 66, 188, 226
Battery backed clock 177
Binary 226
BIOS 226
Bit 227
Block commands 163
Blocks 162
Boot 227
Bootable 227
Branch target 211
BREAK 227
BUFFERS 180

Byte 227
[Ctrl] 19, 228, 229
Cache program 186
CD 114, 124, 227, 229
CD NAME commands 229
CD.. 124
Centronics interface 227
Change Directory 227
Changing a group 96
Changing a group line 98
Changing a program line 100
Changing directories 124
Check 211
Chips 17, 227
CHKDSK 143
Clear screen 224, 227
Click 13
Clock frequency 227
Clone 228
CLS 111, 227, 228
CLS command 111
Cold start 228
Collapse 80
COM 61
Command cancelling 220
Command interpreter 6, 34, 228
Command Prompt 34
COMMAND.COM 59
Commands 6, 236
Compatibility 15, 228
Condition 211
CONFIG.SYS 59, 179
Configure 101, 179
Control key 228
COPY 228
COPY CON 228
Copy diskettes 91
Copying blocks of text 163
Copying disks 228
Copying files 127, 228

241

Index

Correction 228
COUNTRY 181
CPU 228
Crashes
    programs run from Shell 224
Creating a group 96
Creating directories 55, 77, 124
Creating files 166
Creating subdirectories 123
Ctrl key 19, 229
Currency conversion program 208-212
Current directory 229
Current drive 229
Cursor 228, 229
Cursor keys 19, 229

Data security 143
Database 28, 229
Date 44, 105, 177, 229
DATE command 105
DEL 121, 229
DEL *.BAK 229
DEL FILENAME 229
Deleting blocks of text 163
Deleting characters 161
Deleting directories 78, 130
Deleting files 62, 63, 121
Deleting lines 162
Deleting marked text 162
Deleting text 161
Deleting words 162
Descending 84
Dialog box 99
Digital Research 8
DIR 111, 112, 229
DIR command 111
Directories 111
Directory 124, 130, 229, 230
Directory Tree area 32, 35
Disk Copy 76, 91
Disk drive 230
Disk drive problems 223
Disk drives 16, 17

Disk name 230
Disk Utilities 34, 35, 71, 87
Disk Utilities group 87
DISKCOPY 91, 226, 230
Diskettes 17, 230
    new 133
    Root directory 221
Displaying pathnames 75
DOS 230
DOS=HIGH 181
DOSKEY 14, 110
DOSSHELL 30
Double density 231
Double-click 54
Drive change 231
Drive icons 32
Drive letter 32, 231

[Enter] 19, 231
ECHO 176, 196
Edit menu 162
Editing 231
Editor 34, 231
EDLIN 231
Empty directory 231
Enter key 19, 231
Entering text 160
Environmental variables 99
Esc key 19
EXE 61
EXIT 90
Exiting a directory 124
Extension 43, 61, 83, 231
External 232
External commands 14

File 6, 232
File copied to wrong location 221
File extension 111
File list area 35
File management 232
File menu 35, 36
File not found 221

Index

File size 61
File structures 232
File/Copy 57, 59, 73, 74, 75, 92
File/Create Directory... ....55, 77
File/Delete...................... 62, 78, 92, 100
File/Exit 40, 104
File/New................... 94, 95, 97, 101
File/Open 67
File/Properties...........................98, 100
File/Rename... ....63, 78
File/Run... 101
File/View File Contents.....44, 47, 64, 65, ... 175, 179
Filename.........................61, 111, 232
Files...............................28, 180, 230
    Deleting................................ 121
    Rename................................ 121
    Renaming...............................83
    Sort..84
    Undeleting..............................92
FOR ... NEXT 210
Format........................71, 92, 133
Formatting 53, 133, 232
Formatting diskettes.....................71, 133
Function keys 18, 232

Gas mileage calculation program... 205-207
graphics mode 38
Group Title...97
GW-BASIC 199

Hard drive........................16, 17, 232
Hardware 228, 233
HIMEM.SYS.................................. 180
Horizontal scrolling........................ 169

IBM compatible.............................. 233
IF ....THEN 211
INPUT... 206
interfaces...................................6, 233
intuitive user interface......................11
Invalid directory............................. 125

Keyboard.................................. 18, 233
Kilobyte 233

Label...................................211, 233
Languages....................................233
Loop..210
LPT1 227

Main.. 87
Main drive................................230
Main group 87
Mark..211
Marking a block of text 163
MD.............................123, 124, 233
Meg...234
Memory................................... 17
Memory test................................... 30
Menu 35
Menu bar 31
Menu command................................. 35
Microprocessor.......................227, 234
Microsoft Corporation...................... 6, 7
Microsoft Windows....................... 69
Microsoft Word...........................13, 69
Monitor 18
Monochrome 18
Mouse 11, 20, 234
Mouse pointer...............................11, 20
MOUSE.COM............................... 85
Moving between directories 80
Moving blocks of text........................163
MS-DOS 5, 6, 234
    Applications...............................173
    history..7
    innovations 13
    installation 13
    integrated Help................................ 14
MS-DOS Editor 14, 34, 157, 234
    Cursor movement......................169
    Edit/Copy 163, 171
    Edit/Cut....................163, 164, 171
    Edit/Delete 172
    Edit/Paste...................163, 164, 172

243

Index

File/Exit 168, 171
File/New 164, 166, 168, 171
File/Open 171
File/Open 164, 165, 167, 171,
.... 175, 179
File/Print 168, 171
File/Save 164, 166, 167, 171
File/Save As 164, 166, 167, 171
Help/About 172
Help/Getting started 172
Help/Keyboard 172
key reference 170
Menus 171
Options/Display 172
Options/Help Path 172
Search/Change 172
Search/Find 172
Search/Repeat Last Find 172
MS-DOS Editor 226
MS-DOS QBasic 34
MS-DOS Shell 10, 30, 234

New directory cannot be created 222
NIBBLES 204
Non-hard drive systems-installation 215
Not ready error message 218
Numeric keypad 19
Numeric variable 209

Operating system 5, 234
    basic functions 6
Options/Display... .... 40, 57, 162
Options/File Display Options... ...... 83, 84,
.... 86

Parallel interface 234
Parameter 235
Parent directory 49
Password 96, 97
PATH 176, 235
Pathname 126, 235
PAUSE 197
Pause after exit 95, 96
PC 15, 235

Pixels 39
Placeholder 206
Power supply 235
Power-up 30
PRINT 207
Printer 18, 235
Printing a file 168
Processor 235
Program 235
Program list area 34, 35
Program not executable from Shell 223
Program Title 94
Program with parameters 99
Programming language 199
Programs 28
PROMPT 108, 110, 177, 211, 212
PrtSc key 235
Pseudo disk drive 184

QBasic 14, 199, 236
    File/Exit 213
    File/New 205, 208
    File/Open 203, 204, 207
    File/Save 207
    File/Save As 207, 209, 213
    Run/Start 204, 205, 208
Question mark 236, 239
Quick Format 92
Quitting programs 70

Radio buttons 84
RAM 236
RAM disk 183, 236
RAMDISK.SYS 183
RAMDRIVE.SYS 183
RD 130, 236
Real time clock 177
RECOVER 144
REM 196
Remove directory 130, 236
RENAME 121, 236
Renaming directories 78
Renaming disks 236

Index

Renaming files 62, 121, 236
Reset 236
Resident 236
Resident commands 14
RESTORE 91, 151
Restore Fixed Disk 91
Restoring the hard drive 153
Return key 236
ROM 237
Root directory 24, 221, 230, 237
RS-232 237

SAA 200
Saving a new file 167
Saving an open file 167
Saving files 167
Scrolling 34, 111, 169, 237
Selection cursor 33
Serial interface 237
SET COMSPEC 177
SETUP program 13
SETVER 14, 180
SHELL 181
Shift key 237
Single density 237
Single sided 237
Size of a file 44
Slider bar 37
Slot 237
SMARTDRV.SYS 186
Software 199, 228, 237
Sorting 84
Sorting options 84
Source disk 237, 238
Spreadsheet 28
Starting 217
Starting programs 67, 204
Starting QBasic 200
Starting the MS-DOS Editor 157
Startup 238
Startup Directory 95
Startup file 69
Status bar 202

Storage media 238
String variable 209
Subdirectories .. 24, 79, 123, 129, 177, 230
Subdirectory 27, 221, 238
Switch 238
Switch on 30
Switching drives 51
System Application Architecture 200
System prompt ....
.... 6, 90, 108, 175, 177, 228, 238

(Tab) 19
Tabs 162
Target disk 238
Text editor 157, 238
Text mode 38
Text variable 209
TIME 107, 177, 238
Title bar 31
Tree structure 238
Tree/Expand One Level 48
Troubleshooting 217
TYPE 175, 179, 238

Undelete 92
Undeleting files 92
UNFORMAT 14
Unresponsive PC 218
Untitled 201
Upwardly compatible 9
User interface 238
Utilities 239

Variables 206
VDISK.SYS 183
Version numbers 7
VER 225
View/All Files 85, 86
View/Dual File Lists 80
Viewing files 85
Virtual disk drive 184
VOL 239
Volume label 72

245

Index

Warm start.................................... 239
Wildcards..................... 83, 203, 225, 239
Word processor........................... 13, 239
Work area...................................... 201
Write protect................................. 239
Write protect notch..........................52

XCOPY 149
XT 239

Productivity Series Books

DOS 5.0 Complete

Not just another reference book - **DOS 5.0 Complete** is a practical user's guide to learning and using Microsoft's new DOS. It's an encyclopedia of DOS knowledge not only for the computer whiz but for the everyday user.

DOS 5.0 Complete is loaded with helpful hints for outfitting any computer with MS-DOS 5.0. From installing DOS 5.0 to using the new features for file, directory and storage maintenance you'll find techniques and hints here.

DOS 5.0 Complete has dozens of easy to follow examples. This book explains AUTOEXEC.BAT and CONFIG.SYS. The detailed explanations make this the most authoritative DOS book available. The friendly, easy to understand writing style insures that even beginners will grasp the fundamentals quickly and easily. And you'll find a complete DOS command reference.

Topics include:

- Learn the "ins and outs" of using the new MS-DOS 5.0
- Boost your productivity with these practical techniques
- Discover ways to solve your own DOS problems
- Save valuable time with the ready-to-run companion disk.
- Browse the extensive MS-DOS reference section
- Using DOS' new memory management features
- Using the improved SHELL ;for performing your computer housekeeping ;chores
- Using the new DOSKEY utility for faster command line editing and macro power.
- Using EDIT, the new full-screen editor
- Using QBASIC, DOS' new BASIC programming language
- Complete DOS command reference.

DOS 5.0 Complete includes a companion disk with example batch files, detailed explanations, and powerful tips and tricks to help you get the most out of MS-DOS 5.0. **DOS 5.0 Complete** will become THE source for reference information about DOS 5.0.

DOS 5.0 Complete
Authors: Michael Tornsdorf, Helmut Tornsdorf
ISBN 1-55755-109-X.
Suggested retail price $34.95 with companion disk.

To order direct call Toll Free 1-800-451-4319
In US and Canada add $5.00 shipping and handling. Foreign orders add $13.00 per item.
Michigan residents add 4% sales tax.

Windows Software

New BeckerTools 2.0 PLUS for Windows:
Indispensable utilities for every Windows user

If you're a Windows user, you'll appreciate **BeckerTools Version 2** for Windows. **BeckerTools** will dramatically speed-up your file and data management chores and increase your productivity. Where Windows' File Manager functions end, **BeckerTools** features begin by giving you powerful, yet flexible features you need to get the job done quickly. **BeckerTools** has the same consistent user interface found in Windows so there's no need to learn 'foreign' commands or functions. Manipulating your disks and files are as easy as pointing and clicking with the mouse. You'll breeze through flexible file and data functions and features that are friendly enough for a PC novice yet powerful enough for the advanced user. You won't find yourself 'dropping out' of Windows to perform powerful, essential DOS functions like undeleting a file or waiting for a diskette to be formatted. **BeckerTools** has the enhanced applications available at the click of a mouse button. Item #S110 ISBN 1-55755-110-3. With 3 1/2" and 5 1/4" diskettes. Suggested retail price $129.95.

Now includes—

BeckerTools Compress
Defragments and optimizes disk performance.
Optimizes your hard disk performance by defragmenting your files and/or disk. Multiple compress option lets you choose the type of optimization.

BeckerTools Recover
Rescues files and disks.
Checks and repairs common file and disk problems- corrupted FAT's, improperly chained clusters, bad files, etc. Could be a "Life-saver".

BeckerTools Backup
Fast, convenient file backup and restore.
File and disk backup/restore at the click of a button. Multiple select options, optional data compression, password protection and more.

BeckerTools Version 2 Plus is as easy as pointing and clicking with the mouse. **BeckerTools** takes advantage of Windows' multitasking capabilities and **BeckerTools** keeps you informed of its progress as it works.

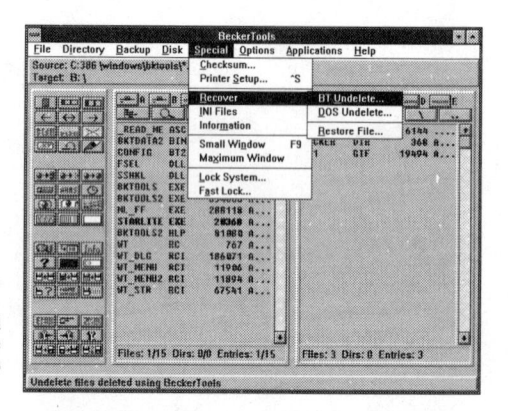

Here are some of the things that you can easily do with **BeckerTools Version 2:**

- Launch applications - directly from **BeckerTools**
- Associate files - logically connects applications with their file types
- Backup (pack files) hard disk - saves 50% to 80% disk space - with password protection
- User levels - 3 levels for beginning, intermediate and advanced users
- Undelete - recover deleted files
- Undelete directories - recover directories in addition to individual files
- Delete files - single, groups of files or directories, including read-only files
- Duplicate diskettes - read diskette once, make multiple copies
- Edit text - built-in editor with search and replace
- Format diskettes - in any capacity supported by your drive and disk type
- Compare diskettes - in a single pass
- Wipe diskette - for maximum security
- Screen blanker - prevent CRT "burn in"
- File grouping - perform operations on files as a group
- Create a bootable system diskette
- Reliability checking - check for physical errors on disk media
- Edit files - new hex editor to edit virtually and type of file
- Dozens of other indispensable features

To order direct call Toll Free 1-800-451-4319

In US and Canada add $5.00 shipping and handling. Foreign orders add $13.00 per item.
Michigan residents add 4% sales tax.

Remove along perforation, complete the information, fold and tape shut.

Name	
Company	
Address	
City	State Zip
Country	Phone or FAX

Qty.	Title	Price

Payment:
- ❑ Visa
- ❑ Master Card
- ❑ American Express
- ❑ Check/ M.O.

Subtotal	
Michigan residents add 4% sales tax	
In US and Canada add $5.00 Shipping per order	
Foreign orders add $13.00 Shipping & Handling per item	
TOTAL amount enclosed (U.S. funds)	

Card No. _____ Exp. Date _____

Signature _____

PLEASE HELP US So that we better understand who you are and what types of books interest you, please answer the following questions and return this prepaid card to us. **THANK YOU!**

Computer:
- ❑ IBM/ PC or compatible
- ❑ PC/ AT or compatible
- ❑ PC 386/ 486
- ❑ Commodore 64/128
- ❑ Amiga
- ❑ Macintosh
- ❑ Other _____

I purchase most computer books from:
- ❑ Retail book store
- ❑ Discount book store
- ❑ Mail order
- ❑ Retail computer store
- ❑ Discount computer store
- ❑ Publisher direct

I learned of this book from:
- ❑ Magazine ad
- ❑ Book review
- ❑ Recommendation
- ❑ Store display rack
- ❑ Catalog/ Brochure
- ❑ Library

Suggestions for new books: _____

This book's title: _____

Comments: _____

Your name: _____

Your company: _____

Address: _____

City: _____ State: _____ Zip: _____

Purchased from (store name): _____

City: _____ State: _____ Zip: _____

Available Book Titles for IBM PC and Compatibles

_____ Assembly Language -Step By Step w/2 disks	$34.95
_____ BASIC Programming Inside & Out w/disk	$34.95
_____ Batch File PowerTools w/disk	$34.95
_____ COBOL for Beginners	$18.95
_____ Computers & Visual Stress	$12.95
_____ Computer Viruses and Data Protection	$19.95
_____ dBase IV for Beginners	$18.95
_____ DOS 5.0 Complete w/disk	$34.95
_____ DOS 5.0 Essentials	$14.95
_____ DOS 5.0 for Beginners	$18.95
_____ DR DOS 6.0 Complete w/disk	$34.95
_____ Finding (Almost) Free Software	$16.95
_____ GW BASIC for Beginners	$18.95
_____ Intro To Windows Programming w/disk	$34.95
_____ Laser Printer Powertools w/disk	$34.95
_____ Lotus 1-2-3 for Beginners	$18.95
_____ MS-DOS for Beginners	$18.95
_____ Novell Netware Simplified	$24.95
_____ PC and Compatibles for Beginners	$18.95
_____ PC File Formats and Conversions	$34.95
_____ PC Intern w/disk	$59.95
_____ PC System Programming w/2disks	$59.95
_____ QuickBASIC Toolbox w/disk	$34.95
_____ Stepping Up to DR DOS 6.0	$14.95
_____ The Leisure Suit Larry Story	$14.95
_____ Turbo Pascal for Windows w/disk	$39.95
_____ Turbo Pascal System Programming w/2 disks	$44.95
_____ UNIX for Beginners	$18.95
_____ UNIX Reference Guide	$ 9.95
_____ Upgrading and Maintaining Your PC	$24.95
_____ Windows System Programming w/disk	$39.95
_____ Word 5.0/5.5 Powertools w/disk	$34.95
_____ Word for Windows Know How w/disk	$34.95
_____ Word for Windows Powertools w/disk	$34.95
_____ WordPerfect for Beginners	$18.95

To order call **TOLL FREE 1-800-451-4319** in US and Canada

BUSINESS REPLY MAIL
FIRST-CLASS MAIL PERMIT NO 5504 GRAND RAPIDS MI

POSTAGE WILL BE PAID BY ADDRESSEE

Abacus
5370 52nd St SE
Grand Rapids MI 49502-8107

NO POSTAGE
NECESSARY
IF MAILED
IN THE
UNITED STATES